MID-AMERICAN
★ FRONTIER ★

JAMES BAIRD WEAVER

Fred[erick] Emory Haynes

ARNO PRESS
A New York Times Company
New York — 1975

0734403

Editorial Supervision: ANDREA HICKS

———◆———

Reprint Edition 1975 by Arno Press Inc.

Reprinted from a copy in
  The University of Illinois Library

THE MID-AMERICAN FRONTIER
ISBN for complete set: 0-405-06845-X
See last pages of this volume for titles.

Manufactured in the United States of America

———◆———

Library of Congress Cataloging in Publication Data

Haynes, Frederick Emory, 1868-
    James Baird Weaver.

    (The Mid-American frontier)
    Reprint of the 1919 ed. published by the State
Historical Society of Iowa, Iowa City, issued in
series: Iowa biographical series.
    Includes bibliographical references.
    1. Weaver, James Baird, 1833-1912. I. Series.
II. Series: Iowa biographical series.
E664.W36H4 1975   973.8'092'4 [B]   75-102
ISBN 0-405-06870-0

IOWA BIOGRAPHICAL SERIES
EDITED BY BENJAMIN F. SHAMBAUGH

JAMES BAIRD WEAVER

JAMES BAIRD WEAVER

FROM AN OIL PAINTING BY
CHARLES A. CUMMING
IN THE HISTORICAL MEMORIAL AND
ART BUILDING DES MOINES IOWA

IOWA BIOGRAPHICAL SERIES
EDITED BY BENJAMIN F. SHAMBAUGH

JAMES BAIRD WEAVER

BY

FRED EMORY HAYNES

THE STATE HISTORICAL SOCIETY OF IOWA
IOWA CITY IOWA 1919

EDITOR'S INTRODUCTION

THERE is much inspiration in the career of General James B. Weaver, because in his day, when the world of politics "was changing and searching out a new orbit", he was a pioneer and a prophet. As a pioneer he gave expression to the thought and feeling of the agricultural West: he was, indeed, the exponent of the democracy of the West, and "the key to his position upon public policies is to be found in his persistent spirit of democracy."

As a prophet General Weaver "voiced ideas and principles in Congress that were little regarded at the time. The contrast between the reception given his views in 1879 and the attitude of the two great parties in recent years towards social politics is the measure of the progress made in the intervening period. The pioneer of 1879 is now seen to have been a far-sighted leader" and prophet.

The ultimate test of prevision is the record of fulfillment. Long before the close of

the nineteenth century General Weaver
stood for more democracy; he stood for prohibition; he stood against the control of
government by the interests; he favored the
direct election of United States Senators;
he favored the taxation of incomes; he
favored the construction of an isthmian
canal; he advocated monetary reform; he
proposed the establishment of a department
of labor; and he saw clearly that militarism
was a policy for keeping the people in
subjection.

BENJ. F. SHAMBAUGH

OFFICE OF THE SUPERINTENDENT AND EDITOR
THE STATE HISTORICAL SOCIETY OF IOWA
IOWA CITY IOWA

AUTHOR'S PREFACE

THIS study of the life of General James Baird Weaver is an outgrowth of the writer's *Third Party Movements Since the Civil War*. A review of the successive minor parties from 1872 to 1912 brought out very clearly the importance of General Weaver's leadership. The work of Bryan and Roosevelt and their influence upon the Democratic and Republican parties is to be explained only by an appreciation of the earlier labors of General Weaver; and a large part of the program of the so-called "Progressive Movement" goes back to the pioneer labors of the same leader, whose platform was essentially one of "social and industrial justice", growing out of conditions existing in the West from 1876 to 1896.

General Weaver's campaigns of 1880 and 1892 were the real precursors of those of Bryan in 1896 and of Roosevelt in 1904. The election of President Wilson in 1912 was in many respects the culmination of Weaver's efforts. He was really the "first progressive". The

platform of 1880, the speeches in Congress from
1879 to 1881 and from 1885 to 1889, the platform
of 1892, and *A Call to Action* are the documents
that form the basis of the Progressive party
platform of 1912.

The materials for the life of General
Weaver are somewhat meager. A large scrap
book filled with clippings and a large letter file
form the greater part of the "Weaver Papers"
preserved by his family. Evidently General
Weaver gave little thought to the *past*. By
nature and temperament an optimist, he looked
forward to the very end of his life. Frequently urged to record his reminiscences in his
later years, he did nothing more than to put
together some "Memoranda" in regard to his
life down to the outbreak of the Civil War.
For his services in Congress, the *Congressional
Record* furnishes ample material, since he was
an active participant in debates and from time
to time made extended speeches in which he
developed fully his policies and measures. His
one book, *A Call to Action,* published during
the campaign of 1892, contains the nearest approach to a systematic presentation of his
views. A careful examination of this volume
will impress the reader with the number of
instances in which General Weaver anticipated

later programs and policies in our political life.

The writer is under special obligations to General Weaver's eldest son, James B. Weaver, Jr., for the generous way in which he has given access to all material in his possession. Likewise the writer is under obligation to the editor of the series, Dr. Benj. F. Shambaugh, for his careful editing and for his advice and encouragement during the preparation of the book. Acknowledgments are also due to Mr. Edgar R. Harlan, Curator of the Historical Department of Iowa, for assistance in the use of newspapers at Des Moines. Dr. Dan E. Clark offered many valuable suggestions; while Miss Helen Otto assisted in the verification of the manuscript, and Miss Ruth A. Gallaher compiled the index.

FRED E. HAYNES

THE STATE HISTORICAL SOCIETY OF IOWA
IOWA CITY IOWA

CONTENTS

PLATES

I

EARLY LIFE AND EDUCATION

1833–1856

THE family of James Baird Weaver was Scotch on his mother's side and German and English in the paternal line. His father's ancestors emigrated to England many generations ago, and thence came to America, settling in the State of New York. Some of the family fought in the Revolutionary War, while others gained distinction in the towns where they lived.[1]

Henry Weaver, the grandfather, was born on April 15, 1761; and on May 1, 1790, he married Susan Ross Crane, granddaughter of Betsy Ross and daughter of a captain in the Revolutionary Army who lived in Elizabethtown, New Jersey. Of this union there were fourteen children. It is through Susan Ross Crane, the paternal grandmother, that the family traces its relationship to Betsy Ross, who made the first American flag at the request of George Washington.[2] Removing from New York to Ohio long before the Indians left that region, Henry Weaver became a leader in the new western community. He fought against the Indians, and at one time commanded a fort which stood upon what is now Main Street in Cincinnati. He served also in the War of 1812, and acted as judge in one of the early courts of Ohio.

It was in the Ohio home that Abram Weaver, father of James Baird Weaver, was born and reared.[3] He married Susan Imlay, daughter of Captain Joseph Imlay who had served with distinction in the Continental Army. James, who was the fifth child among the thirteen children of this union, was born at Dayton, Ohio, June 12, 1833. The father was a skilled mechanic and millwright as well as a farmer. In 1835 the family removed from Dayton to Cass County, Michigan, and settled on a farm in the forest nine miles north of Cassopolis. Here they remained until the summer of 1842, when the farm was sold and the family migrated to the Territory of Iowa.

From the Weaver *Memoranda* it appears that the family reached Keosauqua in October. They "wintered in an unfinished frame house on the farm of James Purdam, situated opposite Ely's Ford on the east side of the Des Moines river, one mile west of the town."[4] According to the treaty with the Sac and Fox Indians "white settlers were not permitted west of Van Buren county prior to May 1st, 1843. The boundary between what was then called the old Black Hawk and the new purchase from the Indians was in part the west line of Van Buren, and Davis county lying immediately west was in the new purchase . . . . But homeseekers under the guise of hunters — my father among them — penetrated the wilds of the west and northwest and selected locations which they intended to and did settle upon as soon as they could lawfully reach them after the clock struck twelve on the night of April 30, 1843.

"About 3 P. M. May 1st", reads the *Memoranda,* Abram Weaver "with his entire family and household goods comfortably packed in a wagon drawn by two good horses, with chicken coop fastened to the rear of the wagon, cow tied behind, trusty rifle and watch dog, halted on a quarter section of virgin soil on Chequest Creek four miles north of where Bloomfield, the county seat of Davis county now stands. The place is now known as the William Dodd farm near the village of Belknap. The county capital, however, was not designated until about one year after this settlement was made", Abram Weaver "being one of the commissioners who located the site. On the 12th day of June following the writer [James Baird Weaver] reached the tenth year of his age.[19]

The first shelter in the new home, continues the Weaver narrative, "was a bark shanty on the bank of the creek. The first house was a large log dwelling built of green timber cut and

hewn from trees taken from an extensive
timber plat on the south part of father's claim.
The roof was made of clapboards riven by
father with an old-fashioned adz. The floor
was made of split logs smoothly hewn and
brought to a straight edge with the adz — a
real puncheon floor as it was called, substantial and strong. The doors and windows
were hung on wooden hinges, all made and
fashioned by father's dexterous hands; so the
family was comfortably housed and prepared
for the winter of 1843–1844.

"In the meantime ground had been broken
and a crop of seed corn, potatoes and other
vegetables had been grown and stored up . .
. . Mother's loom and father's handicraft
had been busy preparing for the approaching
winter, so by early fall all was ready for any
stress of weather that might come. Deer,
wolves, wild pigeons, prairie chickens and wild
turkeys abounded . . . . Sacs and Foxes
and Pottawattamie Indian camps near by were
all very friendly and readily exchanged courte-
sies with settlers. The Indians visited our
home more or less every day until the spring of
1844 when they had mostly disappeared,
'vamoosing' toward the west. Miles of unculti-
vated prairie intervened between the cabins of
the settlers, so that aside from my six brothers
and sisters Indian boys were my everyday play-

mates until the first log school house some two miles away was erected the second year after locating upon the claim. These brawny 'skin-aways', as their parents called them, were sturdy little chaps, fleet, expert with bow and arrow, could climb like squirrels and skip like fauns.''

School facilities are described as ''meager'' in those early days when competent teachers were very rare. ''The first teacher in our locality was Robert Miller, a man of but little education, but a kind, patient and lovable person who made the old log school house with its homely benches, big wide fireplace and greased paper windows seem like a palace for its twenty odd girls and boys gathered daily for instruction under its clapboard roof. That white oak ridge where the homely school house stood is sacred still in my memory. The elementary spelling book which I carried to and from this, my Alma Mater, was obtained at Bloomfield from John A. Lucas, the pioneer merchant, in exchange for a coon skin which I carried to him. That blessed old school book opened first to me the door that leads to the republic of letters. If it could possibly now be found I would treasure it and hand it down to my children. The Friday afternoons we all stood and spelled down were great days and stimulated the youthful ambition to blood heat.

"A lonely Indian trail near our cabin led close by the school house, and it was no uncommon thing as we were going and coming to see wolves both of the large and small variety trot across the trail. This had the effect of stimulating our activity and reducing loitering to a minimum. Wild dogs were almost as numerous in those days as domestic canines are now, with this advantage in favor of the wolves, that they were self-supporting. The fear which they inspired among the children rounded us up like young calves and met with unanimous approval among the teachers in those halcyon days. Neither red haws, ripe plums, hickory, hazel nor walnuts could tempt the children to loiter by the wayside. Punctuality was a virtue with us all. The wolf should have due credit for his contribution to pioneer scholarship.

"We spent five years on the farm. Mother wove on the old loom the jeans and other cloth necessary for family wear and then cut and made our clothes. Each fall father bought sides of upper and sole leather and from these made our boots and shoes. The girls' shoes were made of finer quality of calf skin. All stockings and mittens were manufactured at home from yarn spun on the large and small spinning wheels . . . . Before the open cheerful fireplace there was merry chatter, song, and a thrilling touch of music, father leading with his dear old flute. They were happy days with the children all at home. Everything was natural, and modern conventionalities wholly unknown. Deep snows were a challenge to fun, coon hunting a luxury, shooting wild turkeys and prairie chickens and netting quail almost a daily occurrence. Every necessity of life seemed to be piled right up at our door. The south side of our cabin was always covered in the winter time with coon skins, wolf and deer hides, tacked up to dry. They were regarded as legal tender at the store. Those were charming days when we were all close to Nature's throbbing heart. True, we were forty-five miles from grist mill, and frequently without either meal or flour. But we ground 'grits' on our old coffee mill and fared sumptuously every day.

"When the pioneer preacher came around, as he frequently did, he was always a jolly fellow and after father and mother called the children all in we had enough to make a fair sized congregation, and how those early saddle-bag preachers could sing! With good cheer they hunted up the remote settlers, through rain and sunshine they reminded us of God and duty and invited us all to the big meeting which was always soon to occur at some pioneer home. All formality was discarded at those religious

gatherings. They sang and prayed with
unction. Amen and Hallelujah resounded as a
matter of course.

"After crops were laid by in summer,
through the fall and winter father worked at
his trade, built houses, made furniture, cut
hoop poles, made staves and fashioned them
into barrels, and busied himself with an almost
endless variety of handicraft for which he was
noted throughout the widely scattered neighborhood.

"Finally he was elected Clerk of the District
Court for our county and then we moved into
town. Here our school opportunities were
somewhat improved as they extended over
longer periods of time, and a higher class of
teachers were secured. Our home life was
more varied as we met our neighbors with
greater frequency — a priceless boon in pioneer life. It was a real joy in those days to
meet our neighbors. Hospitality was at high
tide, while only a trace of selfishness could
occasionally be found to mar the generous flow
of good neighborship.

"Soon after moving into town father secured
from the government a contract to carry on
horseback a bi-weekly mail from Bloomfield to
Fairfield, and I was detailed for the job. I
entered upon the work and served for three
years winter and summer. I was forced to

leave school and so pursued my studies as best I could at nights at home. Finally father threw up his contract and then I re-entered the old log school house. My experience as mail carrier was interesting and frequently thrilling, being compelled often times to swim swollen streams, including the Des Moines River and Big Cedar Creek, many times every year, and to engage in battles royal with neighbor boys who gathered along the trail to fret and annoy if possible the lad who rode astride the government saddle-bags. But fair play was always the motto on both sides and that was the only condition required. It was not long until the boys were all my friends and some of them still live to manifest their generous feeling. Caleb Baldwin, afterward Chief Justice of Iowa, and long since passed away, was post-master at Fairfield during this period, and at the same time pursuing the study of law. I frequently rode up to the post-office door and threw the mail bag into his hands. He was a young man of enormous size, weighing three hundred pounds, active and powerful, and completely filled the door as he appeared to receive the bags. . . .

"It is my recollection that I began carrying the mail in the early fall of 1847 and quit in 1851.[5] The Mexican war had occurred while we were on the farm and was over before I became

knight of the saddle-bags, and the old soldiers
had returned, and some of them were domiciled
among us. I took up my elementary studies in
the local school; but news of the discovery of
gold at Sutter's Mill in California in 1848
quickly crossed the continent and became
known to the world. This thrilled and intensely
excited all classes of people, and all the older
pioneers, including myself, caught the fever.
But my parents repressed its rage to the utmost
of their power, and notwithstanding a brother-
in-law, Dr. C. W. Phelps, pulled out for the
Eldorado in the spring of 1849, I was not permitted to accompany him, but continued to
carry the mail until the latter part of 1851.
After quitting the road I attended three terms
of school. In addition, I had begun to study
law under occasional instructors in the office of
Hon. S. G. McAchran, a practicing lawyer at
Bloomfield, during the summer and winter of
1852–1853.

"I was now about nineteen years of age,
strong, and with the rugged experience of the
pioneer lad felt that I was equal to any emergency. Meantime my brother-in-law, Dr.
Phelps, had reached home returning by sea via
New York with a snug quantity of gold, and
was preparing for another trip overland with a
herd of cattle, and would need my help. Fifty
head of steers were secured, all tamed to the

yoke, and I engaged to accompany him as an all round hand and helper.''

Late in March, 1853, the start for California was made by a company of four persons: Dr. Phelps, young Weaver, and two others referred to as ''Mike'' and ''Jack''. The leader of the expedition was Dr. Phelps who had crossed the plains in 1849. His experience with horses on that trip had determined him to change to oxen on this second journey: fifty-two were taken, of which eight worked at a time.

On account of road conditions and swollen streams the party did not reach the Missouri River until about the middle of April. After two days of rest they crossed this river and bade adieu to white settlements. To the youthful traveler the first noticeable feature was the vastness of the country as compared with the narrow limits of his boyhood home. For a fortnight the journey was ''commonplace and monotonous, relieved only by the occasional killing of an antelope for food, or the shooting of a wolf.'' The weather was soft and pleasant for many weeks, except for a sudden sandstorm which surprised the party one morning about ten o'clock and lasted two hours and forty minutes. They survived the ordeal without loss or injury.

While near the Green River country in Utah they experienced some alarm because of the behavior of the Indians, whom they had expected would be friendly and peaceable. Fortunately, however, nothing happened in this region more thrilling than the shooting of a huge cougar by Dr. Phelps. This episode aroused in the party a desire to hunt big game, and so they decided to spend a day or two hunting the grizzly and the lion in the Humboldt Mountains in Nevada near which they would pass. One day's experience, during which they saw two large cinnamon bears and a cougar, satisfied them that a "party consisting of but four men, indifferently armed and inexperienced . . . . were risking life in a hazardous pastime." After crossing the desert and the Sierra Nevada Mountains they arrived at Sacramento on August 15th; and here they went into camp.

"After resting briefly and satisfying our curiosity", wrote Weaver in *The World Review,* "Mike and Jack secured employment and the little party was reduced to the Doctor and myself. Before leaving home, I had resolved to enter the legal profession, and after a brief mining adventure, the desire for gold and the rough life which makes its finding possible, was entirely dissipated, and I was seized with an intense desire to return and take up my studies. The Doctor . . . . was anxious to join me in the return by sea in October. The cattle were readily disposed of at good figures. We then repaired to San Francisco and spent a fortnight exploring the city, hunting up old friends, and informing ourselves concerning the safest and best manned vessel upon which we could embark for New York via Panama. The 'John L. Stevens', a powerful clipper built boat, beautiful to look upon and advertised to clear October 2, was selected and tickets secured. Another ship . . . . was booked to leave the same day and hour, but the 'Stevens' was preferred because of her speed, which resulted from her clipper spread of sails supplementing her steam; and for the further reason that Captain Pierson had commanded her for about five years in the passenger service on that coast."

Except for a severe storm at sea and an experience with brigands in crossing the Isthmus, nothing of moment happened in the course of the journey to New York. The Doctor and his companion each had "belted" about them "about twenty-five hundred dollars in what were then known as fifty-dollar octagon gold slugs." The Panama Railroad was then in operation for a distance of only twelve miles from the Atlantic.[6]

In the year following his return to Iowa young Weaver became clerk for Edward Manning at Bonaparte, Iowa. His employer, who later became one of the richest men in the State, took a fancy to him, and when he indicated his intention of leaving, Mr. Manning offered him increased pay and an interest in the business. Weaver, however, declined to accept the offer, having decided to earn his living by means other than those of manual labor. Ability to speak in public and a taste for discussion and controversy turned him towards the study of law. At the same time the experiences of his early life, coupled with a deep respect for his father, who was both farmer and mechanic, formed an abiding influence in the life of James Baird Weaver: it gave to him an interest in and sympathy with both farmers and artisans that had much to do with the shaping of his career.[7]

In the autumn of 1855 Weaver entered the Cincinnati Law School from which he graduated the following year. His favorite instructor was the professor of legal rights, Bellamy Storer, for whom later he named his first son James Bellamy. The examination preparatory to the receipt of his diploma was conducted by a committee of five; and the certificate, which bears the date of April 14, 1856, was signed among others by Rutherford B. Hayes, who afterwards became President of the United States. While at the law school Weaver's expenses were not high. One hundred dollars, which he borrowed from a friend who charged him thirty-three and one-third percent interest, met the bulk of his expenditures. Such experiences as this one may have had an influence in forming his opinions in regard to capital and the issue of money — opinions which later led him to break away from the Republican party and become an independent party leader.[8]

II

BEGINNINGS IN LAW AND POLITICS

1856–1861

IMMEDIATELY after his graduation at Cincinnati young Weaver returned to Bloomfield and entered into the practice of the law, taking the oath as an attorney-at-law before Judge H. B. Hendershott. Two years later he was admitted to practice in the United States District Court of Iowa at Burlington, the oath being administered by James M. Love.[9] Before he had fairly established himself in the practice of his chosen profession the Civil War broke out; and after 1878 he either held public office or was engaged actively in politics. People who remember his early appearances in court declare he was an able advocate.

At the time when his career was to receive its initial direction the country was agitated by discussions and conflicts over the slavery question. The repeal of the Missouri Compromise by the Kansas-Nebraska Act of 1854 roused the opposition of all those who were hostile to the extension of slave territory and gave to the anti-slavery movement an impetus and support it had never before had. Iowa, bordering as it

16

did upon the territory involved, was vitally interested in the conflicts that followed. Moreover, Iowa had been "a steadfast Democratic State. It had voted for two presidential candidates, Cass and Pierce. In . . . . Congress it had two Democratic senators, one Democratic and one Whig representative. Both of the senators and the Democratic representative voted for the Kansas-Nebraska Bill; the Whig representative did not vote."[10]

The southern half of the State was strongly pro-slavery, while the northern portion had been settled from the regions in the East that were opposed to slavery extension. It was in Iowa that the first election after the enactment of the Kansas-Nebraska Bill was to be held. James W. Grimes who had been nominated for Governor by the Whigs was endorsed by a Free Soil convention. He conducted an aggressive campaign during which he visited nearly every part of the State, driving from county to county in his own conveyance. His election in August by 23,325 votes over his Democratic opponent, who received 21,202 votes, marked the end of Democratic supremacy for thirty-five years. Another result of this election was the choice of an avowed anti-slavery man to the United States Senate. Frémont carried the State in 1856; and two years later Grimes was sent to the Senate.[11]

3

Beginning his active career under such conditions Weaver very naturally became involved in the slavery agitation. His interest was first aroused by a series of debates with George W. McCrary on the Kansas-Nebraska Bill in the country school houses of Van Buren County during the winter of 1853–1854. The discovery, made at this time, that he had a gift for public speaking determined him to study law. Undoubtedly the debates with McCrary, which gave him an opportunity to test his ability, were of great importance in shaping his career.

His own account of these debates described "the eventful period" of his life as beginning with them. He was clerking for Manning at Bonaparte, while McCrary was teaching school in the same town. Weaver, who was then a Democrat, was drawn into a public debate by McCrary who had already become opposed to slavery. Before an audience composed largely of Democrats Weaver "portrayed the danger to the union if slavery was interfered with." He forced his opponent "into a position in which he declared that if it was necessary to preserve slavery to preserve the union, then let the union go. I had him then and the debate was decided for me.".

It was not long after this that Weaver was converted to the Free Soil idea by reading the *New York Tribune* and *Uncle Tom's Cabin*.

"At that time, 1856, there were but six known
Free Soilers in Davis County", writes Weaver
in his *Memoranda.* "Being thoroughly impressed that human slavery was wrong and
wholly bad, and convinced that the Democratic
party was hopelessly committed to the institution, and pledged to perpetuate and extend
it, after consultation with my parents, I openly
left my party in 1857 and announced myself as
a Free Soiler . . . . Of course this called
down upon my youthful head the wrath of every
other Democrat in the locality, but being com-
bative and having anticipated the inevitable
result I did not flinch, but prepared to defend
myself against all assailants.

"The clouds were thickening, events multi-
plying and it became evident to close observers
that the storm would soon break with the force
of an avalanche over the whole country. Re-
cruits began to come into our ranks and soon
we became aggressive and assailed the defenders of slavery in the school houses in every part
of the county."[12]

In the course of this activity, Weaver "went
into Van Buren County and stumped for Mr.
McCrary, who was running for 'floating representative', at the request of H. Clay Caldwell,
afterward judge of the United States Circuit
Court. My speech was at Keosauqua, in the
old court house there. Caldwell was so tickled

over the speech that he kicked a solid walnut table to pieces.''[13]

Once embarked upon a political career in such stirring times, Weaver threw himself heartily into the struggle. His own account of these years in Iowa, as recorded in his *Memoranda,* shows his characteristic enthusiasm and optimism. ''The election of James W. Grimes as Governor in 1854 completely unified the Whigs and Free Soilers . . . . imparted to the new and compact force an aggressive spirit, and made certain the election of Gov. Grimes to the United States Senate in 1858. This promotion of our stout hearted leader electrified his supporters and cleared the way for the great contest for Governor in 1859.

''The Democracy determined to reclaim the ground lost in the Grimes campaign, understood fully the importance of selecting their strongest man, and accordingly placed in nomination Hon. A. C. Dodge who had served in the Senate of the United States acceptably and a gentleman of the highest integrity, possessing no mean military experience on the frontier, and held in the highest esteem throughout the state. In addition to this he was at the time of his nomination our Minister at the Spanish Court.

''The Republicans — this was the name under which the new force was now acting — nominated the Hon. Samuel J. Kirkwood, formerly a Democrat who possessed exceptional skill as a campaigner, and immediately the struggle waxed hot and became fierce. These antagonists were both in their prime and each had seen enough of public life to sharpen their weapons of offense and defense and to give poise in the stress of battle. Kirkwood in those days was like a skilled swordsman, adroit, cool, knew his ground and always aggressive. Dodge was stately, military in bearing, a stickler for the old regimen. He invoked the constitution as interpreted in the Dred Scott decision and plead for the binding character and inviolability of the Fugitive Slave Law. He plead for the Union and predicted dire disaster if the decision and the law were ever repealed. But Kirkwood was the better debater, more impassioned and was abreast with the anti-slavery tide; while Dodge caught by the receding waters of the old feudality which he failed to see could never again flow back, was carried out and engulfed in inevitable defeat. The world was changing and searching out a new orbit.

"The campaign included a series of joint debates between these candidates, and the people came in multitudes to hear. A part of the discussion related to the Fugitive Slave Law. I was present at the Bloomfield encounter and it was a titanic struggle. Kirkwood drew a picture of a slave mother with a babe in her arms fleeing from bondage with her eye on the North Star. In close pursuit was her cruel master with his bloodhounds hard after her, just as she crossed the Iowa line from Missouri. Clenching his fists and advancing toward Dodge he demanded to know if he under such circumstances would turn that fleeing mother and her infant back to her pursuing master. Before the breathless multitude Kirkwood shouted at the top of his voice 'Answer my question!' Dodge replied, 'I would obey the law.' Kirkwood retorted, 'So help me, God, I would suffer my right arm to be torn from its socket before I would do such a monstrous thing!' The crowd broke into a frenzy that resembled the sweep of a cyclone through a forest. Men grew pale and clenched each other in frenzy. The whole audience and everybody were carried off their feet. The moral sense of the multitude had been reached and it was vain to attempt to reverse the deep impression which had been made.

"However, so evenly balanced were the opposing forces in the field that the official returns only gave Kirkwood a fraction of above 3,000 majority in the state over his sturdy antagonist, which demonstrated conclusively that it was skill in debate and presenting the claims of freedom that insured victory in that historic struggle. We were passing through the pangs of a new birth, and for a while it was hard to tell the result. But while the margin was small, it was sufficient to place our young commonwealth permanently in the anti-slavery column and to prepare her people for the historic uprising of 1860, and the deluge just beyond."[14]

Weaver's actual part in the stirring events of the years during which the Republican party was taking shape and while the stage was preparing for the Civil War could not have been a large one since he was only twenty-eight in 1861. One may imagine, however, that he was more than an interested spectator, and that his personal experiences and observations during these years of party change and conflicts left impressions that largely explain his belief in the possibility of the reorganization of parties to serve the interests of the masses of the people.

His active participation in affairs led to his selection as a delegate from Davis County to the Republican State Convention held at Des Moines in January, 1860, to name delegates to the national nominating convention.[15] With Fitz Henry Warren, Jacob Rich, Governor Samuel J. Kirkwood, James B. Howell, James Thorington, Hiram Price, Judge John F. Dillon, Amos N. Currier, and F. W. Palmer he is mentioned as among those who in May, 1860, com-

prised "Iowa's volunteer attendance" at the
Chicago Convention which nominated Lincoln
for the Presidency.[16]   In addition he is named
in a list of fifty-eight "leaders earnestly supporting Kirkwood" in 1859.[17]   He is referred
to as making speeches in the campaigns of 1856
and 1860, and as "fascinated" by the doctrines
of Frémont to which "he gave himself up . .
. . with all the ardor of his mature years."[18]

   To Weaver probably belongs the credit of
being one of the originators of the expression
"the bloody shirt".   His own story of the
origin of the use of the phrase was that a
"preacher by the name of McKinney, a most
pugnacious and forceful man, moved from
Davis county to Texas. He was one of these
fellows who would preach every Sunday if he
had to be the audience himself. Down in Texas
one Sunday he got the negroes together at Ft.
Worth and preached to them. Word was
passed around that an abolitionist was exciting
the negroes to insurrection and the citizens got
together. They took McKinney out and
whipped him with a rawhide blacksnake whip,
cutting his shirt into shreds and lacerating his
body. He returned to Davis county in about
'55 or '56, and an abolitionist meeting was held
and I presided. McKinney had his shirt with
him. A few days later I was at Agency City.
Senator Grimes, James F. Wilson, Edward

Stiles and myself were speakers. I recounted the outrages on McKinney and had the shirt with me. I waved it before the crowds and bellowed: 'Under this bloody shirt we propose to march to victory'. I was a very young man in those days." The effect of such a statement upon an audience gathered together in southern Iowa during those years requires no elaboration. For nearly twenty years after the Civil War "the bloody shirt" was regularly waved in each campaign, and it rarely failed to gain votes for the Republicans.[19]

It was during these years of preparation for his work in life that Weaver married Miss Clara Vinson, a native of St. Mary's, Ohio, who had been teaching school at Keosauqua and whom he met while he was clerking at Bonaparte. Courtship in those pioneer days meant the fording of streams and tramping through the woods. On one occasion young Weaver undertook to make the trip from Bloomfield to Keosauqua; and when he got to Pittsburg he found the Des Moines River "a seething torrent, the ice was breaking up and the river was full of huge cakes, grinding and rocking and almost prohibiting passage. I . . . . got a long pole. With the aid of this, I jumped from one cake to another until I reached the opposite shore." They were married on July 13, 1858, at Keosauqua by Rev. Miltiades Miller.[20]

III

MILITARY RECORD

1861–1865

As soon as the call for volunteers was issued by President Lincoln in April, 1861, a company of volunteers was formed at Bloomfield; and of this company James Baker, who had served in the Mexican War, and James B. Weaver were elected captain and first lieutenant. It was the hope of these volunteers that they would be included in the First Iowa Regiment. Immediately upon the organization of the company, Baker and Weaver left for Burlington in search of Governor Kirkwood to tender to him the services of the new company. At Burlington as they went on board the boat they met the Governor coming off. They retired into the cabin, where commissions were issued to Weaver and others.

The Weaver commission bears the date of April 23, 1861, the name of the company and of the regiment being left blank. The First Regiment being full before the offer was made, the Bloomfield company became Company G of the Second Iowa Infantry. To Weaver a later

commission was issued, under date of May 28,
1861, in which the company and regiment were
given their proper designation.[21]

"Bloomfield was then thirty-five miles from
a railroad, and the patriotic farmers of the
neighborhood brought in their teams and
hauled the embryo warriors to the nearest
station — Keosauqua."[22] The rendezvous for
the troops from southern Iowa was Keokuk;
and as soon as enough companies had arrived
to form a regiment, the Second Iowa Infantry
was organized and mustered into the service of
the United States. "It was the first regiment
of three years' men . . . . sent into the
field, and the first of all to leave Iowa for the
theatre of war."[23]

It left Keokuk on June 13th with instructions
"to take military control of the lines of the
Hannibal and St. Joseph and North Missouri
Railroads." Colonel Samuel R. Curtis stated
in his official report "that he received the order
at one o'clock a. m. and that at five o'clock
a. m." the regiment was on board the steamer.
Landing at Hannibal, Missouri, on the same
day, Colonel Curtis "proceeded to take military possession of the railroads indicated,
using for that purpose . . . . a force of
about 2,700", including his own regiment. "As
he advanced, small forces of the enemy were
encountered and quickly overcome; flags, muni-

tions of war, prisoners and supplies were captured, and loyal and peaceable citizens assured
protection. Leaving detachments to guard the
bridges, buildings and other railroad property
from destruction, he pressed forward'', and
arrived at St. Joseph on June 15, 1861.

In fifty-six hours from the time orders were
received at Keokuk, military possession of the
railroad had been taken and the Confederate
forces that were mustering through that part
of the State were scattered and disorganized.
''The promptness with which the order was
obeyed alone saved this important line of railroad for the transportation of Union troops
and supplies, and prevented a more prolonged
resistance by the Confederate forces in that
portion of the State of Missouri. Colonel
Curtis was promptly promoted to the rank of
Brigadier General and later was given the rank
of Major General.''[24]

The principal points from which the Second
Iowa Regiment operated during the summer
and autumn of 1861 were Bird's Point, Ironton,
Pilot Knob, and Jackson in Missouri, and Fort
Jefferson in Kentucky. Its duties were of the
same character as those which it performed so
well in its first action. ''The fact of principal
interest, however, connected with this part of
the regiment's history, was its unhealthfulness.
When the command returned to St. Louis, in

the latter part of October, there were only about four hundred men fit for duty. The sick list was large in every company."[25]

Remaining in St. Louis during the winter, the regiment was assigned to guard duty at "McDowell College", an institution which was used "as a sort of prison" for persons suspected of secession sympathies. Some of the specimens in the museum having disappeared, the regiment was held responsible. By general order the command was publicly disgraced, and when it embarked for Fort Donelson on February 10, 1862, it did so "without music and with its colors furled." This disgrace, whether deserved or not, was soon wiped out by the bravery manifested at Fort Donelson, where the Second Iowa led the famous charge.[26]

During the year 1861 the war had not been vigorously or skilfully conducted, and consequently the Union arms had suffered during the campaigns. But the successes in the West in 1862 more than reversed the disasters of 1861. The first in importance of these victories was the capture of Fort Donelson on the Cumberland River in Tennessee, which opened the way for the passage of the Union armies up the Cumberland and Tennessee rivers. General Grant, who had just captured Fort Henry on the Tennessee River only twelve miles away, had twenty-seven thousand men, while the garrison of Fort Donelson numbered twenty-one thousand. "The Federal superiority in numbers was more than balanced by the Confederate superiority of position: the fort itself stood on a bluff one hundred feet above the river, dominating also the country to the rear, while well-planned intrenchments occupied the ridges, all approaches blocked with abatis. . .

"Operations against Donelson began with a poor outlook for the Federals. The weather, so mild at first as to lead many of the inexperienced troops to throw away their coats and blankets, became cold and stormy. For a day or two Grant's force was distinctly inferior, and might have been attacked to advantage by an enterprising foe. But his front was bold, and his reinforcements arrived in time." In addition the three Confederate Generals — Floyd, Pillow, and Buckner — were not in harmony, and no aggressive attack was made by them at a time when it would have been most effective.[27]

The Second Iowa Regiment was transported by water from St. Louis to Fort Donelson where it arrived on the 14th of February. Heavy skirmishing had occurred on the 13th, but the first determined attack was not made till the next day by the gunboats under Foote. Meanwhile the army proceeded with the investment, which on the evening of the 14th was practically complete. It was early on the 15th that Pillow attacked the Union right held by General John A. McClernand, and after a furious battle of four hours the Union troops were forced to retire; reënforcements and a new supply of ammunition enabled them to reoccupy their old position and recapture the guns lost in the morning.

Meanwhile General C. F. Smith held the Union left. General Grant ordered him to assault the fort in order to retrieve the situation resulting from McClernand's retirement. He selected as "the storming party" the brigade commanded by Colonel J. G. Lauman of the Seventh Iowa, which was composed of the Second Iowa, the Seventh Iowa, and the Fourteenth Iowa, a regiment of "western sharpshooters", and the Twenty-fifth and Fifty-second Indiana regiments. Colonel J. M. Tuttle with the left wing of the Second Iowa led the advance, and his official report describes the part played by that regiment in the famous charge by which victory was won for the Federal arms.

According to this account the Second Iowa on its arrival had been assigned a position on the extreme left where it spent "a cold and disagreeable night, without tents or blankets." It remained in this position until 2 P. M. of the next day (February 15th) when it received the order "to storm the fortifications of the enemy in front." It proceeded "steadily up the hill . . . . without firing a gun. On reaching the works, we found the enemy flying before us, except a few who were promptly put to the bayonet. I then gave the order to fire which was responded to with fatal precision until the right wing with Lieutenant Colonel Baker arrived, headed by General Smith, when we formed in line of battle again under a galling fire and charged on the encampment across the ravine in front, the enemy still retreating before us. After we had reached the summit of the hill beyond the ravine, we made a stand and occupied it for over an hour." Soon afterwards Colonel Tuttle retired because of an injury, leaving Lieutenant Colonel Baker "in command until the following morning, when the enemy gave signal for a parley, which was succeeded by the enjoyable intelligence that they had surrendered the fort. We were then ordered by General Smith to take the post of honor, in marching to the fort, where we placed our colors upon the battlements beside the white flag of the enemy".

The work of the Second Iowa brought from Major General H. W. Halleck, department commander in the West with headquarters at St. Louis, a telegram in which he referred to the regiment as "the bravest of the brave. They had the honor of leading the column which entered Fort Donelson."

A committee of the General Assembly of Iowa, then in session, was sent to the battlefield to care for the wounded; and on its return to Des Moines it carried the flag that had been used in the famous charge. The flag was presented to the House to be hung near the Speaker's desk till the close of the session, when it was to be turned over to the State Historical Society for permanent preservation.[28]

Lieutenant Weaver was with the regiment throughout its service from June 13, 1861, to the capture of Fort Donelson. He was on railroad guard duty in Missouri from June to October and in St. Louis from October to February. From October 2nd to 12th he took part in an expedition to Charleston, the nature of which is not specially described.[29] In a letter to Mrs. Weaver, written from Fort Donelson, February 19, 1862, he gives a vivid and detailed account of the part played by the Second Iowa in the assault.

According to Lieutenant Weaver's description the regiment landed four miles below the fort during the night of the 13th, and the next morning "bright and early . . . . started over the hills in fine spirits to the scene of bloody conflict. We were ordered by our General Smith to the extreme left of the grand army [which] encircled this indescribable stronghold of secession. The morning of the

4

15th dawned cold and desolate . . . . Early
. . . . that day the battle began to rage
with great fury on the right wing (though they
had been fighting at intervals for nearly two
days) and lasted until about two o'clock when
Gen'l Smith rode up to our regiment and informed them that he expected the left wing of
our Regiment, including our company, to
charge the breastworks of the enemy about
four hundred yards distant from us in full
view. These works were situated on the brow
of a very steep hill all over which the enemy
had felled in wild confusion, heavy timber
which had grown there. Several other regiments had made the attempt to storm the well
planned works of the enemy before and had
failed with terrible loss. Hence the reason for
sending but half of our regiment. It was
enough to sacrifice.

"Col. Tuttle took charge of our wing and
Col. Baker the right wing which was to come to
our support after we had gained the works.
We were ordered not to fire a gun until we had
driven them from their works at the point of
the bayonet. The command of 'forward march'
was given, and at quick time we moved forward to the terrible slaughter and to a more
wonderful triumph. Presently we came within
short range of the enemy's trenches when they
opened upon us a terrible and deathly cross

fire. All around us and amongst us flew the missiles of death and all around and on every side of me men were falling in the agonies of death . . . . But on, on we went without firing a gun or saying a word except those of cheer to our men until we gained the works and then with an awful yell we leaped into the midst of the enemy and here our revenge began. And such a holocaust to the demon of battles! Everywhere could be seen the enemy falling in death while ever and anon some one of our own boys would lay down and give up the ghost. On we went until we gained the second hill. Our right wing was now with us and we were fighting with desperation, but our ammunition was about exhausted and we were compelled to fall back to the entrenchment we had just taken. We came back very slowly and silently. But the enemy had got enough of us and did not pursue. When we got there we found the 7th and 14th Iowa, the 25th and 52d Indiana Regiments occupying the earthworks and eager for the enemy to come upon them. Here we were ordered by Gen'l Smith to form our Regiment outside of the breastworks and to lay under their cover all night ready to fight if attacked and 'in the morning', said he, 'we will advance and drive them from the next tier of works or lose every man in my division'.

"We formed over near those who remained

and there we lay without shelter or fire until daylight. During the time we looked around for our dead and wounded . . . . About daylight we were supplied with ammunition and it was expected that we were going to move forward. But the enemy, thank God, began to 'sound the bugle for the parley', and presently we saw moving everywhere white flags. It was Sabbath morning and we supposed they wanted to bury their dead. But no, it was unconditional surrender. And then such a shouting! Our flag was moved from the breastworks, and in a few minutes our regiment was informed that the General desired to give the 2nd Iowa the distinguished honor of moving into the fort first and of planting our flag upon the ramparts of their citadel. Here I wept like a child. We marched in and such a sight! 25,000 prisoners were there formed to receive us. Voltaire Twombly, our flag bearer, unfurled our banner on the walls. But I shall have to stop. I was struck on my right arm but it did not hurt me. My cap was shot through and my head grazed but through the providence of God I was saved. Thank God! Let us ever worship Him.''[30]

An interesting letter from John A. Duckworth, then second sergeant in Company G, to the editor of the ''home paper'' at Bloomfield gives an account of the same events. It refers to Lieutenant Weaver during the assault as passing "quickly from right to left, reminding us of our duty, and charging us to 'keep cool' ". Of incidents it mentions Colonel Baker and Lieutenant Weaver as each receiving a ball through their caps.[31] Colonel Tuttle, in his official report, refers to Weaver and eight other lieutenants by name as deporting "themselves nobly throughout the engagement."[32]

"Of the six hundred and thirty officers and men who formed the storming party, being all of the regiment fit for duty at the time", thirty-three were killed and one hundred and sixty-four were wounded. The losses of the Second Iowa were higher by more than one hundred percent than those of the regiment standing next in number of casualties, the Twenty-fifth Indiana. From Company G the losses were six killed and twenty-two wounded.[33]

General Grant believed that in the confusion following the fall of Fort Donelson a good leader, well supported by the united Union forces in the West "could have marched to Chattanooga, Corinth, Memphis, and Vicksburg". The Union armies, however, were not united, and General Halleck seems to have been suspicious and jealous of Grant, with the result that the victory was not immediately followed up. After a costly delay, which had given the Confederates time to rally from the confusion that followed the unexpected defeat, the Union troops moved up the Tennessee to attack "the strategic points on the Mississippi and Alabama frontiers". At the end of March it appears that Grant had about 33,000 men "at and near Pittsburg Landing", while twenty miles distant Johnston and Beauregard occupied Corinth with 40,000 troops. Buell with about 30,000 was marching to join Grant. Would the Confederate General attack before the two Union armies united?[34]

The Second Iowa remained nearly a month in the vicinity of Fort Donelson, and then embarked for Pittsburg Landing where it arrived on the 19th of March. The men encamped about one mile from the landing and remained there in quiet till Sunday morning, April 6th, when it took part in the Battle of Shiloh which lasted during that day and the next.[35]

This battle was the result of an attempt on the part of the Confederate generals to redeem the losses due to the fall of Donelson. Believing that no offensive would be taken by his opponents so soon after their defeat, Grant neglected defensive measures and thus exposed himself to attack. The Confederate army left Corinth on April 3rd, but stormy weather and bad roads caused the delay of the attack planned for April 5th to the next day. During the afternoon of the same day the advance

guard of Buell's army arrived in the neighborhood, but did not push on to Pittsburg Landing
since Grant did not anticipate a fight at that
point. The result was that the first day's
battle witnessed 40,000 Confederate troops
confronting 33,000 Union troops.

The contest on the first day continued twelve
hours and was a Confederate victory. Nevertheless the outcome was a disappointment since
the plan was to capture the Union army, or at
least to drive it from the field in complete confusion. On the next day the Confederates had
to meet the fresh troops of Buell who had
arrived late on Sunday, April 6th. At two
o'clock, after eight hours of fighting, the Confederate commander gave the order to retire,
and this was accomplished in good order; no
effective pursuit was made by the Union
forces.[36]

It was under the command of Lieutenant
Colonel Baker that the Second Iowa participated in the Battle of Shiloh, since Colonel
Tuttle, having won the rank of Brigadier
General at Donelson, had been placed in command of a brigade composed of the Second,
Seventh, Twelfth, and Fourteenth Iowa Infantry. During the first day's battle it formed
part of the Second Division, commanded by
General W. H. L. Wallace. Beginning early
that day the enemy made repeated attacks for

about six hours. By that time the troops on each side had given way so as to give the enemy an opportunity to turn both flanks, and consequently General Wallace gave orders for the whole brigade to fall back. "The Second and Seventh retired through a severe fire from both flanks, and reformed, while the Twelfth and Fourteenth . . . . delayed by their endeavors to save a battery which had been placed in their rear, were completely surrounded and compelled to surrender."

The two regiments that had escaped capture formed, along with fragments of other regiments, "an important part of the line of last resistance at Shiloh on the 6th of April, and again the regiment occupied a post of honor. On Monday, the 7th, the Second Iowa was placed under the orders of General Nelson [General Wallace was killed April 6th] and made a bayonet charge in a most gallant manner, the enemy giving way before them. It will thus be seen that the regiment well sustained at Shiloh the record it had made at Donelson." The entire loss of the Second Iowa was between seventy and eighty men.[37]

Lieutenant Weaver described the battle in a letter written to his wife on April 9, 1862. In this account he stated that "the enemy under Beauregard, one hundred thousand strong, made a most vigorous attack . . . . Our

force was somewhat surprised but from 6
o'clock A. M. until dark, the battle raged all
along our lines (five miles in length) with the
greatest fury. Buell had not yet reached us.
The enemy greatly outnumbered us and the
slaughter was of the most horrid character and
magnitude on both sides. The enemy had
driven us slowly back during the entire day,
though our men contested every inch of ground
they passed over with a zeal worthy the highest
admiration. Nothing could be heard during the
entire day but a continuous roar of artillery
and musketry. About sun down we succeeded
in checking the enemy's advance and after a
most awful battle between our artillery and that
of the enemy in which we fearfully worsted
them, the battle closed for the day, both armies
lying within gun shot of each other. During
the night Buell's force came up and formed in
our front in a masterly manner all along the
lines. At daylight we made an attack upon the
enemy . . . . Then came on the bitterest
contest ever witnessed on this continent. But
the enemy could not stand. At 4 o'clock P. M.
we had him completely whipped and driven
pell mell in perfect rout. The day is over, thank
God, and the entire rebel army in the West
badly, fearfully, routed and all cut to pieces
and completely demolished. We captured
nearly all their artillery and small arms in

great quantity. The enemy retreated in perfect disorder, throwing away all they had. Report from our headquarters says that Mitchel with about 40,000 men has taken Corinth with about 13,000 prisoners. All is ours. No more fighting in this woods for us of any consequence. Company 'G' had nobody killed. Wounded, Capt. Moore, severely, in both legs, not dangerous . . . . The balance of the company are all safe. Our wounded are getting along well and are not in the least danger. . . .

"We had killed and wounded about 8,000, the enemy about 10,000. The field is covered with dead for miles in length and breadth. I do not pretend to state the precise number of killed or wounded on either side, although the enemy suffered vastly more than our forces. . . .

"Our regiment did not suffer very badly, although they have suffered enough God knows. We had 72 wounded and 7 killed, 5 missing. We had five captains and lieutenants wounded, none killed. The 12th and 14th Iowa were most all taken prisoners the first day and are yet in their hands. . . . Have not got any pay yet. Col. B. is safe . . . . On the battlefield just before our regiment became engaged I took out the little testament you gave me and read a psalm. It did me good.''[38]

After the battle of Shiloh it appears that

General Halleck assumed personal command of the main army at Pittsburg Landing and began "with pick and spade" a slow advance upon Corinth. Beauregard with greatly inferior forces held him at bay for a long time and finally left "only the shell of his camp." Corinth was occupied by the Union armies on May 30th, and Halleck was called to Washington in July to become general-in-chief, leaving the Western forces in charge of Buell and Grant.

The Federal armies now dominated a vast area, including Kentucky, most of Tennessee, a section of Alabama, and a smaller portion of Mississippi; "but the population was hostile; the lines of communication ran through long, unfriendly distances from Louisville, the faraway base on the Ohio River . . . . The inhabitants showed their hostility by communicating misleading intelligence, by cutting off stragglers and small detachments, by swooping down in guerilla bands even upon heavy columns drawn out in a long march."

In September Grant sent to Buell two divisions to aid in the defeat of the Confederate invasion of Kentucky and Tennessee; "he still had forty-six thousand men in the two armies of the Tennessee and Mississippi, but they were much scattered, guarding posts and communications in a hostile country." There were considerable Confederate forces in and near Vicksburg; and Memphis, "an unfriendly city", must be held "as the base to which transports brought" supplies. The Army of the Mississippi lay at Corinth with 23,000 men under General W. S. Rosecrans. Most of the active work of dealing with the Confederates fell to Rosecrans during this period. On September 19th at Iuka, Alabama, a fight occurred between the Federal forces and a part of the Confederate army. Early in October the combined forces of the enemy attacked Rosecrans at Corinth — the opposing armies being about equal in strength. The fight continued for two days, October 3rd and 4th, when the Confederates were allowed to retire without effective pursuit.[39]

The Second Iowa Infantry remained in camp near Pittsburg Landing till the campaign against Corinth began. Its record during this period was devoid of noteworthy incidents. It joined in the pursuit of the Confederate army after the evacuation of Corinth, which involved several days of hard marching. Afterwards it went into camp near Corinth. The next operation of any importance by the Second Iowa was a march to Iuka; but the men did not take part in the battle there on September 19th. During this period Colonel Tuttle had been made a brigadier-general, Lieutenant Colonel

James Baker had become colonel, and Lieutenant Weaver had been promoted to major, on the eve of the battle of Corinth.[40]

The circumstances under which Lieutenant Weaver received his commission as major were described by him to his son only a week or ten days before his death. He was "in charge of the outside guard on the picket line on the evening of October 2, 1862. While thus engaged Col. Baker . . . . rode up to Lieut. Weaver and said to him, 'Lieutenant, you are placed under arrest.' . . . . he saluted the Colonel, drew his sword and reversing it, handed it to the Colonel, at the same time saying, 'what does this mean?' Col. Baker then drew from his pocket a paper which he handed to Weaver. On being opened it proved to be his commission as Major of the Regiment. Col. Baker then said to Weaver 'I had this done because I know that if anything happens to your superior officers I can depend upon you to take care of the Regiment'." The commission as major was dated July 25, 1862.[41]

From a different angle John M. Duffield, captain of Company G from which Weaver was promoted, gives a more detailed account of the circumstances of his promotion and also of his later appointment as colonel of the regiment. "On the 2nd day of October", writes Duffield, "as well as I remember, the word came to the camp that Lieutenant Weaver had been commissioned Major of the regiment, and that I was ordered to relieve him. He was then in charge of the outside guard, and I was ordered to go and relieve him, and take his place in command of the guard. The next morning when I returned to camp, I saw there was great dissatisfaction among the line officers because of a Lieutenant having been promoted to Major over all of the Captains of the Regiment.

"This feeling seemed to exist until the battle of Corinth which took place on the 3d. day of October. On that day Colonel Baker was mortally wounded, on the 4th day of October Lieutenant [Colonel] Mills was mortally wounded, and the command devolved on Major Weaver who had only two days before that been First Lieutenant, and had never been in command of a regiment, or maneuvered a regiment. Major Weaver seemed to realize the responsibility that rested upon him, and displayed the greatest courage in directing his men, in keeping close to the line of battle, and encouraging his men to advance on the enemy. When we had driven the enemy from the field, a reënforcement of the enemy under Colonel Johnson of the 18th Arkansas advanced on us. Major Weaver rode up and down the line waving his revolver over his head, and calling upon the men to bring the enemy's colors down, and

LIEUTENANT JAMES BAIRD WEAVER

SECOND IOWA INFANTRY

COLONEL JAMES BAIRD WEAVER

SECOND IOWA INFANTRY

every time that he shouted . . . . he fired at
the man carrying the colors with his own revolver. When the sergeant carrying the colors
fell, the enemy fled, and Major Weaver was the
only man I saw in that charge on horseback;
all the other officers had dismounted. Afterwards, when I was asked who that young officer
was that so gallantly rode up and down the line
encouraging his men, I told them it was Major
Weaver who had only two days before been
promoted from the First Lieutenancy from the
company which I commanded in that battle.
The man who asked me the question, then remarked, that that was one of the bravest men
he ever saw.

"Ten days after that battle the line officers
met together to recommend someone for Colonel of the Regiment, and I believe that General
Weaver received the vote of every officer . .
. . for Colonel, and I am satisfied that his
bravery in that battle was what removed the
prejudice that seemed to exist by reason of his
having been promoted over other officers a few
days before."[42]

The official report of the part taken by the
Second Infantry in the battle of Corinth was
made by Major Weaver. According to his
account the regiment went into the engagement
"with three field, two staff, and twenty-one line
officers, and three hundred and twenty men,

making an aggregate of three hundred and forty-six. In the first day's battle near White House, which was most stubbornly contested, the loss of the regiment was very heavy, particularly in officers . . . . an aggregate of forty-two killed, wounded and missing in the first day's engagement . . . . total killed, wounded and missing in both days' engagement, 108. . . .

"Colonel Baker fell mortally wounded on the first day, at the very time his regiment was charging on the retreating enemy with the greatest enthusiasm and fury. He remarked as he was being borne from the field, 'Thank God when I fell my regiment was victoriously charging'. Lieutenant Colonel Mills was wounded in the second day's engagement, while fighting with the most conspicuous courage and coolness . . . . Colonel Baker expired on the morning of the 7th at 11 o'clock and Lieutenant Colonel Mills on the 12th at 7 o'clock . . . . After the fall of Lieutenant Colonel Mills, ... the command devolved upon myself."[43]

Two letters to his wife written by Major Weaver from Corinth and dated October 6th and 12th supplement his official report. In one he writes that he assumed "command in the forenoon of the 2nd day of the fight and took the Regiment triumphantly through". In the

other letter he refers to the death of Colonel
Baker and indulges in some reflections naturally produced by the experiences through which
he had been passing. His deeply religious
nature is clearly displayed in this letter.[44]

After Corinth the Second Iowa, now reduced
in numbers by heavy losses, continued in service in Tennessee, Alabama, and Georgia,
during the fall and winter of 1862 and the spring
and early summer of 1863. For a whole year it
participated in no general engagement, but
formed part of the forces under General G. M.
Dodge, which indirectly assisted General Grant
in his campaign against Vicksburg by "keeping
open communications between Middle and West
Tennessee, in preventing raids, and in many
other ways". In the summer of 1863 the encampment was moved to Lagrange, Tennessee,
and late in October to Pulaski where it went
into winter quarters.[45]

From Pulaski the regiment started upon its
last great campaign, that of Atlanta. It left
Pulaski on April 29, 1864, and on May 9th
began skirmishing with the enemy in Georgia.
From that date till the fall of Atlanta in September it was almost constantly "within the
sound of skirmish or battle". On May 14th
and 15th under the command of Colonel Weaver
it took part in the fighting which accompanied
the crossing of the Oostanaula River near

5

Resaca, Georgia. "The regiment was the first
one thrown across the river after the pontoons
were laid, and . . . . by threatening the
enemy's communications, caused Resaca to be
evacuated." This was the last enterprise in
which Colonel Weaver commanded, as his three
year term of enlistment expired May 28, 1864,
when upon being mustered out he returned to
Bloomfield.[46]

After the fall of Atlanta the regiment joined
in the march to the sea, during which it "had
little fighting, except . . . . when General
Rice crossed the Ogeechee River in face of the
enemy and had a brisk engagement, in which
the Confederates were quickly and handsomely
whipped with considerable loss. The Second
lost two men slain and as many wounded in
this brilliant affair. A fortnight afterwards
the grand army entered Savannah in triumph."
Late in January, 1865, after about a month
spent in the city, the march northward began.
The last battles of the regiment were fought
near Columbia and Lynch's Creek, South Carolina, in February. At the latter place "many
of the men fought in their 'birth-day suits',
having stripped to cross the stream", and en-
countering the enemy's cavalry before com-
pleting the crossing. At Bentonville, the last
of General Sherman's engagements, the regiment was in the reserves.

The Second Infantry marched by Goldsboro, Raleigh, Petersburg, and Richmond to Washington where it took part in the grand review in May, 1865. Remaining in camp near the city till early in June, it then proceeded to Louisville, Kentucky, where it was mustered out of service on July 12th. From Louisville the regiment moved to Davenport "where it was received by the citizens *en masse,* and welcomed back to the State by the Hon. Hiram Price, Representative in Congress. Colonel Howard responded briefly, and the regiment marched to camp for the last time, and was soon finally disbanded."[47]

Colonel Weaver had been mustered out May 27, 1864, at the expiration of his term of enlistment, and honorably discharged from service. Consequently he had no part in the later activities of the Second Iowa around Atlanta and on the march northward. He returned to Bloomfield and entered actively upon the practice of his profession. His military experiences "made a deep impression upon his character. He ever remained a warm defender of those who had taken part in defending the Union and both in public and private life remained loyal to his comrades." He was "brevetted Brigadier General United States Volunteers, March 13, 1865, 'for gallant and meritorious services and conduct on the field of battle'."[48]

Captain A. A. Stuart, in his volume on *Iowa
Colonels and Regiments,* describes Weaver "as
a good and brave officer", and adds that "there
are few who were as cool as he in battle.   At
Shiloh, while the 2d and 7th Iowa were running
that terrible gauntlet, on the afternoon of the
first day's fight, Captain Moore, of company
G, was shot through both legs and disabled.
Lieutenant Weaver stopped, picked him up, and
bore him from the field.   Under the circumstances, not one man in five thousand would
have imitated his example.   He is a member of
the Methodist Church, and is one of the few
officers who abstained from the use of liquor in
the service."[49]

IV

COMMANDER OF THE POST AT PULASKI

As has been stated the Second Iowa Infantry was stationed at Pulaski, Tennessee, from November, 1863, to April, 1864, during which time Colonel Weaver "was assigned to the command of the post at Pulaski by order of Gen. G. M. Dodge, commander of the left wing of the 16th army corps. . . . Gen. Dodge issued an order and made it public, in which he stated that his army was in need of supplies of every kind, and that if the people would bring in supplies, vouchers would be rendered for the same without making any inquiries as to the loyalty or disloyalty of the parties. The people brought in their supplies and vouchers were given, and they were all paid by the assistant commissary general, Cyrus C. Carpenter.

"During my administration as commander of the post", reads the Weaver statement, "a large number of refugees came within our lines. They came from the Confederate army in Alabama and elsewhere. They were totally without supplies and destitute, and at that time they could not be allowed to depart without restraint. Gen. Dodge issued an order commanding me [Weaver] to make a levy of $2000, as I now remember, from wealthy citizens living in the vicinity, for the purpose of paying for supplies necessary for the sustenance of these refugees. In obedience to that order I issued an order reciting the authority under which I was acting, and served it upon certain parties . . . . The money collected was paid direct to Col. Cyrus C. Carpenter, assistant commissary general . . . . and did not pass through my hands, if I remember correctly, and the wants of the refugees were supplied. In no event was one cent retained by myself . . . .

"I did not dispossess any one of their dwelling houses and appropriate the same for officers quarters during my stay in Pulaski. My headquarters were in the Court House and I boarded with a private family, that of Mrs. Ballentyne. The officers of my regiment lived in their tents in line with their respective companies. The several divisions, brigades and regiments encamped at Pulaski were not under my authority — not even my own regiment — while I was in command of the post . . . . My association with the people was as peaceful and fraternal as possible during the existence of hostilities, and remarkably so in all that region of the country."[50]

The foregoing statement made by Colonel

Weaver was in reply to charges of cruelty and oppression directed at him by political opponents during the campaign of 1892. His speechmaking tour in the South was disturbed by threats of violence, and he was compelled to give up his appointments in Georgia where systematic opposition was encountered. The basis of this hostility was a revival of sectional feeling aimed at a political candidate who threatened to weaken the dominant party control in the South. Its spirit was shown by the remark of one of the residents of Pulaski who, addressing a reporter sent to investigate the charges, referred to Weaver as that "darned Yankee Colonel."[51]

In a letter addressed to Weaver at the time, General Dodge declared that "twenty-five or thirty years after the war they propose to punish in the South a good soldier, which you were, for simply obeying orders from a superior officer; it does not make any difference to me whether the orders were good or bad or cruel. It is a very singular thing because a soldier obeyed an order in the Federal army he should be denounced in the South where their orders were far more strict than ours.

"Then, again, it is very singular to me that Giles County, Tennessee, should object to any order, because, as you know I commanded there. I did not force the oath upon any person. I said to those people — knowing them to be all in sympathy with the South — that if they would send in to our different posts what they had to sell we would buy it from them, but if we went after it we would not pay for it.

"Now, the refugee order was an order from General Sherman to me and I gave it to you. General Sherman planted himself upon the ground that these were their own people. And if because they were Union people they forced them out of their line into ours, that the Rebels in our lines should take care of them."[52]

Another account of Colonel Weaver's conduct as commander of the post at Pulaski was by a resident of the place written twenty-eight years later in reply to an inquiry by the editor of the *The Weekly Toiler* of Nashville, Tennessee. The writer referred to Colonel Weaver "as a Christian gentleman" whom he had known well, as his tent had been on his "premises, within sixty feet of my dwelling house, for one whole winter. His tent was his headquarters until he was ordered to the courthouse, which was in full view, to take command of the post, which duty he performed until his regiment was ordered to Chattanooga. He was commander of the post say about half the winter of 1863–4, but his tent was not taken down until he made his final move. . . .

"I had built my house in the edge of a grove

of tall trees, the nearest grove to the town of Pulaski, looking to the eastward. It was a grand grove and I felt proud of it. On the evening of the day that the 2d Iowa took possession of and encamped in my grove I sought Col. Weaver and plead for my grove, telling him that I had been raised in the country amongst the trees, and had it not been for that grove I should not have remained in the country; and more than that, that I intended to preserve it for the benefit of others as well as for myself. Just at that moment I spied some soldiers passing, each with a couple of fence rails on his shoulder. I remarked if my fences are burned they can be replaced but if this grove is destroyed I can not live long enough to grow another. Col. Weaver straightened himself to his full heighth and declared with emphasis, 'It shall not be cut' . . . . He did not go back on his word. He gave me to understand that he did not make war upon the citizen.''[53]

A reporter for *The Weekly Toiler* also interviewed Mr. A. J. Ballentine, a prominent citizen of Pulaski, with whose mother Colonel Weaver boarded during his stay in that town. His reply to a question for information ''about this rascal Weaver'' was a vigorous one. ''Young man, if you want to hear anything in the way of abuse of Gen. Weaver never come to a

Ballentine after it. As for me, I never saw
Gen. Weaver, and was opposed to him during
the war and am against him now [1892]. With
all that, I can never say a word against a man
who protected my mother and sister as Gen.
Weaver did while he boarded with them. He
knew that my mother had four sons in the Confederate army, yet he treated her with the
greatest respect. I was in the army at the time
and know nothing of Weaver, as an officer or as
a gentleman. All I know is that mother said
he was a gentleman, and a kind-hearted, brave
soldier. So, you see, young man, when my
mother (she's been dead two years now) tells
me that this man was a nice man, it is hard for
me to believe otherwise. I remember one morning after the close of the war that she asked me
to see after some papers she had. They proved
to be vouchers for supplies given to Weaver.
I took them very reluctantly and told her she
would never realize anything on them. A few
weeks later she asked me about them, and I con-
fessed that I thought so little about them that
I had lost them down at the store. Gen.
Weaver, however, came to the rescue, and tried
to get the money for us. My brother was with
the general in congress and I have heard him
speak of Weaver often.''[54]

V

Defending the Home Country

Iowa, like all States near the boundary between slave and free territory, suffered from disturbances caused by sympathizers with the South. So-called Copperheads opposed the war and urged peace much as do the pacifists of the present. Under the mask of opposition to the war, "Knights of the Golden Circle, draft evaders, deserters", and other more disreputable characters committed all sorts of outrages, not even stopping short of murder. The first open violence occurred in Keokuk County in August, 1863; while in October of the same year Fremont County witnessed similar outbreaks. In October, 1864, "outrageous murders were committed in Sugar Creek Township, Poweshiek County."

Murders of Union men also took place in Davis County at about the same time. "Twelve young men, dressed in Federal uniform, mounted on splendid horses, and armed with from two to seven revolvers each, entered the county near the southeast corner, on the morning of the 12th of October, 1864." They rode through

the county, robbing the farmers along their
route and threatening all sorts of violence.
Many of the people of Bloomfield were at the
county fair, and when rumors of the raid
reached there, it resulted in the breaking up of
the fair and the return to town of the men. An
attack was "momentarily expected; men were
placed on the tops of houses, as look-outs, to
watch and warn us of approaching danger.
Men, women, and children were hurrying to and
fro . . . . All was hurry, bustle, and confusion; all were willing and vied with each
other in getting ready to meet the danger . .
. . But there was no one to take command,
and bring order out of chaos. The voice of a
citizen was heard above the din and confusion,
proposing that Col. J. B. Weaver, late of the
2d Iowa Infantry, take command of all the
militia, and that every man would yield prompt
and implicit obedience to his command. A
universal shout of approval rang out along the
lines, and confidence was seen and felt in the
cheerful obedience to every order issued.

"A company of mounted men, led by Col.
Weaver . . . . started in pursuit late in
the afternoon, leaving the command of the
militia, for the defense of the town", to Lieutenant Colonel S. A. Moore who was "materially assisted by Capt. Gray, Capt. Minge, and
a large number of returned soldiers, whose

nerves had been trained to steadiness at Fort
Donelson, Shiloh, Pea Ridge, siege of Vicksburg and other fields, made glorious by their
valor.'' The force under Colonel Weaver followed the trail until midnight, when they were
in Missouri, five miles behind the raiders.
Finding it impossible to overtake them, ''they
reluctantly retraced their steps homeward.''

Preparations were made for the defense of
the county seat. Rumors came that the Confederate army was on the western ''side of the
Missouri river; the valley of the Des Moines,
with its immense supplies of provisions and
forage, was surely [its] destination unless met
and driven back by the federal army . . . .
The inhabitants of the county were fully
aroused to the importance of the occasion;
companies, armed and unarmed, were called
out, and performed cheerfully the guard and
patrol duties assigned them.''

An order was issued by the Governor's aid-
de-camp ''to Col. Weaver, instructing him to
take command of the entire militia forces of
the county, and to put as many men on duty on
the border as he thought the public safety required. One hundred mounted men and two
commissioned officers were detailed by the
Colonel, and assigned to duty along the south
line of the county, with instructions to patrol

the roads day and night. Twenty-five men were
detailed to do duty in the county seat, and instructed to arrest every suspicious-looking
stranger that could be found in the vicinity.
The same instructions were given to the troops
on the border . . . . Over one hundred
persons have been arrested and turned back to
Missouri, at one post (Savannah). Ceaseless
vigilance was the order of the day. A chain of
couriers was appointed, reaching to every
school district in the border townships, and
every precaution taken to guard against
surprise.

"On the evening of the 21st day of October,
1864, a courier arrived . . . . from Pulaski, with the intelligence that a body of
twenty-five mounted men had been seen that
morning, some three or four miles from Milton,
in Van Buren county. Some forty men were
immediately mounted on horseback, many of
them 'pressed' for the occasion, and started in
the direction of Milton, fifteen miles distant,
under command of Col. Weaver." On the way
information was received that the raiders were
encamped six miles south of Milton. At Milton
they found "the militia of Troy, Pulaski, and
other posts of the county, with the forces in the
vicinity". About daylight the next morning
the force reached the place where the raiders
were supposed to be encamped only to find that

they had left there about nine o'clock the preceding evening. "The command was again
mounted, and started in pursuit; but with some
nine hours the start of us, it was impossible to
overtake them. Their tracks indicated that
they had divided into small squads, taking as
many different roads. We scoured the country
for some twenty miles in Missouri, and failing
to find them, returned".

From that time to the evening of November
seventh there was comparative quiet, although
"the number of strangers constantly passing
and attempting to pass through the county"
gave rise to the fear that "Southern fugitives"
would concentrate "somewhere near the border,
and make another raid for pillage and murder."

On November 7th six persons entered the
county from the east, traveling in pairs. Two
of them stopped at a house and "in a rude,
boisterous manner demanded something to
eat". On the refusal of the lady of the house
"to get dinner for them, they helped themselves
to what they could find in the cupboard, and
left." They went to another house and put up
for the night. Three men of the neighborhood
determined to arrest them and went to the
house where they were staying. In the struggle that followed one member of the arresting
party was killed and one wounded, while one
of the strangers was injured but managed to

escape. The militia arrived in a short time and pursued, but in the darkness the men made their escape. Their horses and equipment were captured. "Their saddle-pockets were filled with powder, balls, percussion-caps, bullet-molds, horse-shoe nails. Everything about their equipages indicated that they were rebel bushwhackers or Confederate soldiers."

The news of this outrage reached Bloomfield quickly. "The militia were called out, the roads were patrolled and guarded in every direction. Quite a number of strangers had been seen during the day in different parts of the county. Many believed that an attack was contemplated the next day, the day of the Presidential election."

Arrests were made, and at one time there were as many as thirteen men in jail. Two United States detectives "came along, and being arrested and confined with the prisoners obtained much information of value . . . . in regard to the future movements in contemplation by the bands of scoundrels who have infested northern Missouri since the rebellion. The prisoners were all sent to Missouri and placed in the hands of the proper authorities. Nine contraband horses, with their equipments," were captured by the militia and sold. The belief was very prevalent that "large numbers of rebels" were "quietly wintering in

Iowa with a view of recruiting their horses and recuperating themselves preparatory to a concentration at some point in the spring.''[55] The people along the southern border of Iowa were urged to be on the alert and to question all strangers whom they met. Every loyal man was advised to have at least one revolver in addition to the arms furnished by the State and to carry this with him at all times ready for immediate use.

VI

A Republican Leader

1865–1877

Colonel Weaver's military record gave him a
position of leadership in Davis County and
southern Iowa which entitled him to consideration in the councils of the Republican party of
the State. The party that had carried the war
through to a successful conclusion occupied a
peculiarly strong place in the support of the
people, while the Democracy was weakened by
its connection with slavery and disunion. In
1865 the *Burlington Weekly Hawk-Eye* declared
that "the vastly preponderant sentiment of the
soldier is with the Republican ticket . . . .
Governor Stone is sure of an overwhelming
majority. His associates on the State ticket
are destined to win; and the Legislature will
hardly have a copperhead in it to represent a
miserable band of plotters and traitors." The
same paper a few months later described "the
military element in the Legislature" as "very
strong. It is our opinion that fully one-half
the members have served in the army."[56] The
same conditions that produced a line of soldier
Presidents after the war opened official posi-

tions all over the country to the men who had
served in the army.

General Weaver's own ability and interest in
politics, which had developed before the outbreak of the war, inclined him to take advantage of the favorable situation. Within about
a year after his return to civil life he was a
candidate for nomination as Lieutenant Governor before the Republican Convention, standing second in the number of votes received on
the first ballot. Benjamin F. Gue was the successful candidate for the nomination. Out of a
total of nearly 900 delegates Gue had the support of over 500, Weaver came next with from
250 to 255, George W. McCrary received 80,
and another candidate recorded 32. Upon a motion made by Weaver and seconded by McCrary,
the nomination of Gue was made unanimous.[57]

After the election in October it appears that
Weaver sent a letter to the *Burlington Weekly
Hawk-Eye* enthusiastically expressing his in-
terest in the victory of the Republican party.
The letter ran as follows: "Dear 'Hawk-Eye'.
— Davis county is thoroughly redeemed: 150 to
200 majority for the whole union ticket, both
State and County. Who can do better than
this?"[58]

The next year Weaver's activity is recorded
in his signature to the call for a convention in
the first Congressional district as a member of

the committee representing Davis County.[59]
At the October election he was the successful
candidate for district attorney in the second
judicial district which was then made up of
Davis, Appanoose, Wapello, Monroe, Van
Buren, and Wayne counties. The election was
for four years.[60] Soon after the election he
sent letters to the *Burlington Weekly Hawk-
Eye* and the *Gate City* of Keokuk. He called
the attention of the *Hawk-Eye* to the fact that
Davis County gave "J. F. Wilson 300 majority
over Fitz Henry Warren, *Preacher* to Guatemala — State and county ticket from 250 to
280. Who has done better? You will see that
we have doubled our last year's majority." In
his letter to the *Gate City* he wrote: "The
Copperheads refused to vote for Warren because they heard he was Minister to Guatemala.
'Preachers,' they say, 'should not meddle in
politics.' Fatal for Warren."[61]

In 1867 General Weaver was appointed by
President Johnson to the office of assessor of
internal revenue for the first district of Iowa,
in which he served the government for six
years — or until the office was abolished by an
act of Congress in 1872 providing for the abolition of the offices of assessor and assistant
assessor on or before June 30, 1873. Previously
there had been a collector and assessor in each
collection district. These districts were estab-

lished by the President and could not exceed in number in any State the number of its representatives in Congress. The assessor divided his district into a convenient number of assessment districts, in each of which an assistant assessor was appointed by the Secretary of the Treasury upon the nomination of the assessor. After 1873 the duties of the assessors devolved upon the collectors, and the new system proved more efficient and economical.[62]

General Weaver's ability as a public speaker was forcibly described in the *Burlington Weekly Hawk-Eye* in 1871. In September he had addressed a Republican meeting at Burlington where, according to the account, "he spoke for an hour and a quarter, comparing the platforms of the two parties in this State, contrasting the histories, the purposes, and the principles of the two parties in the country, and advocating the reasonableness of the claim of the Republican party for a continuance of its beneficent rule and the absurdity of Democratic pretensions. This portraiture in both cases was striking, and his reference to the deeds of the Republican party and the development of its great central ideas of liberty and progress were eloquent and thrilling, and stirred the blood of his hearers into repeated outbursts of applause.

"Gen. Weaver was listened to with close

attention, and made an excellent impression upon those who heard him. We have not room for a complete synopsis even of his speech, but must content ourselves with this general reference to it, and in advising all our readers to improve the first opportunity they have to listen to this able defender of the Republican faith."[63]

By the year 1872, if not earlier, General Weaver had come to be regarded as a prospective Congressman to represent the first district following Wilson and McCrary, and later the sixth district when Davis County had been set off from its old connections. In 1872 he was one of the presidential electors, representing the sixth district.[64]

It was in 1874 that General Weaver came within one vote of receiving the nomination for Congressman in the sixth district. On the informal ballot he had thirty-two votes to his principal opponent's twenty-four — two other candidates receiving eleven votes. On the first formal ballot the two leading candidates had thirty-two and twenty-six votes respectively and one other candidate had eight. But on the second formal and final ballot Weaver received thirty-three votes, while his successful opponent, Judge E. S. Sampson, had thirty-four votes.

Weaver had been regarded as the probable

nominee and there were many charges made both by Republicans and Democrats that he was defeated by unfair means. One delegate was reported to have desired to change his vote before the final ballot, but the chairman of his delegation refused to announce it. The friends of Weaver were so aroused that they sent a committee to Sampson to urge him not to accept the nomination, while at the same time his opponents sent a committee to the candidate to urge his acceptance. The convention was held at Ottumwa and Judge Sampson was holding court at Fairfield. Both committees started from Ottumwa on the evening train to interview the candidate. One of the members of the committee, disappointed by Weaver's defeat, telegraphed Sampson not to accept the nomination till he saw the committee. Both committees conferred with the candidate, who took the matter under advisement and a few days later announced his acceptance.[65]

The Iowa State Register in referring to the nomination of Sampson declared that "no better selection could possibly have been made, unless, indeed, General Weaver had been chosen, and that would have been a choice undoubtedly as good, but perhaps no better. General Weaver gave Judge Sampson close and gallant contest, and lost the prize by only one vote. That the General did not succeed will be

regretted by thousands and tens of thousands
of his devoted friends and admirers in all parts
of the State. Outside of the District, the feeling was largely and warmly in his favor, and it
was generally supposed that there was little
doubt of his success. It would have pleased us
to chronicle here his nomination.''[66]

The *Bloomfield Democrat* declared that ''the
nomination was secured by such trickery that
numbers of the Republicans refuse to support
the ticket'', and that many Republicans ''believed, and justly too, that Weaver had been
most villainously cheated out of a nomination.''
Later this paper described the nomination as
coming to Sampson ''by the meanest kind of
wire pulling, by political chicanery, and by the
use of dishonorable transactions.'' Another
editorial in the same paper stated that recently
Sampson had ''assured Gen. Weaver himself,
while the twain were riding in a railroad coach,
together, that he (Sampson) would not in any
manner stand in the way of the other's aspirations. We have received this information from
Republican sources, and have every reason to
believe it authentic . . . . Weaver is honestly entitled to the nomination. Thru scul-
duggery Sampson was boosted ahead of him.''

Again a week later the *Bloomfield Democrat*,
commenting upon a statement that ''what defeated Weaver . . . . was the same thing

that defeated Harlan, the *Methodist Church*",
declared that "the people have concluded that
the Methodist Church cannot run this country.
This is only an excuse; the true reason was that
Weaver would not pledge himself to continue
the present set of Federal officials in their com-
fortable quarters, if he should be elected. He
didn't propose to go into the race handicapped
with Warden and Hedrick and Hamilton; so
these worthies and the rest of the ring proceeded to slaughter him and place the nomination where it *would* do good. The Methodist
Church may do for a scape-goat, but the *true*
reason for Weaver's defeat is the one we have
given above."[67]

Apparently Weaver was regarded as the
logical nominee in the sixth district in 1874.
His personal strength is shown by the fact that
he later carried the district three times as an
independent candidate. Clearly there was distinct and interested opposition to him. His
ability and independence explain this opposition as satisfactorily as it can be accounted for
by a study of contemporary political conditions.
The opposition in the Republican party to able
and fearless leadership that has defeated it
from time to time was already gathering
strength in 1874. It was to be one of the factors in driving Weaver out of the party a few
years later.

In 1875 General Weaver was the leading candidate for the nomination as Governor before the Republican State Convention. He made a vigorous campaign and won a majority of the delegates. The opposing candidates were John Russell, John H. Gear, Robert Smythe, and W. B. Fairfield. Weaver had aligned himself fearlessly ''with the elements which were demanding the vigorous control or entire suppression of the saloons, and the public control of the railways and other semi-public corporations.'' When his opponents found that ''he was going to be nominated, unless some strong new feature or issue, or some new and stronger man, could be introduced on the scene, there was much of canvassing all night long the night before the Convention met, to devise a winning plan and accomplish Weaver's overthrow.''

His most active opponents were ''the liquor or saloon people''. The corporation representatives ''were also nearly all opposed to him, but not nearly so earnestly nor so unanimously as the saloon element.'' Various proposals were considered, among them one to nominate General G. M. Dodge; but it was known that he would not accept because he did not want the office and because of his friendship for General Weaver. After canvassing this possibility ''the saloon people began to turn to

Kirkwood, and yet morning came without any regular programme having been reached to present his name or to work the stampede from Weaver."[68]

The convention met in Des Moines on June 30th at Moore's Opera House, "with the house so crowded that several of the delegations had to be seated on the stage. There was much gossip and speculation among the delegates as to what was to be done, and the whole Convention was plainly nervous and expectant of something sensational going to happen. There was no chosen leader to take charge of the Kirkwood boom, or to openly antagonize the Weaver majority."

Senator Frank T. Campbell nominated General Weaver; and then in turn John Russell of Jones County, John H. Gear of Des Moines County, Robert Smythe of Linn County, and W. B. Fairfield of Floyd County were named. At this point in the proceedings Dr. S. M. Ballard arose to nominate Ex-Governor Kirkwood; and General Trumbull of Dubuque inquired if he had authority to present the name. Dr. Ballard, "a veteran white haired Republican of imposing form", replied: "I have the authority of the great Republican party of Iowa". This statement was greeted with tremendous cheering, and Russell and Gear immediately withdrew their names, declaring they

would not oppose the "Old War Governor".
Senator Campbell asked if friends of Kirkwood
had not received a dispatch from him saying
that he was not a candidate. This inquiry was
replied to by cries that it made no difference.
Dr. Ballard moved to nominate by acclamation,
but the motion was opposed and withdrawn.
An informal ballot was taken and resulted in
the casting of 268 votes for Kirkwood, 200 for
Weaver, 111 for Smythe, and 33 for Fairfield;
a total of 612 making 307 necessary for a choice.
A formal ballot was next taken, but before the
vote was counted, delegations began to change
to Kirkwood, whereupon Captain John A. T.
Hull, of Davis County, moved to make the nomination unanimous, an action that was greeted
"with thundering applause."[69]

The stampede of the convention away from
Weaver so greatly desired by the anti-prohi-
bition and pro-corporation delegates had been
accomplished; but the result was probably
brought about by "instantly utilizing a way
opened to them in a time of great need" and
not by originating the movement. "The Convention in its highly wrought condition and
excitement was hypnotized, as so many large
popular bodies frequently are, and enough of
General Weaver's delegates were swept off
their feet and carried along by the storm to
furnish the votes needed to make a majority

for Kirkwood . . . . Before the next day
had come, and the spell was over, many of those
who had helped to do it, deeply regretted it,
and would have undone it if they could."

A combination of circumstances in connection with the adroit use of the name of the
"War Governor" without his knowledge, swept
the nomination that "General Weaver had so
ardently coveted, and had so clearly and honestly won . . . . out of his hands and his
whole course in life [was thereby] changed."

After General Weaver's death in 1912 James
S. Clarkson, long the editor of *The Iowa State
Register* and prominent in the Republican
party of the State, recorded his recollection
and judgment of the convention of 1875. He
felt at the time, and had felt ever since that
Weaver "was treated unjustly . . . . and
given ample provocation for the course that he
afterwards took. I have always believed, too,
that the unjust action of that Convention
caused in the end as much of loss to the Republican party as it did to General Weaver. For
at that time he was already one of the two or
three strongest men in mental force, debating
power and popular influence in the Republican
party in Iowa; and if he had been given the
nomination for Governor then, for which he
had an unquestionable majority of the delegates when the Convention met, he would have

been elected, would have made a strong and popular Governor, and would almost surely have been afterwards elected United States Senator and would have made such a great career in the Senate, as a parliamentary leader and debater as to have added greatly even to the great power and renown which Iowa, through its unusually able men in Congress between 1861 and until about 1908 enjoyed — a renown and a power which were equalled by no other delegation in Congress except that of the State of Maine.''

Mr. Clarkson believed that General Weaver was compelled to leave the Republican party ''in vindication of his self-respect''. He never blamed him ''for the course that he took''; and ''in the inner circles of the Republican party, and among fair men everywhere, this view was taken. It was a most serious sacrifice to him, for he had a nature which prized and treasured personal friendships as being really the sweeter things in human life, and the most of his friendships were among the Republicans. His original aspirations were all within the party of his first choice. His illustrious career as a soldier, and the devotion to him of all Union soldiers but added to this. At different times and in different ways, but of course always without publicity, many of us in the Republican party sought to open the way for the self-respecting return of the General to the party. But the right way could never be opened; and besides the General once he had entered upon his new career of fighting the Republican party, because of its growing tendency no longer to keep human rights and human interests above all property rights and property interests, felt that it was his duty to stay at the new post in the new field.''

In concluding his tribute, Mr. Clarkson declared that it was ''to the eternal credit of General Weaver that the main motives and desires of his life always were to serve his fellow man. Generously endowed by nature, in both mental and physical force, he could easily have won fortune and success in several fields. . . when the call of duty came, however, and he became convinced that the government was drifting into the control of the special interests and the privileged classes, and from Lincoln's ideal of a 'government of the people, by the people, for the people,' he did not hesitate to make the sacrifice and give up all his personal ambitions and go to the defence of the people. Then he became one of the forerunners, and I think the greatest of them all, in the great popular movement to resist this tendency to make our Republic a government of money, by money, for money, and not of men, which is now nation-wide, and so valiantly led by Roosevelt and other gallant spirits following on these higher paths where Weaver led. Millions of fair men who opposed the General then, and honestly thought him visionary or seeking personal power and renown through new and untenable issues, find it a pleasing duty to themselves to do him justice now.''[70]

The evening session of the Republican convention that nominated Kirkwood as Governor in 1875 completed the State ticket and adopted a platform. A spirited discussion was carried on in regard to temperance, the currency, Southern questions, and a third term for the President of the United States. The chief controversy, however, was waged about prohibition, to which the platform as reported by the committee on resolutions made no reference. By a delegate from Keokuk a resolution was proposed for which General Weaver immediately offered a substitute, declaring that ''the Republican party of Iowa is opposed to the repeal of the prohibitory liquor law of this State, and will stand by its record on that question.'' A motion was then made and adopted to refer both proposals to the committee on resolutions with instructions to report ''forthwith''.

A little later the committee brought in a substitute of its own to the effect that it was the duty and right of the State ''to provide such legislation upon the subject of the liquor traffic as will best protect society from the evils of intemperance." Colonel Henderson proposed to leave the matter to the General Assembly and to the people. Attention then was given to General Weaver's substitute. Mr. Potter of Scott County protested against its adoption, since it would drive 20,000 Republicans out of the party; and he urged the reference of the question to the people. In reply General Weaver said that 40,000 Republicans would leave the party if the platform did not confirm the record of the party. "I warn you not to defy the temperance sentiment in the Republican party". Potter replied with a warning against crippling the Republican party by adopting the prohibition test, and he was supported by another delegate from Scott County. Judge Nourse spoke in favor of honesty in the platform. He opposed the committee's resolution for it meant nothing; "the resolution of Gen. Weaver" was "the only one" that had "any ring to it." Delegates from Floyd and Dubuque counties favored temperance, but objected to crowding it down the throats of those opposed to it. Finally, "the resolution and all its amendments were laid upon the table — the vote on both sides being heavy and strong, but the majority clearly and largely with the ayes."[71]

The attitude of opponents of prohibition on

7

the position taken by General Weaver is clearly illustrated by editorials which appeared in the *Bloomfield Democrat*. One editorial declared that "when Gen. Weaver comes to be nominated for the State Senate next fall, the naturalized citizens of this county will remember that he said . . . . 'The time has come for American civilization to assert itself against European dictation.' Properly interpreted, this means that a foreign born citizen has no right to drink a glass of beer against the protests of a native American cold-waterite. The Gen. may yet have cause to regret this enunciation of know-nothing sentiments."

Another editorial in the same number of the same paper, referred to General Weaver in connection with a comment of the *State Leader*, which said that "it is time we hear from General Weaver of Davis county. If Kirkwood is for license how can General Weaver support him in the face of his speech made in the state convention?"[72]

Late in August of the same year General Weaver was nominated for State Senator from Davis County by acclamation. After the other candidates had been named, "Weaver was vociferously called for"; whereupon he arose and spoke as follows:

Gentlemen of the Convention: I thank you for the nomination you have to-day given me. I assure you

that it is appreciated on my part, because it came
from those with whom I have lived from my child-
hood, and for the further reason that it was entirely
unsolicited on my part. No member of this Convention can say that I have asked directly or indirectly,
for this nomination. I have lived among you 33
years, and this is the first time that my name has
been before a Convention in this county. I wish to
remark right here, that as you have taken the responsibility of nominating me to-day, upon you will rest
the responsibility of electing me; but while I lay upon
you this responsibility, I shall, at the same time do
everything in my power, during the canvas to secure
my election, and the election of the whole ticket. We
must have no scratching at this election, if we can
help it. Let us by united work secure a triumph in
Davis county this fall. The people of this county,
Democrats, alike with Republicans, have a common
interest, in securing good officials and good government. I promise you, gentlemen, if elected, to do the
very best I can for the interests of this country.
There is one thing, however, which I wish clearly
understood — one thing that I intend to live and die
by — *I am a prohibitionist.*

"Under cover of the applause which greeted
this declaration, the Gen. retreated, to give way
to Power [the nominee for Representative],
who said that he was not a speech making man,
but that he endorsed the principles advanced
by Weaver, and would represent the principles
of the party, this winter, if elected."[73]

The campaign opened immediately. According to the *Bloomfield Democrat,* which referred
to the Republican convention as "Hull's Convention", the "Ring Ticket was nominated",
and the "Bloomfield Clique have it their own
way". A meeting at Pulaski on September 20th,
at which the Democratic candidates began their
canvass, was attended by fully as large a
crowd "as the one addressed by General
Weaver, the week before." Senator H. A.
Wonn, who was a candidate for reëlection,
replied to Weaver's questions as to his course
in the State Senate. He showed that "instead
of voting 'first, last, and all the time' for the
railroads, as had been charged by Weaver, he
gave repeated votes for measures which were
intended to curtail the power of those corporations. Mr. Hotchkiss [candidate for Repre-
sentative] followed in a reply to Weaver's
speech, and made a very telling argument
against the position taken by the would-be Senator. Weaver's statement on the currency
question was shown up by quotations from the
decisions of the Supreme Court." A crowd of
Republicans led by Hull, the county chairman,
were described as conducting "themselves in a
boisterous and sacreligious manner in the
church. When Gen. Weaver spoke he had the
consideration to ask that no demonstrations of
that character be made."[74]

Early in October the same paper contained comments upon the campaign to the effect that "Weaver goes about the county saying that under the operation of the present railroad law the people of Iowa have saved a million of dollars in the past year". It also was stated that "Wonn, in the Senate, voted for a substitute to the present railroad law, which provided that railroads should charge only reasonable fare; yet the *Republican* charges that he voted in the interests of the railroads."[75]

After the election the *Democrat* declared that "Weaver stepped into nomination for Senator at the County Convention, by acclamation, but stepped out by one hundred and thirty-nine majority in ballots." Another editorial in the same paper reminded its readers that they must not forget their "allies, the Liberal Republicans and Anti-Monopolists who stood shoulder to shoulder with us . . . . Along with these allies of the Democracy we wish to thank those Republicans who had no stomach for ring rule and clique dictation, and aided our cause with their votes."[76]

A week later the *Democrat* described the election as "the best fight the Democracy of Davis county ever made within our recollection . . . . The strongest man the Republicans could select as their leader, Gen. Weaver, conducted the most thorough canvas ever made

here, and was defeated. Preponderance of
votes did the work . . . . Every available
vote in the county was in the ballot boxes."[77]

Still another reference in the same paper described "the gubernatorial election" in Davis
County as "a mere matter of form, an event of
no moment. The grand center of attraction
was Weaver. Weaver was the perfect embodi-
ment of radical Republicanism, and radical
Republicanism loved and caressed, petted and
worshiped the General; but dear friends, all
sublunary things are uncertain.— Fortune is a
fickle Goddess. Weep no more, dear friends;
the way is yet open; the Democracy are mag-
nanimous in time of victory; so throw away
your broken sticks, abandon your false idols
and ye shall be received with outstretched arms
of welcome".[78]

The attitude of the Republican papers was
reflected in the statement that Weaver "has the
entire Republican press of the State to aid in
salving his political wounds".

One paper was quoted as saying that the
"defeat of no man in the State will be more
generally regretted than that of General
Weaver . . . . he could and will wield
more *Real* influence in the State Senate, than
fifty like the gentleman who has defeated him
. . . . the people of Davis county . . . .
will regret their unwise act in defeating the

man who could do more in the Legislature than
any other man in their midst.''[79]

General Weaver's defeat for the nominations
for Congressman in 1874, for Governor in 1875,
and in the campaign for the State Senate
showed conclusively that there was some strong
influence in the State opposed to his advancement. At the same time it is equally clear that
he was regarded by the rank and file of his
party as an able and conscientious leader. His
military career had been highly creditable, and
he was popular with the men who had served in
the army. Apparently he had the qualities,
and the conditions in general were favorable to
his success. The key to the situation seems to
be found in his views on temperance — views
which created a solid and unyielding opposition
and prevented his further advancement in the
party.

So notable was the succession of defeats that
the *Burlington Hawk-Eye,* a Republican paper,
asked the question in November, 1875, whether
Weaver was to be forced to leave the party.
It referred to him as "really too good a man
to be thus driven about from one end of the
ring to the other." The *Henry County Free
Press* was quoted as "aptly" saying that "if
there is one man in the State of Iowa who is
justified . . . . in becoming a 'sorehead',
that man is Gen. Weaver." Recent political

history was reviewed to show that before 1874
he had been successfully side-tracked for nominations that he had good reasons to assume
were coming to him. He was regarded as the
prospective successor to Wilson and McCrary
in the first district, but Gear who wanted to be
Congressman used his legislative influence to
throw him into the sixth. Later he was defeated for the nomination from that district by
Loughridge and Sampson. Again, in the State
convention in 1875 "Gear and Kirkwood
double-teamed against him, and though he led
on the first ballot, he lost the prize."[80]

In spite of these repeated disappointments
there were no immediate indications that General Weaver seriously considered leaving the
Republican party. In January, 1876, he was
described as "in Des Moines, one of Harlan's
chief Lieutenants, foremost among the workers
at the Harlan headquarters", and doing all
that he could to make him again United States
Senator.[81]

In July *The Iowa State Register* printed a
card from Weaver in regard to his candidacy
for Congress in the sixth district against Judge
Sampson. He wrote that he had "always conceded the Judge's right to a second nomination,
if his course in Congress was satisfactory to his
constituents. And I now concede his right,
under the two term rule to the nomination, if,

in his opposition to the repeal of the Resumption Act, and in his opposition to making silver coin a legal tender for all sums, he expresses the will of the Republican voters of this District. With one exception I have neither talked nor written to a single delegate concerning this matter, and then only in reply to a letter received from him. Please do me [the] justice to publish this letter". Another item in the same number of the same paper called attention to the card and declared that the writer "had no idea that he [Weaver] entertained any notion of being a candidate until the 10th inst., though, as we learned, his friends had then been working in his interest for some weeks."[82]

About the same time a number of citizens of Appanoose County wrote to him asking his opinion on "the resumption question and other financial matters. His reply was frank and manly as his answers always are". The correspondence, which was published at the time, developed more fully the general ideas presented in his card sent to *The Iowa State Register*. He described the Resumption Act as "a violation of all the natural laws of trade" and as "a costly experiment to the whole country . . . . It is causing daily, fearful and rapid contraction of the currency, which was barely adequate to the business interests of the country before contraction began . . . . The idea that we will be ready in 1879, to commence business in this country upon an exclusively gold basis . . . . is a proposition too absurd to be entitled to any but mirthful consideration."

He referred to the declaration of the Republican State convention of 1874 for a "policy of specie resumption at such a time as is consistent with the material and industrial interests of the country, to the end that the volume of currency may be regulated by the natural laws of trade." He called attention to the fact that the last Congressional convention of the sixth district endorsed this policy and added a statement in favor of "regulating the issue of currency so as to promote a return to specie payment without producing a derangement of business." Expressing the opinion that these declarations represented "the uniform doctrine of the Republican party in Iowa for years" and that there was nothing in them "inconsistent with the National Republican Platform", he added a brief comment upon the silver legislation of Congress, which he described as "a crime against Providence, and the common sense of the age. This is in keeping with the plan of the eastern gold jobbers, of both parties, to bring the west to their feet as suppliants when the crash shall come."[83]

Again, in September there was what *The*

Iowa State Register called a "laconic correspondence" between General Weaver and the
Greenback Congressional convention in the sixth
district. Porte C. Welch telegraphed from
Oskaloosa to General Weaver as follows: "Will
you accept the Congressional nomination on the
Indianapolis platform, waiving choice for President?" To this inquiry General Weaver
replied: "No, I am for Hayes and Wheeler,
Silver and Greenbacks". In reply came the
question whether he would "accept the nomination on the Indianapolis platform and vote
for Hayes if you want to?" To this telegram
signed "Moore and Ballard", he sent the
answer "No".[84]

Evidently during 1876 Weaver had no idea
of leaving the Republican party. A receptive
candidate for a Republican nomination to Congress, he abruptly declined to consider a Greenback nomination. His opinions in regard to
the currency seemed to him consistent with his
continued membership in the Republican party.
He closed the campaign of that year with a big
speech at Bloomfield the night before the election. As one of his admirers later expressed
it, he was then "a red-hot Republican".[85]

In 1877 he was mentioned as among the
strong men in the field for the nomination for
Governor against John H. Gear, who was regarded by some Republicans as almost sure to

be nominated by acclamation. Yet there are no
indications that Weaver was as keenly interested as in 1875. He attended the State convention and was one of the vice-presidents.
Mr. Gear was nominated upon the first formal
ballot.[86]

General Weaver was "entirely satisfied"
with the position taken by the Republicans upon
the temperance question, and he so declared
himself in a letter to *The Iowa State Register*.
He referred to his "well known" opposition to
the nomination of Mr. Gear, and said that he
would support him "unreservedly", and that
he had faith that he would "do nothing to
undermine the expressed will of his party."
He urged the temperance people to "move up
their forces and occupy the vantage ground
already conquered. *Consolidate your forces by
letting the world know that you intend to be
reasonable.*" He did not regard the action of
the convention as "a compromise between Mr.
Gear's supporters and the temperance men",
but as "an independent, honest and bold enunciation, introduced and supported by men who
were opposing Mr. Gear's nomination."[87]

The letter in which General Weaver expressed himself satisfied with the position of
the Republican party upon prohibition and in
which he declared his intention of supporting
Mr. Gear was dated at Bloomfield, July 11,

1877. From the same place he wrote Mr. Gear on August 29th the following letter:

Differing, as I do, so widely with the Republican party upon questions of finance, I find it impossible for me to go before the people and advocate a continuance of that policy. Neither do I feel that it would be right for me to remain silent and withhold my protest against what I conceive to be a gigantic wrong. I wish, therefore, to be released by you from my pledge of personal support, assuring you, sincerely, that my action is not dictated by considerations personal to yourself. I shall act with the Independents.

Two days later Mr. Gear replied from Burlington as follows:

Yours of 29th at hand. You ask me to release you from your "pledge of personal support". Your offer of support was of your own free will and accord — I accepted it as frankly as it was offered and am free to say that I was gratified by your offer.

I release you from your promise but regret — not on personal grounds — that you see it to be your duty to leave the republican party in which you have done such loyal service to train in other camps. The republican party has done much for the country and this is ample evidence to me that it can in the future do better by the country than can the "Independents" or any other party organized on what seems to me to be a false basis.[88]

General Weaver's final break with the Republican party, with which he had been identified almost from its birth, and in which he had attained a position of leadership, was a dramatic event fraught with results little understood at the time and for many years thereafter. His own political experience had brought home to him the fact that the Republican party had ceased to be one of high ideals, whose interests were primarily for the people. Partisanship, office-seeking, and corruption had replaced the self sacrifice and devotion of earlier years. Especially was it true that corporation and financial interests seemed to be more and more in evidence. The fight for prohibition had apparently been largely won when the party adopted the policy officially in its platform of 1877, and Weaver himself seems to have been satisfied for he urged the extremists to be reasonable.

He had been giving careful attention and study to currency and financial problems for several years. These questions had attracted popular interest through the fall in the price of silver and because of the controversies over the resumption of specie payments. The formation of a Greenback party in 1876 was the result of the failure of the two great parties to satisfy the demands of those who were opposed to the demonetization of silver, and who favored the continued use of greenbacks. Both Hayes and

Tilden were known to be hostile to the views of the "Independents". The distresses due to the effects of the business depression beginning in 1873 and the difficulties involved in contraction were real reasons for a careful consideration of the monetary situation. Bankers and business men failed to grasp the needs of the situation. Political compromises combined with the increasing influence of corporations and financial interests gave rise to suspicions of officials and government. General Weaver's retirement from the Republican party and his alliance with the Greenbackers was only a conspicuous incident in a period when many persons were taking similar steps. The near approach to defeat of the Republicans in 1876 showed that the opposition to that party was widespread and influential.

In September and October, 1877, General Weaver took an active part in the State campaign upon the Greenback side. Of course he was fiercely assailed by the Republican press as a renegade, no opportunity being neglected to ridicule and denounce him. At Oskaloosa, on September 21st, he engaged in a joint debate with Marcellus E. Cutts, a Republican "of great ability and a man of most extraordinary and brilliant talents." According to an account of the meeting in the *Oskaloosa Herald,* reprinted in *The Iowa State Register,* each speaker was to have half an hour and the whole debate was to consume three hours, thus giving each one of the debaters three opportunities to present his case. Cutts opened the discussion, and maintained his position with great success, while Weaver entirely failed to meet his telling points. His part was described as a complete failure, and he was advised "to skip Oskaloosa and — Cutts", when he came that way again. Weaver's well known ability as a public speaker makes his reported collapse in this connection quite unlikely.

In the same number of *The Register* there was printed a dispatch from General Weaver to the editor, dated September 25th, in which he referred to the statement that Cutts "used" him "up" at Oskaloosa. His comment was, "Ask all the people of Oskaloosa outside of the *Herald* office as to the truth of that. Have Cutts do it again" in Des Moines on October 6th. According to *The Register* Weaver was still "smarting under the argumentative battering ram of Hon. M. E. Cutts at Oskaloosa, and he probably wouldn't have felt so bad if *The Register* had not sent the fact broadcast over the State." It should be noted that Weaver was the challenger for the second debate — an indication that he was not so completely defeated as his former Republican friends would like to have it appear.

The second debate at Des Moines, in the opinion of *The Register,* was also a "failure". It was, however, "not all his own failure; it simply illustrated the utter fallacy and the complete weakness of the Greenback party . . . . With all proper candor, and with all due respect to Gen. Weaver, who is a most estimable gentleman and an able speaker, it is to be said that his portion of the debate . . . . was literally a continuous confession of the sophistries of his cause, and of his inability to meet argument with argument, and to match logic with logic." Reference was made to the packing of the hall with Greenbackers "to come to the relief of Weaver in case of distress, and by interruptions and questions to try to throw Cutts off his line of argument and consume his time". According to this report of the meeting all these efforts completely failed, and the victory of Cutts over Weaver and his supporters was overwhelming.[89]

The accounts of the two contests between Cutts and Weaver are so plainly partisan and unfair to the latter that little dependence can be placed upon them. They represent the attitude of persons who had no sympathy with or understanding of Weaver's point of view. Their hostility was also increased by the bitter controversies aroused during the campaign — a campaign made more acrimonious by Weaver's

8

recent defection. His prominence in the Republican party and his remarkable ability upon the platform made his loss more keenly felt. Hence his work for the Greenbackers was systematically and persistently underrated and subjected to sarcasm and ridicule.

As already suggested, Weaver's unusual power as a public speaker makes it very unlikely that he failed to give a good account of himself in these debates. At any rate, in the opinion of many persons who heard them, they were the sensation of the year, and General Weaver was regarded as having the advantage. Cutts was a master in "sardonic ridicule and irritating invective", and the contest between him and Weaver was a battle of wits conducted with great ability. So many people would not have remembered them and the great attention which they attracted had they been as one-sided as partisan Republican accounts would have us believe.[90] Certainly the lapse of time would not have transformed the vanquished into the victor. Weaver was a pioneer and his position was beyond the comprehension of those who saw only the partisan aspects of the situation. They could not conceive of any other motives than those with which they were familiar. Their only weapons were ridicule and misrepresentation.

After his election to Congress in 1878 General

Weaver devoted himself largely to public affairs: his time in the public service was limited, but he was constantly in demand as a public speaker and he was active in every political campaign. Consequently, his career as a lawyer was subordinated to his public activities. Before 1878, and after his return from military service in 1864, his work as a lawyer seems to have been "rather notable". From 1866 to 1870 he was district attorney and therefore a party to every suit of importance during those years. Judge Robert Sloan of Keosauqua, who was circuit judge in the district from 1869 to 1880, recalls that Weaver had good success, and adds that "the lawyers opposing him . . . . in all the important cases, were of more than usual ability and very resourceful, and a victory for the state, could only be won by arduous effort on his part.

"As I remember", continues the Judge, "he was regarded as an able prosecutor, but not a *persecutor,* and gave good satisfaction throughout the District. He was very courteous to opposing counsel and the Court, and quite successful in examining witnesses, and very able in argument of a case to the jury, and eloquent when the case was such as to justify it. In civil cases, he displayed the same qualities as in criminal cases. After the close of his term as District Attorney, he was engaged in practice

in Bloomfield, but at the same time devoted
much of his time and attention to politics and
public speaking, in which he greatly excelled,
and by reason thereof was not as close a student of the law as he would otherwise have
been. Had he devoted himself to the law, there
is no doubt in my mind that he would have become one of the leading lawyers of the state.
He displayed excellent ability while he remained in the practice, and was entitled to high
rank among the lawyers of the District of that
day, and there was no better bar in the state
than the bar of the Second Judicial District.''[91]

VII

FIRST SESSION IN CONGRESS

1879

THE political situation in 1878 in Iowa and in the country as a whole was such as to put the Republican party in a position of defense. Inevitably some corruption had resulted from long continuance in power; and business depression had reacted upon it. No constructive currency legislation since the Civil War had been undertaken: not even the resumption of specie payments had been accomplished. There was intense opposition, especially in the West, to the proposed resumption for which the Republicans were responsible; inflationists demanded a larger circulation, which was to be made up of silver or greenbacks. The administration of President Hayes had given satisfaction neither to the politicians nor to the independents.

Under such conditions there seemed good reason to hope for the success of a coalition of Democrats and Independents. General Weaver had taken an active part in the campaign of 1877 — which was a State campaign. The chief center of interest in 1878 was, of course, in the Congressional contests. There was considerable talk of the Democrats endorsing the Greenback nominees for Congress, and General Weaver was regarded as a candidate for the Democratic nomination in the sixth district.[92] The leading Greenbackers favored fusion with the Democrats, but there was a good deal of opposition to it in the rank and file of the party — especially among the editors of Greenback papers.[93]

General Weaver seems to have been a consistent believer in fusion. Throughout his career, when conditions promised a measure of success, he favored the union of the forces of the opposition. The most conspicuous instance was in 1896 when he urged the union of Populists and Democrats in support of Bryan. In part this attitude was prompted by his political intuition, and in part it was due to his disinclination to go to extremes. Thus as a prohibitionist he urged reasonableness in 1877. Acting on the theory that the surest progress was always gradual, he was constantly attacked by the extremists for his compromises with some branches of the opposition.

Actual and effective fusion in 1878 was brought about in only two Congressional districts in Iowa — the sixth and seventh. In the former Weaver was elected over his old opponent, Sampson, by a vote of 16,366 to 14,308; in the latter, the Des Moines district, E. H. Gillette was elected by a vote of 16,474 over the Republican candidate who received 15,546 votes. On the State ticket four Democratic candidates were withdrawn late in September and four Greenback candidates substituted; but this fusion arrangement was of little importance since it did not result in any successes at the polls. The significant victories in Iowa in 1878 were those of Weaver and Gillette in the Congressional districts.[94]

As already noted, General Weaver had been a candidate for Congress in the sixth district for a number of years. Defeated in 1874 and 1876 by Sampson for the Republican nomination, he carried the district in 1878 by a plurality of over 2,000. The victory, coming as it did so soon after his change of parties, was a notable one. Undoubtedly· it was facilitated somewhat by his personal record and the belief that he had been unfairly treated in the past by his former party associates. At any rate his success was a personal endorsement of which he might well be proud. It indicated clearly his personal strength, and also showed that there was a very considerable support for the point of view in politics which he represented.

The Republicans made a great deal of talk about what they called the "Corrupt Weaver

Bargain" with the Democrats. They claimed that he had agreed to give up "the platform he had helped to make at Toledo" and act with the Democrats in everything except finance. In return for these concessions the Democrats were to nominate no candidate for Congress in the sixth district, thus leaving their party members free to vote for General Weaver. It was said that he wanted a direct nomination by the Democrats, and was disappointed when he did not receive it. The bitter partisanship of the period makes it difficult to disentangle truth from falsehood. Undoubtedly there was some understanding in regard to joint action, since General Weaver was at the Democratic convention at Ottumwa and was invited to speak but declined because some of his Democrat friends and some of his Greenback associates thought he had better not do so.[95]

Judge H. H. Trimble, one of the Democratic leaders, in answer to a letter of inquiry in regard to Weaver, described him as having left the Republican party for good because he regarded it "as having sold out to the bond-holding and gold interests of the world, and as utterly abandoned to all popular interests and rights." He had not given up "his convictions as to slavery and the war, but regards that as *finally settled.*" He was fully satisfied with Hayes's policy as to home rule in the South.

JAMES BAIRD WEAVER

CANDIDATE FOR CONGRESS 1878

If elected, runs the Trimble letter, General Weaver "expects to labor for a reform in finances, and will co-operate with such men, as believe with himself in regard to finances, and when he cannot find, on any given measure, such men, will act with those who come nearest his views. He expects to co-operate with the Democrats as against the Republican organization, and will assist the Democrats in the organization of the House." He was a Democrat before the Civil War and had always been opposed to a protective tariff.

"He is not an extremist on currency," continues the letter, "does not believe in unlimited inflation, and thinks we ought to have an increase of currency, either by full silver coinage or more greenbacks; is opposed to making the nation pay interest, directly or indirectly, on its currency, and is opposed to any policy looking to the creation of a perpetual debt."[96]

At the time of his first election to Congress in 1878 these views probably represent General Weaver's opinions stated in a conservative way to avoid unnecessary offense to possible supporters who might differ in unessential matters. The distinctive features of his views centered around finance.

Two editorials in *The Iowa State Register* expressed the opinions of his former party associates in regard to his election to Congress.

The first described the election of General Weaver as "not so objectionable as that of Gillette, for the General has far more to commend him personally, and much more to fit him for service in Congress, and is in every respect more a man of honor". A second editorial compared the results in Iowa and Maine, in each of which States two Republican Congressmen were lost, and pointed out the "striking coincidence" that in both States "one of the two Greenbackers elected" was "a man of good record and honor personally, and with the qualifications of integrity and capacity to fit him for Congress, like Weaver here — and the other, Murch, like Gillette here . . . . an avowed Communist, a dishonest agitator".[97]

Probably the extreme statements about Gillette were due to the fact that he had defeated the candidate of the party of which *The Iowa State Register* was the official organ. The remarks about General Weaver represented the feelings of former party associates who had had ample occasion to observe his ability and qualifications. In addition, Gillette was a wealthy Easterner who had made his home for only a short time in Des Moines and could therefore be regarded somewhat as an intruder. In any event General Weaver's opponents were compelled to admit his preëminent fitness for service in Congress.

In December, 1878, a Greenback conference called by the State Committee met at Des Moines to discuss fusion with the Democrats. The conference lasted all day, and in the evening a public meeting was held at the Court House. There were a number of speakers, including General Weaver who declared that clubs must be formed in every township in Iowa for the next campaign: organization must be the motto. Opponents of fusion said only a few persons were invited who were known to favor fusion. The only reporter present represented *The State Leader,* the official organ of the Democrats. A chairman of the State Committee was chosen outside of the membership to get a man favorable to fusion. The conference was described "as a fraud, a cheat and a swindle".[98]

The Forty-sixth Congress was called in special session in March, 1879, because of the failure of the preceding Congress to pass the necessary appropriation bills — an outcome of the conflict between the executive and legislative branches of the government over the President's policy in regard to the South. As in the two preceding Congresses the Democrats had a majority in the lower House; there was also a small representation of Nationals or Greenbackers, to which group General Weaver belonged. The combined Republican and Greenback membership of the House was only 144, while the Democrats had 149 members; and so the organization of that body was effected without the aid of the Greenbackers,[99] who cast their votes for Hendrick B. Wright for Speaker. James A. Garfield was the Republican candidate; and Samuel J. Randall, the successful Democratic nominee.

In the committee assignments General Weaver received appointments upon the committee on elections and the committee on expenditures in the Treasury Department.[100] It was evident from the first that his position in Congress must depend entirely upon his personality and ability unaided by party affiliations and seriously handicapped by his connection with an independent or third party. A member of a minority of a minority had little chance for a display of his ability, and little hope of recognition upon his merits.

General Weaver's first speech was made on April 4, 1879, in the debate in the committee of the whole upon the army appropriation bill with special reference to the use of Federal troops at elections in the South. The debate was a continuation of a controversy which had arisen in the preceding Congress and involved particularly a discussion of the new policy in regard to the South. It had been the occasion for the failure of the last Congress to enact the usual appropriation bills. General Weaver's participation in the discussion enabled him to make plain his own position and that of the Greenback group upon this as well as upon other more or less connected subjects.

By way of introduction Weaver declared that the people of the country had "witnessed for many years with painful impatience the continuation of . . . . sectional strife." He then referred to the fact that "the same eternal broil" had been kept up during the two preceding Congresses. "And now in this first and extraordinary session of the Forty-sixth Congress, when the people are confidently looking for substantial relief, the same old difficulty is again introduced and weeks of precious time are being wasted in the discussion. . . .

"I have changed my mind entirely as to the remedy necessary to drive away from the politics of this country this disturber of our peace. I . . . . was a republican for twenty-one years. As soon as I obtained my majority almost I joined that party and fought in an humble way both at home and in the field to ingraft upon the laws of the country the measures which I believed were rightfully advanced by that organization. But in my opinion no remedy applied merely to the surface of this wound will give the people permanent peace. We must have constitutional treatment that will remove even the cause of the disease, and this makes it necessary to have a change of physicians."

Congressman Weaver next expressed amazement at the reference of a member of the House the day before "to the hereditary right of the democracy to rule", and the comparison of "that party to the children of Israel in their wanderings from Egypt to the promised land . . . . Upon reflection I thought there might be some similarity, but I did not know but he had mistaken the army of Pharoah for that of Israel. Let us, however, notice the similarity between the children of Israel and the democratic party. The democracy have succeeded in getting their Joshua into the Senate and their Caleb into the House, but thousands of their carcasses have fallen in the wilderness on their way to the Canaan of their hopes. And I say to him and to the gentlemen on that side of the House that their Moses in 1880 will die on Mount Nebo, especially if he should be a hard-money Moses. . . . The new Moses, if he represent sectional strife and the financial views which are now starving the people of this country, will perish also without realizing his exalted hope; but not because he struck the rock from which the water was to issue, but because he and his friends have joined hands across this aisle with the hard-money men on the republican side of the House to dry up the fountains of the prosperity of the people.''

"Sir, gentlemen talk about revolution — the eloquent gentleman from Ohio [Mr. Garfield] did so on last Saturday in the most adroit and forcible manner. I say to this House that if by the continuation of sectional strife and the withholding of substantial relief you force the people to much longer 'eat the bread of idleness', it will not be long before they will thirst for the 'wine of violence'. There is where the danger of revolution is to be looked for. It does not come from the defeated confederacy, it does not come from the gentlemen on my right, primarily; but it comes from the uneasy masses who are out of employment to-day, and out of food and destitute of raiment. It comes from those through whose enforced idleness the country is now losing more per diem than it cost to put down the rebellion at its most expensive period.

"Sir, I want it distinctly understood that cotton is no longer king in this country, nor is gold, but that the laboring-man, the industrial classes are sovereign, and their behests must be obeyed, and be obeyed speedily. It is unquestionably the duty of the industrial classes, by means of the ballot, to speedily take the Government into their own hands, but in doing so to do justice to all.''

Returning to what he called "this unpardonable sectional strife", Weaver stated that he believed that the old parties were incapable of giving relief to the country. It takes "ten or fifteen years to develop the leaders of a great party, and fully as long to shake them loose again; and it is never done, and history will bear me out in that statement, except by movement from without that crushes the organizations over which they dominate. This is the only method through which the people can gather the fruitage of advanced civilization. . . . . A new organization must do it, and the Lord is raising up that party now. The workmen are all at work in the quarries, and every block in the temple shall be peace. As an humble representative of the national greenback party, I feel great solicitude that it shall commence to build on solid foundations; and I say here to the gentlemen on the right and on the left that the national greenback party wants neither soldiers nor bulldozers at the polls".

After several interruptions and questions, to which Congressman Weaver replied amid laughter and applause, he closed his speech by saying that unless there was passed at that session, "first, a law for the unrestricted coinage of silver; second, a law for the substitution of greenbacks for national-bank notes; third, a law stopping the further increase of the bonded debt and providing for the speedy payment of the debt now outstanding; fourth, a law liberating the five hundred or more millions now lying idle in the Treasury; fifth, give to the people an opportunity to escape from the impending loss of their homes; unless these things be done at this session, very few of the gentlemen who occupy seats upon this floor will ever see them again.

"Our people out West do not like the combat to which you summon them, nor the feast that you set before them, nor yet the contrast that exists between the inflation mortgages upon their farms and the resumption hogs they are forced to sell. There is too great a contrast between them. There is a screw loose in Federal legislation, and the people have found where it is. They have learned that these parties [Republican and Democratic] are recreant to their trust and are not legislating for their interests.

"Let us act as Representatives of the whole people, and not as politicians, nor for the rings and cliques of the country."[101]

This first speech in Congress was very illuminating. It not only gave General Weaver an opportunity to declare his views upon public questions, but it also gave him a chance to display his ability as a debater. His ready use of scriptural references and quotations was espe-

cially noticeable: his deeply religious nature
was never concealed in his public service. The
success of his first appearance may be inferred
from statements made in Iowa papers in which
it was declared to be the first time the sixth
district had been heard from in Congress since
its organization in its then existing form.
Indeed, such was the impression made that
Congressman Weaver was invited by the mayor
and other citizens of New York to speak at
Cooper Institute on April 30th.[102]

General Weaver had voiced ideas and principles in Congress that were little regarded at
the time. The contrast between the reception
given his views in 1879, and the attitude of the
two great parties in recent years towards
social politics, is the measure of the progress
made in the intervening period. The pioneer
of 1879 is now seen to have been a farsighted
leader.

Again on April 10th Weaver took part in a
debate in regard to the proper disposition of
$10,000,000 held in the Treasury to redeem
fractional currency. The debate was an incident in the discussion of appropriations for the
Pension Bureau in connection with the legislative appropriation bill. On account of an
impending deficit the Secretary of the Treasury
had proposed an issue of four per cent bonds.
Opponents of this recommendation urged that

the $10,000,000 referred to was idle money, and could safely be used because of the small amount of fractional paper currency in circulation, and also because the Secretary of the Treasury was authorized to exchange $10,000,000 of subsidiary silver coins for the $10,000,000 of paper money. Mr. James A. Garfield and Mr. John A. McMahon of Ohio were the principal speakers. Weaver supported the position taken by Mr. McMahon who argued for the use of the $10,000,000; while Mr. Garfield opposed it on grounds of sound financial policy.

Congressman Weaver thought it "unquestioned that the $346,000,000 of legal-tender notes outstanding" included "the $10,000,000 held in the Treasury for the redemption of the fractional currency", and that the Secretary of the Treasury was "abundantly able to redeem all the fractional currency" as it came in with fractional silver. The suggestion of Mr. Garfield that the law passed on May 31, 1878, requiring the Secretary to pay out greenbacks as they came in under the Resumption Act, was simply a law to make certain what before was uncertain was not true. "The resumption law was a bold attempt to convert every greenback into interest-bearing debt and then to destroy them . . . . under the resumption act the Secretary of the Treasury was destroying the greenbacks, every one that came into his hands. This law was passed . . . . to prevent the further destruction of greenbacks; and it further provides that he should pay them out and keep them in circulation. This amendment does not change existing law. Why keep on hoarding them? Why keep them there to redeem fractional currency when there is no necessity, when you have plenty of fractional silver currency to redeem them? It is a mere trick of the Secretary to avoid the plain object of the law and to circumvent public sentiment.

"Now, the policy of the gentleman from Ohio [Mr. Garfield] is this: to issue bonds to get money to pay the arrearages of pensions, while ours is to issue the idle greenbacks now in the Treasury and save to the people this enormous and unnecessary increase of the public debt."[103]

On May 8, 1879, Weaver interposed remarks in a debate upon a free coinage bill. Congressman H. G. Fisher of Pennsylvania, a hard-money advocate, opposed the measure upon the usual grounds that gold would be driven out of circulation and the country would have only silver. He referred sarcastically to a bill introduced by a Greenbacker, Mr. Gilbert De La Matyr of Indiana, asking for $1,000,000,000, saying that he wanted the same amount for a few constituents "for the laudable purpose of constructing a narrow-gauge air-line railway to the moon, to ascertain whether or not that luminary is made of green cheese.'' Mr. Fisher declared that he wanted to say to the gentleman from Iowa that he was elected by his constituents upon a gold platform and that he had carried his district the first time it was ever carried by the Republicans. In reply Weaver said, ''That is good. I carried mine the other way for the first time.''[104]

General Weaver's longest speech during the first session of his service in Congress was delivered on May 9, 1879, in connection with a discussion over a bill for the free coinage of silver. He declared, in beginning his address, that the consideration of ''systems of finance for a great government'' was an important matter, but that he had not been highly impressed with the manner in which those opposed to the bill had discussed the question. ''They seem to regard the bill as an unwarranted intrusion upon the rights of somebody. They attack it alternately with levity, sarcasm, and abuse. It is a question that ought to be discussed in the light of the Constitution, the necessities of our people, and the present condition of public affairs.''

Two facts, he said, impressed him forcibly at the commencement of the discussion: ''silver and gold have been used as money from the foundation of human society'', and there is "about an equal amount of gold and silver bullion in the world." Opposition to the remonetization of silver can only be based upon "the position that there is too much metal money in the world . . . . The annual gold product throughout the whole earth at this time is about $100,000,000, (and it is rapidly declining,) barely enough, if we could command it all, to pay the annual interest of the bonded debt of the United States alone. If we are to demonetize silver, and have no power to create a legal-tender paper money, it will be readily perceived that the proposition is to hitch the car of American progress and American civilization to this decreasing product, and this will lead us into inevitable decline and pauperism."

General Weaver maintained that Congress had no power to prohibit silver coinage and that the law passed in 1873 was consequently unconstitutional. In referring to the more recent claim that the demonetization of silver in 1873 was "an accident, and was not intentional", he said that if the excuse was a true one, the proposal to reinstate silver as legal-tender money would not be opposed. "The animus of the demonetization of silver is disclosed by the opposition which its remonetization has met with and is now meeting with. In reality and in truth, silver was demonetized in the interest . . . . of a certain class of men in this and in other countries.

"It is very remarkable, when you come to read the history of the demonetization of metal money, that that metal which is the more abundant is always demonetized . . . . it is a remarkable circumstance that demonetization in the Old World is coincident in point of time with demonetization in this country. And the war upon silver is made by the same class of men the world over, namely, those having fixed incomes and who complain that the value of their incomes will be depreciated in proportion to the increase in the value of property. I want these facts to be well understood by the people who own the great bulk of the labor and property of this country. I want them to distinctly understand that the conflict is between money on the one hand and all other kinds of property on the other. . . .

"I am as much opposed as any member here to worthless money, to depreciated money, but unquestionably it is the interest of the great mass of our people that we should have cheap money and dear property; I do not mean worthless money, but I mean cheap money as compared with the property which it buys. Property is held by the many and money by the few; and if the Government is to be administered in the interest of the many, then my proposition is correct. I want good money, but cheap money and dear property. We have just the reverse of this to-day; we have cheap property and dear money. Money to-day is master and king in America, and property goes begging and is at a discount.''

In the next place reference was made to the fact that England, ''the greatest bondholding nation upon the earth,'' was the first to demonetize silver. ''The money dealers of Germany, England, and the United States own the bulk of the funded debt of the world, which now amounts to about thirty-two thousand millions, mostly contracted in flush times.

''Capitalists readily saw that if they could strike down as legal-tender money one-half of the metal money of the earth and make this enormous funded debt payable in gold alone, it would be greatly to their advantage. The people should thoroughly understand this also. They are beginning to understand it, and are everywhere and almost unanimously demanding that silver shall be thoroughly reinstated. Thus we are brought face to face with the great fact that demonetization was the result of a great international conspiracy, inaugurated by men who had fixed incomes as against, and to the detriment of those who own the great bulk of the property of the world.''

After a number of questions were asked and answered, General Weaver turned to a consideration of the national banking system and showed that if it was to be permanent "then of necessity the bond system must be permanent also . . . . Hence you have ingrafted upon this Government as another step in the great conspiracy the system of permanent national banks and permanent national debt". As another reason for opposing national banks he referred to their power to contract the currency at their pleasure in accordance with the demands of trade. He maintained that the elasticity obtained at the option of the banks constituted one of the greatest objections to the system.

General Weaver also declared that "resumption was another step in the great scheme which included the demonetization of silver. The resumption act was one of the trinity of infamies fastened upon the American people by that diabolical plot. What was the plea for that act? It was that we should pay our honest debts, that we should pay the debt created by the greenback. This was the plea of the republican party all over the country; that the Government ought to pay its honest debts. I wish to show right here and now the hypocrisy of that declaration. I say that the resumption act was not passed for the purpose of paying our honest debts, but for the purpose of increasing the bonded debt of the country."

In conclusion he referred to the abusive

methods used by the opposition in Congress and by the press against the Greenbackers. "It makes the syndicate and subsidized press as mad to see a greenbacker in Congress as it does a bull to shake a red flag at him."[105]

A contemporary newspaper account of Congressman Weaver's speech will give some idea of the impression made by him in Congress during his first session of service. According to this report his speech in April "made him such a reputation as a debater and a man of ability" that he was sure of an attentive hearing whenever he desired to speak. When it became known that he had prepared a careful speech reviewing the whole scheme of Republican bank and bond legislation, there was a general desire to hear him. As soon as he began to speak members from all parts of the house crowded into the seats near him. His own seat was "next to the center aisle, three seats from the front, the most available place in the House." The galleries were well filled at the beginning and the numbers increased as he proceeded.

"As the speaker gradually opened the theme", continues the account, "and step by step, exposed and denounced the wicked legislation of the Republican party, drawing hearty applause at every turn, it was amusing to see the syndicate fellows on the Republican side

wince and gnash their teeth. Finally, angered
to a perfect fit of frenzy, they began to interrupt the speaker with questions. But they were
answered so quickly, candidly and effectually,
that they could not retain their anger, and as
many as ten or a dozen would be up propounding questions at the same time. Finally, Gen.
Weaver, who preserved his good temper
throughout, remarked that he was perfectly
willing to answer all the questions that anybody
might care to ask, but he suggested that it
caused too great confusion to have the whole
syndicate propounding questions at the same
time. This raised a general laugh and took the
wind completely out of the whole horde.''[106]

It was on May 15, 1879, that Congressman
Hiram Price of Iowa commented upon Weaver's
speech which had been delivered during his
absence. In the course of his remarks he mentioned the fact that he had the printed speech
before him. He wanted to show, he said, that
''the whole tendency of the debate'' was ''to
create unrest, uneasiness, dissatisfaction, uncertainty'' in monetary and commercial affairs.
He was ''a silver-dollar man, and in favor of
the silver dollar of 412½ grains.'' He refused
to allow Mr. Weaver to interrupt in a five-
minute speech. He could take his own time and
he would answer any speech or question that he
might ask. He reiterated his statement that

such a debate as they were engaged in was unsettling the business of the country and making the people uneasy and dissatisfied. "To-day a day's labor will buy more of anything that a man eats or wears than it ever would at any time in the last fifty years of the history of this country."[107]

During the voting upon various sections of the silver coinage bill on May 21st General Weaver offered an amendment directing the Secretary of the Treasury to pay out "without discrimination standard silver coin belonging to the Government that may at any time be in the Treasury the same as gold coin in liquidation of all kinds of coin obligations against the Government." After much opposition to the presenting of this amendment from Republican leaders like Mr. Garfield and Mr. Reed, a vote was taken which resulted in 143 yeas, 75 nays, and 67 not voting.[108]

The next day during some heated remarks a hard-money representative referred to the government as "a damned scoundrel", if it paid interest on its bonds in depreciated currency. He added that he did not "use the word in a profane sense, but as a pulpit expletive." At this point General Weaver made the point of order that the gentleman was "swearing like the army in Flanders"— a sally that was greeted with laughter by the House.[109]

Again on June 18th Congressman Weaver was allowed five minutes in the debate upon the bill providing for the exchange of trade-dollars for legal-tender silver dollars. He remarked by way of introduction that it was amusing to listen to "the conflicting views" upon metal money. One member thought the silver dollar of 412½ grains was not of equal value with the gold dollar, and would be willing to cut down the gold dollar to equalize them. He did not have personally "any very serious objection", but he would like to inquire how the bonds issued since 1870 could be paid since they were payable either in gold or silver dollars of existing weights. A change in the gold dollar would leave only the silver dollar with which to pay interest upon the bonds. "That, I think, would be a capital joke on the bondholder, and I rather like it."

Next he paid his respects to his colleague from Iowa, Mr. Price, whom he described as growing eloquent in the closing hours of the session in favor of unlimited coinage of silver after voting against the Warner Silver Bill a few weeks before. Mr. Price interrupted to warn him against misrepresenting his position, and to say that he had never stated that he was in favor of unlimited coinage of silver. In reply Mr. Weaver remarked that "at the risk of my personal safety, then, let me put my colleague on record before the people of Iowa as being opposed to unlimited coinage. The gentleman may take that form of the dilemma if he likes, and that will not be very safe for him in Iowa.'' Mr. Price answered that he had stated his views upon the question before the people of Iowa.

Congressman Weaver then took up the proposed redemption of the trade-dollar with standard dollars. ''What! Propose to redeem a dollar of 420 grains with one of 412½ grains? Why will not the gentleman be consistent and come out and admit frankly . . . . that it is the fiat that he wants and not more grains of metal?'' In reply to questions as to whether he did not think that paper money could be ''made as good by the simple fiat of the Government as metal money'', he stated that he was ''in favor of gold, silver, and legal-tender paper money, of equal legal-tender qualities, and made so by the fiat of the Government.'' His opponents were ''in favor of gold, silver, and national-bank currency — particularly the national bank part of it.''

Asked what he would have his greenback money based upon, Weaver replied that he wanted it founded ''upon the gold, the silver, the wheat, the corn, and everything else in the country, including the public credit.'' Several other questions brought out from Weaver the rejoinder: "One at a time, if you please. Verily, the voice of the greenbacker stirreth up my friends on the right."

"Now, there is great difficulty in regard to cutting down the amount of gold in the dollar", continued Weaver. "As I remarked, if you reduce the amount of metal in the gold dollar it will be said you cannot pay the bond in gold. And if you add to the amount of silver in the silver dollar, then you take away, for the third time, from the people the right to pay the bonded debt according to the contract. It is high time for this Government to do away with this bartering with creditors, and say, 'There is one dollar for all, rich and poor alike; and it shall pay all debts to the rich and the poor, whether he be a bondholder or a bondpayer'. We want a dollar of the Government established by law, and not by barter with crafty public creditors . . . . I adhere to the old standard of 412½ grains for a silver dollar and 25.8 grains for a gold dollar, and then I would have the royal loyal greenback as my paper dollar. It came to the rescue of the Government when silver and gold, like cowardly traitors, fled away and hid until the battle was over."[110]

During this first session General Weaver introduced ten bills, six of which had to do with pensions or relief for soldiers or their

dependents and one related to the removal of
cases from State courts to United States courts.
The remaining three measures had reference to
the currency: one directed the Secretary of the
Treasury to pay out standard silver coin without discrimination; another authorized the
Secretary of the Treasury to issue $600,000,000
of United States notes to be known as lawful
money of the United States; and the third gave
the same official power to issue $50,000,000 of
fractional currency. The bills introduced by
him, as well as the part which he took in debate,
indicated that his paramount interest was in
currency and financial matters.[111] He represented ably and constantly opinions that had
been gradually taking shape for a number of
years. Some of these opinions have been
proven, by later developments and through
wider observation, to be mistaken. Thus, the
myth about the ''Crime of 1873'' as a part of a
world-wide conspiracy to strike down silver is
no longer seriously regarded. But the fundamental truth of the danger to democracy from
the concentration of wealth and financial power
is now generally recognized.

General Weaver was a pioneer with the
viewpoint of the agricultural West. At the
same time he was without the experience to
judge broadly as to financial and business
developments in the older industrial and com-

mercial parts of the country. Instinctively, and in the main accurately, he felt that financial and commercial interests could not safely be left to deal with matters of vital concern to the masses of the people. The details of his diagnosis have many times been shown to be erroneous, but his main conclusions have come to be generally accepted. Even in the case of his emphasis upon the currency, many observers and authorities admit that a more liberal policy might have avoided some of the difficulties actually experienced. Political reasons rather than economic forces have too often determined national policies.

VIII

SECOND SESSION IN CONGRESS

1879–1880

DURING the second session of his Congressional service, lasting from December 1, 1879, to June 7, 1880, the rôle taken by General Weaver was similar to that assumed by him in the first session. On December 3, 1879, he introduced what came to be known as the Weaver Soldier Bill, described to be "for the relief of the soldiers and sailors who served in the Army and Navy of the United States in the late war for the suppression of the rebellion, and to restore to them equal rights with the holders of Government bonds." The bill was read twice and referred to the committee on military affairs. A week later he asked "unanimous consent to present a petition signed by about twenty thousand ex-soldiers or their immediate friends." Although not specifically mentioning it, the petition requested relief along the lines suggested by the bill introduced by Congressman Weaver.

The petition declared that the soldiers had been paid in "a depreciated currency" worth, during the greater part of their terms of service, "from forty to seventy cents on the dollar in coin"; that the government had since described "the payment of the bondholders in the same money" as "dishonesty and repudiation"; and that the bondholders did not have "a claim either in law or equity better than the men who offered their lives that the nation might live". The petitioners, therefore, believed that the government was "honestly and justly indebted to the soldiers for the difference between the value of greenbacks and gold at the time of payment with 6 per cent. interest, compounded semi-annually", and that Congress should provide for the payment of such differences in "a full legal-tender greenback, not to be fundable into bonds of any rate or class." Such action, it was declared, would give "immediate and direct relief to one million of the defenders of our Government in its hour of trial and danger, and indirectly to forty millions of American citizens by reason of the impetus given to all industrial pursuits".

Congressman Weaver requested that the petition without the names be read and that it be referred to the same committee to which his soldier bill had been referred. He also announced that "at the proper time" he would address the House in support of the petitioners.

On December 18, 1879, General Weaver rose

to a question of privilege in regard to a para-
graph in the *New York Tribune* of the day
before which described the numerous petitions
recently received from ex-soldiers as all alike
and suggested that he was the author of them.
Viewing the item as a reflection upon his character "as a Representative of the people",
Weaver declared that he was not the author
and was not "the exclusive medium of their
presentation to the House . . . . I hurl
back the imputation as a slander by this Wall
street journal upon myself and the brave men
who have petitioned for equal rights with the
holders of Government bonds." In conclusion
he remarked that "at the death of Horace
Greeley the *New York Tribune* lost its reputation both for honesty and intelligence."

About a month later Congressman James W.
Singleton of Illinois presented a petition from
five hundred officers, soldiers, and sailors from
Greene County, Illinois, asking for the passage
of the Weaver Soldier Bill. The petition contained resolutions, adopted at a mass-meeting
held in the county, requesting their "Senators
and Representatives in Congress (without regard to political parties) to support this most
just and righteous measure", and urging organization "all over the nation" and the keeping
of a record of the action of members of Congress as to their attitude toward the measure.

The bill received no further consideration in the House, and consequently General Weaver probably never delivered his promised address in its favor, although there was printed in the appendix to the *Congressional Record,* under date of May 10, 1880, a speech entitled *Human Life versus Gold,* and described as "on the bill for the relief of the soldiers and sailors . . . . . and to restore to them equal rights with the holders of Government bonds."[112]

The most dramatic episode in Weaver's second session in Congress was his long struggle for recognition by the Speaker in order to present two resolutions. In the first of these resolutions it was declared to be the sense of the House that "all currency, whether metallic or paper, necessary for the use and convenience of the people, should be issued and its volume controlled by the Government, and not by or through the banking corporations of the country". The second resolution opposed the refunding of the public debt, urging that it should be paid "as rapidly as possible", and "to enable the Government to meet these obligations, the mints of the United States should be operated to their full capacity in the coinage of Standard Silver Dollars, and such other coinage as the business interests of the country may require".

These resolutions, embodying fundamental

financial principles from the point of view of
the third party group in the House of Representatives, were drafted by Weaver, and on the
first Monday in January, 1880, he asked to be
recognized by the Speaker in order to introduce
them.   Under the rules of the House at that
time it was proper for any member on Monday,
if he could secure recognition of the Chair, to
move the suspension of the rules and place upon
its passage any measure which he might desire
to offer.

Recognition of Mr. Weaver was refused by
the Speaker because the Democrats did not wish
to be placed upon record, immediately before
the Presidential election, upon what they regarded as "mere abstractions." Each Monday
for thirteen weeks the struggle continued.
After a few weeks it began to attract general
attention.   Crowds filled the galleries on Mon-
days and the newspapers severely criticized
"the aggravating perseverance of the author
of the resolutions."   The Speaker received
many letters, some praising him for his firm-
ness and others denouncing him as a tyrant.
The illustrated weeklies also contained "gross
and uncomplimentary" caricatures of General
Weaver.   Finally, on March 6, 1880, *Harper's
Weekly* published a full page cartoon by Nast,
representing Weaver "as a donkey, braying to
the utter consternation of the House.   The

Speaker was represented as standing with his
back to the author of the resolutions, members
as holding their hands over their ears, others
as endeavoring to crawl under the desks, and
the Mace as having been blown violently from
the hands of the Sergeant-at-Arms while he was
vainly attempting to hide from the storm.''[113]

The first reference in the *Congressional Record* to these resolutions is to be found on
February 27, 1880, in a debate upon the revision of the rules. Weaver referred to them
as having frightened the House for five weeks,
saying that they represented the opinion of
ninety-nine out of every hundred members of
the Democratic party west of the Alleghany
Mountains. He then had them read as a part
of his remarks, and afterward declared that he
''well understood'' why the leaders of the
Democratic party, ''being in the East for hard
money and in the West for soft money,'' did not
want to be put on record ''on the eve of a presidential election. But these resolutions are now
before the country, and I shall be found standing here inserting the thorn in the flesh every
Monday from now until the adjournment of
Congress, unless sooner gratified, seeking recognition. I am determined that gentlemen in
this House shall be put upon the record on
those resolutions and their public professions
tested.''[114]

March 1, 1880, Congressman Weaver rose to make a "parliamentary inquiry". After considerable controversy with the Speaker and other members, he mentioned the cartoon by Nast, "a gross misrepresentation", showing the Speaker with his back toward him. Mr. Garfield asked which figure represented Mr. Weaver, who replied: "The large figure with the long ears, of course, represents me. You know that the ass in the Bible saw the angel before Balaam, his rider, saw him."[115]

Finally at the beginning of April it became apparent that the long struggle would soon end. Rumors that recognition would be given the first Monday of the month became current, evidently emanating from the Speaker himself. Then a new problem appeared as under the rules a yea and nay vote could not be secured unless demanded by one-fifth vote of the members. There were but thirteen of the National party so that assistance was necessary to obtain a vote after recognition had been conceded by the Speaker. In this emergency Mr. Weaver and his associates appealed to Mr. Garfield to help in obtaining a yea and nay vote. They pointed out that the Republicans were already on record against the propositions contained in the resolutions, while the Democrats at home usually favored the propositions, but always avoided being put on record in regard to them.

After consultation with his colleagues Garfield replied that his side of the House would support the demand for a yea and nay vote.

It was on the first Monday in April that General Weaver was finally recognized. He made "the necessary motion to suspend the rules and demanded that the vote be taken by yeas and nays. Upon statement of the demand by the Chair the Greenback members, General Ewing, of Ohio, and Mr. Tillman, of South Carolina, rose to their feet followed by the entire Republican side of the House. The yeas and nays were accordingly ordered." Immediately with a few exceptions, the Democrats left the hall and gathered in the cloak rooms for consultation. On the first call of the roll only three or four Democrats responded, while the Republicans voted almost solidly in the negative. On the second call there were 84 yeas and 117 nays, 91 not voting. The affirmative vote consisted of eleven Greenbackers, one Republican, and seventy-two Democrats, mostly from the South and West. The negative vote was composed of Republicans, reinforced by eastern and middle States Democrats.[116]

In the debate upon the resolutions Mr. Garfield said that he had never heard the provisions contained in them until they were read that day. They had, however, attained "some historical importance by being talked about a good deal in the newspapers, and by blocking the other business of the House for some weeks." After a brief analysis of the resolutions, he asked how the $780,000,000 falling due "this year and next" were to be paid. "Print it to death — that is the way to dispose of the public debt", according to the resolutions. He urged "both parties" to show their courage by destroying "the triple-headed monster of centralization, inflation, and repudiation combined."

Replying to the leader of the Republicans, Congressman Weaver declared that he reckoned himself "most happy in having an opportunity of witnessing a vote upon these resolutions" which had "so attracted the attention of this House and of the country for the past three months." He was not surprised at the opposition of the gentleman from Ohio, for he understood "very well that that gentleman and his party" stood "in the road blocking the progress of the people toward financial reform." With reference to the criticism directed at the resolutions, he pointed out that "the national greenback party is opposed to the violation of the public faith, and is squarely opposed to the repudiation of any portion of the public debt. We are in favor of the payment of the debt according to the contract, and we are the only party that desires ever to pay it." In answer to the question where the government could get the money to pay the matured bonds, he said: "first, from the surplus revenues properly increased by a judicious income tax; second, by the coinage of silver." Explaining more fully his meaning, he declared that the government bought silver with the surplus revenues and manufactured silver dollars, and the $4,000,000 worth monthly that might be purchased under the existing law, would pay off the debt in half the time that it was proposed to fund it for. He called attention to the fact that they were paying off the debt then "for electioneering purposes at the rate of two millions a week", and did not feel it. There was ample surplus revenue for the purpose; all that was needed was the disposition to pay.[117]

During the second session of the Forty-sixth Congress it appears that General Weaver introduced ten bills, nine of which were for pensions or for the relief of soldiers and their dependents. The tenth measure was the so-called Weaver Soldier Bill. He also introduced five resolutions — two of these being the propositions about which he made his long fight for recognition by the Speaker. Of the other three, one was his minority report from the Committee on Elections, of which he was a member, recommending that the seat occupied by

William F. Slemons from the second district of
Arkansas be declared vacant; another requested the Secretary of the Treasury to report to
the House his action in anticipating interest
payments upon the public debt as provided for
by a joint resolution passed in March, 1864;
and the third recommended the employment of
an "additional page for the convenience of the
House."[118]

These bills and resolutions indicate his two
chief interests — justice to the soldiers who
had served in the Civil War and currency and
finance. Frequently he combined them in one
measure — as in his Soldier Bill in which he
proposed "to restore to them equal rights with
the holders of Government bonds."

His speeches and incidental remarks illustrated the same tendencies. On January 22,
1880, he spoke upon the bill then under discussion requiring the reserves of national banks to
be kept in gold and silver coins. He pointed
out that under the proposed measure banks
might keep their entire coin reserves in subsidiary silver and trade-dollars. Those coins
were consequently "exalted above the greenback", which was a legal tender for all
amounts. Such a proposal was "a discrimination against the greenback and inimical to the
interests of the people . . . . and in favor
of the bondholder. It is the same old obnoxious

class legislation over and over again . . . .
The greenback is the only reliable dollar in
America to-day. It stays at home, and is al-
ways as good as gold.''

The claim of the opposition that the country
owed ''three hundred and forty-six millions of
legal-tender war debt'' was refuted by reference to the act of Congress of May 30, 1878, by
which ''the greenback became the perpetual
legal-tender money'' of the United States. He
admitted the statement of the opposition that
President Lincoln approved of the issue of
greenbacks because there was no other re-
source. ''Gold, silver, and the Shylocks of the
country failed the Government in the hour of
its trial, and we were compelled to resort to
legal-tender paper. It was the fiat of the Government to save the nation's life; and the same
fiat is doubly necessary to-day to save the
liberties of the people . . . . The issue
fairly before the people is this: Shall we have
in this country legal-tender paper issued by the
Government, or shall the people depend upon
banking corporations for their circulating
medium? Shall the Government or the banking
corporations control the volume of the currency? Let gentlemen meet that issue fairly
and squarely. The issue is between the corporations and the people. Shall we depend
upon banking corporations for the volume of

our currency, and in that way give the banks
the control of all values in this Republic?''

He referred to the opposition of "the gentleman from New York [Mr. Chittenden]" to his
soldier bill; "he stooped over and shook his
little fist in my innocent face! . . . . The
gentleman goes into hysterics the very moment
he mentions the soldiers' bill. He regards it as
an assault upon the peculiar interests which he
represents. But he is not the only gentleman
who is seriously annoyed by it. A very distinguished gentleman, a citizen of the State of
Illinois, a distinguished ex-soldier and philolo-
gist [John A. Logan] said . . . . that the
bill introduced by General Weaver . . . . to
equalize the pay of soldiers was the worst piece
of 'demagogy'—'demagogy' is good — ever
introduced into an American Congress.''

Mention was also made of a letter of a member of the House from Missouri in which it was
said that the author of the soldiers' bill was
not in earnest and that the bill would not pass.
"Sir, let me say that the author of that bill and
the more than five hundred thousand men who
stand behind him were never more in earnest
than now. They were not more earnest when
storming the heights of Fort Donelson or fighting the bloody battles of Shiloh, Gettysburgh,
and the Wilderness. And this House must give
the relief asked for, or these men will send a

Congress here that will grant them their prayer.''

General Weaver next paid his respects to his ''colleague from Iowa [Mr. Price]'', who had spoken a few days ago. He had told them that ''France had $426,000,000 of silver money, and 60 per cent. more than that of gold. That would give France $19 *per capita* in gold, $12 in silver, and she has $12 *per capita* in paper, making in all $43 *per capita* for the entire population, while in this country we have not to-day $8 *per capita* in actual circulation, although we have a population 50 per cent. greater than France, and an area of territory eighteen times larger than the territory of that country.'' He pointed out that his ''colleague'' had ''occupied every sign in the zodiac upon this question of finance, and no man can tell from what he said in his speech whether he favors this bill or is opposed to it . . . . But my colleague lauds the greenback! There is one thing I do not want him to do. He must not try to crawl into bed with the greenbackers without first taking off his republican boots and overcoat.''

In conclusion he declared that the bill was calculated ''to take the greenback out of the reach of the people and place it in the hands of those who will hoard it. Under the law as it now stands they can not do this as well as they

could desire. The people have some little protection. But if this bill becomes a law they will
be largely deprived of the legal-tender paper
dollar. It will disappear from circulation . .
. . the attempt has been made in this House
since the assembling of Congress to suppress
the discussion of the financial question. It cannot be done. The pressure is from without. It
comes from the people, who are masters of the
situation. They are discussing it in every village and hamlet, in every public meeting, in the
workshops, and even in the churches, and they
will continue to discuss it until it is settled in
their behalf.''[119]

Another speech by Weaver was printed in
the appendix to the *Congressional Record*
under date of May 10, 1880, with the title of
*The Irrepressible Conflict — The People vs.
Privileged Classes*. It is described as having
been made while the House had under consideration the bill ''to facilitate the refunding of
the national debt''— although it may never
actually have been delivered. In this speech he
maintained that the ''system of funding the
public debt, now the ruling policy of this Government, affords the most startling evidence
of the domination of the privileged classes, and
marks our total and melancholy departure from
the teachings of the founders of our Republic.
It is not a plant of American growth, but is

borrowed from the effete aristocracies and monarchies of the Old World. This system has been ingrafted upon our simple republican polity by men who are hostile to democratic institutions, and who believe in an aristocracy of wealth whose privileges and exemptions guarantee to the few the greatest possible accumulation of property and the widest control of public affairs . . . .

"All legislation looking to the perpetuation of our national debt, and of the national-banking system which feeds and fattens upon it, should be universally discouraged and denounced as a crime against the people, and all laws looking to their existence should be immediately repealed."

"Such has been the management of our finances, that it is conceded we cannot pay at the date these bonds become redeemable. The pretext upon which they were issued was, that the Government was not then able to pay, but would certainly be at the expiration of the time for which they were then to be issued. The expectation that we would ever be able to pay all these bonds at once was never for a moment entertained by the managers of this funding scheme, and if the people ever entertained such an idea they have been signally disappointed.

"The national party is opposed to funding this debt. We say that it is our great duty to

11

demand that it shall be paid. How can it be done, and when? We answer:

"First. By applying the surplus revenue to its extinguishment, which now amounts to over $50,000,000 per annum after defraying all expenses of the Government.

"Second. By paying out the silver now in the Treasury, amounting to $70,000,000. Twenty-three million dollars of this consists of subsidiary coin 7 per cent. light, which would have to be coined over into standard dollars.

"Third. By operating our mints to their full capacity in the coinage of standard silver dollars.

"Fourth. By levying a judicious income-tax upon the wealthy, who now bear none of the burdens of taxation.

"Fifth. By substituting legal-tender greenbacks for national-bank notes and canceling the bonds now held by the Treasury to secure their circulation."

In conclusion General Weaver declared that "national banking and the funding system are counterparts of each other. The two must perish together, and perish quickly. They are twin monsters, brought hither to crush out liberty on this continent. Aware of the danger, the people have organized a party for self-defense. This party believes in the power of the Government to make all the money necessary for the use of the people, and in the right of the nation to pay off its debt whenever it has the money. No human power can stop the progress of this new movement. It is broad and national in its doctrines and purposes. It eschews sectionalism, and demands for the humblest individual in the land a free ballot, fair play, and equal rights before the law. The old factions will not allow us to succeed if by any means, fair or foul, they can defeat us. In California they strike down free speech with fine and imprisonment. In other sections they confront us with slander and misrepresentation. The bulldozers of one section join hands with the money kings of the other to crush the people's party, and to keep laboring-men from voting their untrammeled sentiments. But 'your covenant with death shall be disannulled and your agreement with hell shall not stand.' You have the chains forged necessary to rob industry of its reward. But you shall be disappointed. You would like to see the sun rise and set on a nation of slaves. But the people perceive your purpose and are awake to the danger.

"May God in his infinite mercy help the taxpayers of this country to look into this question, and nerve them to rebuke their despoilers; may He send upon our people that high type of patriotism and courage that will crush all parties, and men, and laws that stand for the enslavement of the people!''[120]

No matter what might be the nature of the measure upon which General Weaver was addressing the House, he seems usually to have turned to some phase of the subjects that mainly engaged his attention. In February, 1880, in speaking upon a bill regulating the removal of causes from State to Federal courts, with which he expressed himself as ''in hearty accord'', he took up the subject of corporations. He regarded the right of corporations to appeal to Federal courts in the trial of cases brought against them by individuals as a serious grievance, and in violation of the constitutional principle that the citizen should be tried by a jury of the vicinage.

He pointed out that the founders of the government ''threw around the cradle of the young Republic certain safeguards. One of these safeguards was that there should be no titles of nobility in this country; another that the right of primogeniture should not obtain here, that there should be no entailed estates, so that the wealth of the country should diffuse itself among the people according to natural and beneficent laws. They did not contemplate the creation of these corporations that are as real entities as are individuals — ideal persons that never die, and yet possess the power to acquire and hold property equally with real persons. They did not . . . . contemplate the rise and progress of these legal Goliaths. . . .

"The existence of such corporations seems to be necessary to the progress of our civilization; they are inseparable from it; but they should not be clothed by legislation with exclusive privileges over the citizen. The people must put hooks into the jaws of these leviathans, and control them.

"The accumulation of capital in the hands of these corporations of itself gives them immense power and tremendous advantage over individuals. But if you, in addition to that, load them with exclusive privileges by law — the privilege of shirking and shunning the ordinary tribunals in which the common people have to litigate their rights — and if you allow them the power and the privilege of dragging the citizen to remote tribunals, then, indeed, you more than double or treble their power. The corporation should seek no exclusive privileges, and the citizen should be just to the corporation. . . .

"What objection . . . . can be urged against compelling corporations to come into the State courts? The only one I can imagine is that there is a prejudice in the minds of the people which precludes justice in the State courts . . . . If there is prejudice existing

to-day in the minds of the people against corporations, it grows out of a deep-seated conviction on their part that the legislation of the
country has been in favor of the corporation
and against the citizen. Let the citizens . .
. . know and understand that there are to be
no exclusive privileges, that the corporations
are simply to go into the State courts and there
assert their rights as any other citizen; that of
itself will disarm any honest man of prejudice. . . .

"There is no such thing as shutting the eye
. . . . to the fact that there is a growing
tendency to-day in this country to concentration
of power in the hands of the few. I do not
charge in my remarks that this is the result of
any deliberate scheme of legislation; it is not
necessary here for me to do so; it is a fact
nevertheless. And whenever this Congress or
this House has the opportunity to strike down
that tendency, and to reduce all classes of
citizens to an equal footing, and to remand
them to common rights, they should avail themselves of the opportunity."[121]

Weaver's position in the House was an unusual one; for the first time there was a group
of members who did not belong to either of the
two great parties. They were too small in numbers to hope to have much influence, but they
believed that they represented a considerable

proportion of the people of the country, and
consequently felt obliged to assert themselves.
Their official designation was "Nationals", but
they were variously referred to in the House as
the "party of the center" and as a "third
party". The former appellation was taken
from the location of their seats (six of them
including Weaver had seats on the center
aisle); the latter came from the traditional
division of our people into two parties following the accepted English arrangement. Any
divergence from settled principles was described as a third party; all legislative arrangements presumed two parties and two only.[122]

Early in his Congressional career General
Weaver seems to have been recognized as the
leader of the third party group. His ability as
a speaker and debater, and his prominence as a
soldier and in the Republican party before he
joined the Independents pointed to him as the
most promising member for such a rôle. Toward the end of the second session the time of
final adjournment was under consideration.
The Speaker ruled that fifteen minutes should
be allowed to the member representing the majority, and the same amount to the one representing the minority, and he added that "the
gentleman from Iowa [Mr. Weaver] claims that
he ought to be recognized to have a portion of
the time, and therefore the Chair would sug-

gest that a part of it, say, five minutes, should be allowed to him." In reply to a question the Speaker said that it was the custom "to recognize representative members."

There was considerable opposition to the ruling, but it was finally followed and General Weaver spoke against adjournment. He described the funding bill as "a menace to the labor and industry of this country, and threatens the whole country with a calamity more terrible than a plague, pestilence, or famine. The fate of that bill is extremely doubtful if the vote can be reached now. The vote in this House on the 5th of April on the currency and debt resolutions placed the funding bill in great peril. This is well understood. But it is just as well understood that if its friends can carry it over until after the presidential election, they will pass it and fasten that debt perpetually upon American industry. That is one of the main reasons for this hasty adjournment.

"Again, the right of petition has been denied and abridged to the American people during this session. Petitions bearing the signatures of more than six hundred thousand soldiers have been stowed away in a committee-room in this House unheeded. These soldiers petition for justice and the equalization of their pay. They ask the Government to fulfill its solemn contract made when the country's life was in hazard. But there is no disposition on the part of a majority of this House to regard their petition. Fifteen years have now passed away since the close of the war, and yet the bounties and back pay due to soldiers and the pay of teamsters and others who served in our armies for the preservation of the Union are unsettled and utterly neglected. Hundreds of claims have been adjusted, even under existing law, but Congress has thus far failed to make the necessary appropriation to pay them.

"During these fifteen years that have elapsed since the war closed the Government has been giving away to rich corporations vast empires of our public domain and throwing the wealth of the country into the laps of the opulent and powerful. But there is no disposition to be just, much less generous, to the soldier, his widow, and orphan.

"I enter my solemn protest against the final adjournment until Congress does justice to the men who saved the flag that throws its protecting shadow over the Speaker".[123]

These remarks are an excellent illustration of the way in which Weaver made use of every opportunity to emphasize his favorite principles. In season and out of season he called attention to those measures which he regarded as of vital importance. Most of his effort seemed wasted at the time — practically no results were obtained. His work was that of a pioneer, misunderstood and ridiculed. But it was destined to bear fruit in due time, although not always in the form which he proposed. Many times he was mistaken in his detailed proposals, but he was sound in his hostility to special privilege as opposed to the best interests of the masses of the people.

He made two basic contentions: that the gold production of the world was inadequate to furnish the circulating medium for the trade of the world, and that the control of the volume of money in circulation should be by the government and not by the bankers. As to the first of these contentions, it should be remembered that the circulating medium per capita in the United States and the world has been tripled since 1896 by the opening of the Rand and Alaskan mines, and by the introduction of processes for the reduction of low grade ores. Furthermore, the control of the currency has been definitely placed by the enactment of the Federal Reserve Act in the hands of the Federal government.

IX

First Campaign for the Presidency

1880

The records show that General Weaver was granted leave of absence "indefinitely" from June 7, 1880, by the House of Representatives, Congress itself adjourning that year on June 16th.[124] No reason was given for the action; but it was understood that such leave would allow him to attend the Greenback National Convention which was to meet in Chicago on June 9th, and by which he was to be nominated for the Presidency. His prominence in Iowa as a Republican leader before his change of parties, supplemented by his activity in Congress for two sessions, made him inevitably one of the most promising Greenback presidential probabilities in 1880. He seems to have been very optimistic in regard to the prospects for the Greenbackers playing an important part in the election.[125]

There was clearly a chance that the new party might hold the balance of power in the next Congress as it had hoped to do in the Forty-sixth Congress. The narrow escape

from defeat in 1876, together with the dissatisfaction of many Republicans with the administration of President Hayes, gave encouragement to the hopes of success of the Democrats.
In any event the new party might find itself in
a position of advantage. No selection of President by the electors might throw the election
into the House, and in such an event the Greenbackers would hold a place of great strategical
importance, and might conceivably dictate
which one of the leading candidates should be
made President. Political uncertainty in 1880
favored the Greenback party.

In 1879 occurred the biennial election for
Governor in Iowa, John H. Gear being a candidate for reëlection. Weaver was reported to
have decided against fusion with the Democrats,
and to have said that the Greenback vote in the
State would amount to 75,000. He also believed
the Greenbackers would carry the South in
1879. An editorial on an interview with him in
The Iowa State Register in September described him as "the leader of his party in this
State and a popular candidate of it for the
Presidency next year." Weaver announced
that the "great guns" of the party — Solon
Chase and Congressman Murch of Maine,
James Buchanan and Congressman De La
Matyr of Indiana, and "Old" Jesse Harper of
Illinois — were coming to Iowa to help elect a

Greenback congressman in the Fifth District to fill the vacancy caused by the death of the member elected in 1878. Success in this contest would strengthen the Greenbackers in Congress as well as prepare the way for the campaign in 1880. Weaver himself had taken part in the campaign in Maine, from which he had just returned.

His estimate of the Greenback vote in Iowa was too optimistic — the actual count was nearer 45,000 than 75,000. But 1879 witnessed some near successes in Maine and Massachusetts that made his predictions actually more reasonable at the time than subsequent events now lead us to believe. In Iowa, too, the Greenbackers received the largest vote ever cast for a third party in that State — thus partly justifying Weaver's optimism.[126] On the eve of the campaign of 1880 there was really some ground for the belief that the situation of the Greenbackers corresponded to that of the Republican party in the early days of its existence.

In January, 1880, a National Greenback Labor conference was held in Washington, attended by one hundred to one hundred and twenty-five delegates exclusive of the Greenback Congressmen. Most of those present were representatives of State and local Greenback organizations with a few from trade and labor unions. The gathering was composed of lawyers, editors, workingmen, and farmers, representing many different shades of political and social reform. After the chairman of the National Committee had called the conference to order, Congressman Murch of Maine was made permanent chairman. The purpose of the meeting was to decide the time and place for the next national nominating convention, and after considerable discussion Chicago was selected as the place and June 9th as the time. Besides adopting the usual resolutions the conference endorsed Weaver's bill for the equalization of soldiers' pay and bounties; but immediately afterwards Weaver himself appeared and asked the withdrawal of the endorsement, since in his opinion the matter was not suitable for consideration at that time. His request was promptly complied with.[127]

A few months later General Weaver was said to favor General Benjamin F. Butler of Massachusetts as the best man for the Greenbackers to nominate for President; and Congressman De La Matyr agreed with him, declaring that with Butler as a candidate the election would be thrown into the House and the Democrats would vote for Butler in preference to a Republican.[128]

Early in June, 1880, Weaver, Gillette, and Senator David Davis of Illinois, had an extended conference in Washington upon the political situation. It was hoped by Weaver and Gillette that Senator Davis would consent to become the candidate of the Greenback party for the Presidency and the meeting was arranged with that object in view. The conference occurred in one of the committee rooms of the House of Representatives and lasted for about three hours. Senator Davis declared that he felt grateful for the mention of his name as "the candidate of the industrial people, and was in accord with most of their purposes; but he was not in a situation to accept the nomination and must decline, and we were instructed to see that his name was not placed before the convention. We plead with him to yield, but without avail."[129]

In May, 1880, the Iowa State Greenback Convention met at Des Moines. Resolutions to present General Weaver as the first choice of Iowa Greenbackers for President to the National convention were objected to; but upon the explanation being made that only a recommendation to the delegates was intended, the resolutions were adopted upon motion of L. H. Weller "with three cheers and a tiger." General Weaver, Congressman Gillette, Daniel Campbell, and M. H. Moore were chosen delegates at large.[130]

The National Greenback Convention met at Chicago on Wednesday, June 9, 1880, and con-

tinued in session until early Friday morning
Considerable confusion attended its organization because of the very varied elements of
which it was composed. Almost every phase
of radical opinion of the time had representatives anxious to have their peculiar views
recognized. Supporters of woman suffrage
and socialism were especially active in their
efforts; and there were divisions among the
Greenbackers themselves, some favoring fusion
with the Democrats and others opposed to compromise of any kind. Woman suffrage was
given a hearing, but no reference to it was made
in the platform. Forty-four delegates from the
Socialist Labor party were admitted to the
convention at their own request in order "to
make common cause against the common enemy
— the money power."

Apparently General Butler was most generally thought of as a candidate for President at
the beginning of the convention — at any rate
he seems to have been the second choice of a
very large number. Edward P. Allis of Wisconsin also had "a good deal of strength among
Western delegates." Later the sentiment of
the convention turned to Weaver. Nominations began at one o'clock Friday morning and
continued for three hours. Congressman Gillette nominated General Weaver and six other
candidates were named. At four o'clock an

informal ballot was taken and resulted as follows: General Weaver, 226; Hendrick B. Wright, 126; Stephen Dillaye, 119; General Butler, 95; Solon Chase, 89; Edward P. Allis, 41; and Alexander Campbell, 21.

Before a formal ballot was taken the names of Wright, Dillaye, Allis, and Campbell were withdrawn. When in the balloting it appeared that General Weaver had over 500 votes, States rapidly changed their votes; and when the results were announced at six o'clock, he was declared to be the unanimous choice of the convention for President. B. J. Chambers of Texas was quickly nominated for Vice President. Escorted by a committee that had been appointed to request his presence, General Weaver appeared and accepted the nomination in a "few neat and timely words." At 6.45 A. M. after an all night session the convention adjourned.[131]

A committee authorized by the convention and composed of S. F. Norton, E. P. Allis, Solon Chase, S. D. Dillaye, and E. H. Gillette, wrote General Weaver "that the Greenback Labor party of the United States, represented by 830 duly elected delegates from 36 States of the Union, assembled in National Convention . . . . reposing special trust and confidence in your integrity as a servant of the people, unanimously nominated you for the office of

12

President of the United States . . . . We also notify you that the convention, realizing the fact that the press, the pulpit, and public speakers, are to such an extent in the service and under the control of our political opponents, that our limited force of newspapers and public speakers, are at a disadvantage, in point of numbers, in the work of discussing the questions of finance and labor reform, passed a resolution urgently requesting you to devote your time to personally addressing the people at public meetings during the campaign.''

On July 3, 1880, from his home at Bloomfield, General Weaver formally accepted the nomination ''as a solemn duty''. After referring to the importance of the union of ''the various Greenback and Labor elements into one compact organization'', he declared that ''the admirable platform adopted by the convention'' met with his ''cordial approval. It is comprehensive, reasonable and progressive — containing those principles of economic reform essential to the preservation of the liberty and the prosperity of the whole people.''

An adequate circulating medium was, in his opinion, at the basis of the prosperity of the people of the country. Such a medium could only be issued by the government and should not be controlled by banking corporations. The existence of the national banking system depended upon the continuance of a national debt, both institutions having been borrowed from the English monarchy. He urged the payment of the public debt as rapidly as possible, and maintained that the surplus revenues and the idle coin in the Treasury, together with that which would accumulate under the silver law of 1878, would be sufficient to pay off the debt within the next six years. The only excuse for funding the debt was to perpetuate the national banking system which, with other corporations, was "fast swallowing up the profits of labor, and reducing the people to a condition of vassalage and dependence. Those monopolies, of whatever class, headed by the associated banks, are interlocked in purpose, and always act in closest sympathy."

General Weaver believed that "the great problem of our civilization" was "to bring the producer and consumer together", and to do this, besides an adequate currency, the "rigid regulation of inter-State commerce and transportation" was necessary. As both of these were in the control of monopoly, the producer and the consumer were being ground into "poverty and ruin". He was "especially thankful" that the platform was "open, bold, and unmistakable on these great questions", because the Republican and Democratic platforms were either "silent" or "pronounced in favor of the monopolies and against the people".

As to other items in the platform he referred particularly to the fact that an area of the public domain "larger than the territory occupied by the great German empire" had been "wantonly donated to wealthy corporations", while a bill to enable poor people to reach and occupy the public lands had been "ridiculed and defeated" in Congress. The public domain should be sacredly reserved for actual settlers, and where corporations had not complied strictly with the terms of the grants, the lands should be reclaimed. *The Iowa State Register* described this proposal as "the Socialistic land resolution adopted by the recent national convention of the Greenback-Labor party" in noting the receipt by the national executive committee of the Socialist Labor party of a letter in which Weaver expressed approval of the resolution.[132]

As to the immigration of persons from foreign countries General Weaver thought that those "seeking homes and desiring to become citizens of the United States, should be encouraged, but the importation of Chinese servile laborers" should be strictly prohibited.

He pointed out that the bondholders had been paid in gold, while the soldiers and sailors had been paid for their services in greenbacks.

The soldiers had been taxed to pay the interest on the bonds, while the bondholders had gone free. During the existing Congress all efforts for relief had failed because of the rigid rules of the House of Representatives, and the dictatorial power lodged in the hands of the Speaker.

In this letter of acceptance General Weaver took occasion to declare that "one of the grand missions" of the Greenback party was "to banish forever from American politics that deplorable spirit of sectional hatred, which for base purposes" had been kept alive by the Republican and Democratic leaders. "Let us have a free ballot, a fair count, and equal rights for all classes — for the laboring man in Northern manufactories, mines and workshops, and for the struggling poor, both white and black, in the cotton fields of the South."

Finally, he urged "united action of all industrial classes, irrespective of party . . . . to re-establish in the administration of public affairs, the old time Democracy of Jefferson and Jackson, and the pure Republicanism of Abraham Lincoln and Thaddeus Stevens."

In answer to the desire of the convention that its candidates "visit the various sections of the Union and talk to the people", he replied that it was his "intention to comply with this request to the extent" of his ability.[133]

This letter of acceptance embodied Weaver's

views upon public policies on the eve of the presidential campaign in 1880. His fundamental interest, as has been already indicated, centered in finance, including the currency, banks, and the public debt: he favored the use of greenbacks and silver upon an equality with gold. As a Western man he also felt the need of the regulation of transportation, and he believed he discerned a connection between the money power and the railroads. He anticipated by many years the idea of "interlocking directorates." He saw another field of activity of the corporations, especially of the railroads, in the public lands, and here he anticipated in part the later policy of conservation of natural resources. He felt that the soldier had been discriminated against in favor of the bondholder, but he discouraged a continuance of sectional controversy between the North and the South. He hoped for the union of all the forces of democracy in his day just as before the Civil War there had been a union of all the forces opposed to slavery. In his day he saw in the place of slavery the money power and industrial monopoly. Weaver was the first real leader in a movement which has gone on increasing in momentum, but which has by no means as yet attained the goal to which he looked.

The campaign of the Greenback candidate

seems to have begun in July: it ended only with election day. He covered the country from Arkansas to Maine, and from Lake Michigan to Mobile. In July and August he spoke in Alabama, Georgia, Arkansas, West Virginia, and Indiana. Late in August he went to Maine, speaking in Faneuil Hall, Boston, on his way there, and at Cooper Union, New York, on his return. In October, at Des Moines, he described his campaign to date by saying that he had been speaking in the open air for nearly one hundred days, sometimes twice a day; had made more than one hundred speeches; had travelled 20,000 miles; had shaken hands with 30,000 persons; and had addressed 500,000 people in fifteen States. At Terre Haute, Indiana, he had an audience of 30,000, and at other places in that State he had spoken to 8000, 10,000, and 12,000 people. Notwithstanding continued rain, Cooper Union in New York City was packed to its utmost capacity. His campaign in Maine was described as a triumphal march. People were said to have travelled over two hundred miles to hear him at Portland, and then were greatly disappointed because his time was limited by the lateness of the hour.[134]

Late in September the charge was made that the Greenback canvass was being "manipulated in the interest of the Republican party, and

General Weaver's expenses borne in large measure from the Republican campaign fund." The author of the charge, Dyer D. Lum, assistant secretary of the Greenback National Committee, described a meeting of the Executive Committee in New York in July at which, besides the chairman of the National Committee, Congressman Murch of Maine, General Weaver, Lee Crandall, Edward Daniels, Geo. O. Jones, and Lum himself were present. They "were also assisted with the advice and counsel of Senator John P. Jones of Nevada." At that meeting General Weaver proposed the name of Geo. O. Jones to raise funds for the campaign.

When General Weaver was in New York on his way from the South to Maine, Lum claimed to have called his attention to a rumor that Jones had received $5000 from the Republican fund. Weaver was described as replying "that it made no difference how much had been received, for his tour of Alabama and Arkansas would have been simply impossible without the aid Mr. Jones extended to him." General Weaver was accompanied from New York to Boston by Mr. Jones, and on that trip it was arranged that Weaver should oppose fusion in Maine, and create disaffection between the Greenbackers and Democrats. Lum declared that every act of Weaver recently had aimed to injure the Democrats.

In addition Lum referred to visits made by him to Republican leaders, including General Chester A. Arthur, from whom he obtained information as to sums of money given to Jones and by Jones sent to Weaver. Information as to the existence of this plan had come gradually, and in his desire to protect the party from scandal he had hitherto remained silent. Now that the policy was becoming a matter of general suspicion, and other persons were protesting, he felt that he ought not longer to remain silent. Consequently, he regarded it as his duty to give the information that he had to the chairman of the National Committee, who had not been in close touch with the campaign since the July meeting.

In reply to these charges General Weaver declared that Lum's statement was "base, treacherous, and false in all of its essential features." He then gave a list of the moneys received by him since his nomination for President. These amounted to $1,695, of which $800 had come from Mr. Jones. Out of these funds he had paid the expenses of his "long and laborious campaign", and he had contributed $570 to party expenses in various States. The remainder $1,125 had fallen short by $100 of paying his actual expenses. He knew "personally" that the national executive committee was in debt several hundred dollars for documents sent out to the people. He had given a careful statement of the sums received and the immediate sources, but he did not know, and had not asked where the money originally came from, and he did not care in the least. He did, however, "most positively assert" that he had "never requested, either directly or indirectly, personally or through another, contributions from the Republican committee, its agents or friends; nor have I the promise or hope of receiving any money from such source. The people of this nation have heard and read my speeches during the campaign, and can certify whether they have been delivered in the interest of the Republican party . . . . I treat both [parties] alike, and compel them to face the record they have made. I am making an open fight for the integrity of my party and the welfare of the people against both the old rotten organizations. I defy all traitors in Christendom to injure me in the least."

The next effort of the opponents of General Weaver to discredit him took the form of a forged letter, purported to have been written by him to Gillette early in September. In this letter the opinion was expressed that most of the Greenbackers who had come from the Republican party would return to that party; and so the problem was how to hold the Democratic vote. The letter answered that it was "only by the breaking of that party we can hope to succeed. If we can hold that vote it will probably elect the Republican candidate, but we must be cruel in order to be kind and may possibly throw the election in [to] the House where our chances would all be equal. Should the fusion in Maine be successful . . . . to which I am indifferent; as it would only inure to the success of the Democrats in the October States and elect their ticket in November, our position would not be enhanced but threatened.''

The forged letter was published in the latter part of October in the *New York Star,* a Democratic paper. As soon as he heard of it, General Weaver issued a sworn statement in which he branded the document as ''an unqualified forgery throughout.'' He had never written such a letter and had not ''entertained such sentiments or thoughts''. Congressman Gillette also immediately denied ever receiving such a letter from Weaver, and declared that from conversations with him he knew that he did not hold such opinions. Mrs. Gillette had conducted her husband's correspondence during the period when the letter was supposed to have been written, and she added her statement to those of General Weaver and Congressman Gillette.

The trick of the Democrats seems to have had for its purpose the winning of the election by weakening Weaver so that he would not get as many Democratic votes as he might otherwise obtain. The Democrats were dissatisfied because Weaver did not favor fusion with them in 1880. They had hoped that he would follow the same policy in the national campaign as he had followed in the Congressional election. Apparently Weaver believed that there was a chance for the Greenbackers to develop strength enough to dictate to the old parties and possibly even displace one of them. At Des Moines in October he predicted the election of from twenty-five to fifty Congressmen, and he thought that they would "crowd the old parties close in some States on the electoral ticket".[135]

In connection with these charges the *Iowa State Press,* a Democratic paper, declared that General Weaver had not done anything to favor the Democrats during the entire campaign. He had urged fusion with the Republicans in Alabama, but had denounced fusion with the Democrats in Maine. Recently the most prominent Greenbacker in Pennsylvania, and Congressman Murch of Maine, had denounced his policy in the present campaign.

General Weaver wrote to the Pennsylvania Greenbacker, Frank Hughes, in answer to his published charges that he was opposed to fusion. He was "in favor of an open, straight fight against the Democratic and Republican wings of the Money Power", and had "no choice between them. If you have, take your choice and go where you belong.

"It is impossible for the Greenback party to overthrow the old parties by forming an alliance with them to place them in power. Nor can an honest man have any respect for a party organization that will do so.

"You, sir, have the right to differ with me in opinion; but you mistake the sentiment of the Greenback voters . . . . if you think they are in favor of dividing our electoral ticket anywhere with either of the old parties."

"As to your insinuation that I am actuated by sinister motives in anything said or done by me during the campaign, I denounce you as a slanderer and calumniator."

About the same time *The Iowa State Register* said editorially that General Weaver made mistakes, but was never charged with corruption. It was added that he never made a fusion in which he could not dictate the terms.[136]

In the election in November, General Weaver received 308,578 votes as compared with slightly over 80,000 cast for Peter Cooper in 1876. The ten States contributing the largest number of votes in the order of votes cast were Missouri, Michigan, Iowa, Texas, Illinois, Pennsylvania, Kansas, Indiana, New York, and Kentucky. Only two of these States were eastern:

the Greenback Labor party was chiefly western. [137]

The election of 1880 was the first national election in which a third party had had aggressive leadership attempting to create a new party. General Weaver seems to have believed sincerely in the possibility of such a manifestation of strength by the Greenbackers that the Republican and Democratic parties would be compelled to recognize their importance. Of course he was disappointed in the immediate outcome, but the result that he undertook in one way has to a considerable extent been brought about in another manner: instead of the creation of a new party there has been the permeation of both the old parties by the ideas for which he stood. The social and industrial emphasis in the politics of the present goes back to Weaver as the pioneer. Social politics had its source in the campaign of 1880 — a campaign that ranks historically with those of 1896 and 1912. His actual canvass, in the extent of territory covered, and the number of people to whom he appealed directly, was not excelled until the Bryan campaign of 1896. He estimated that he had spoken to a million people in sixteen States.[138]

Shortly after the election in November there was a meeting in Chicago of a half dozen prominent Greenbackers of the northwest. During the conference, which was for the purpose of consultation, a reporter of the *Chicago Tribune* interviewed General Weaver, who said that the "Greenback party has reason to feel proud of the result [of the election] so far as it is concerned. We did not expect to elect our Presidential candidate, but we expected to establish ourselves as a party to be respected." When he was asked how he accounted for the falling off of the Greenback vote in Indiana, Illinois, Ohio, and Michigan, he replied that there was no falling off if the country as a whole was considered. The vote four years before was only 80,000, while for the present year it would be from 300,000 to 500,000. The States referred to were "neutral ground when the two great parties were fighting for their lives, and that fact drew many votes from our party. Many men were afraid of the Solid South, who otherwise would have voted and worked for us. They were afraid to throw their votes away while that question remained unsettled. Now the Southern question is forever settled. Now the Democratic party is dead. The Solid South is broken."

In reply to an inquiry as to how he expected the break in the South would be effected, he said: "Through the Independent party — the Greenback party. I believe the question of a free ballot was settled at the last election, but I believe that this settlement will not be accomplished by the Republican party. The South will never accept the Republican party, but they must accept the Republican idea. History is repeating itself, and we expect to be the new party built on the ruins of the dead Democracy.''

The reporter then asked General Weaver about his future course, and he answered that he should make his ''fight solely and squarely against the Republicans. We shall insist on a discussion and settlement of the great economic questions . . . . The Republicans, under the leadership of John Sherman, and the Democrats under Senator Bayard, will insist on the demonetization of silver and the retirement of the greenback. We shall oppose that, and I believe that the Republicans of the West will be unanimous in defense of silver and the greenback. If they dare to press this question — and I believe they intend to — we shall gain thousands of Republican and Democratic votes, and will surely succeed on that issue. We shall not press for expansion, but we shall urge the displacement of the National bank-notes by the greenbacks. The Republicans, I believe, will, as soon as they get into power, pass the Funding act, putting off debate under the previous question if necessary. What I should advocate would be to pay off the bonds in silver, from the surplus revenues, thus giving the bondholder coin of the standard in use at the time the bonds were issued. The people do not want a simple gold currency, and any attempt of the Republican leaders to pass such a measure will cause a stampede to our party. I should not increase the circulation except by the silver coined according to the amount fixed by law."

In concluding the interview, General Weaver said: "I can tell you one thing. We are in accord with the Republican idea on the National question. Every good Greenbacker spells the word 'Nation' with the biggest kind of an N."[139]

Soon after the Chicago conference General Weaver issued an address to the "National Greenback Labor Voters of the United States" on the results of the election. The main features of this address were a claim that "near five hundred thousand votes" were cast for the party's candidates, and an earnest appeal to his supporters to reorganize for the next campaign. *The Iowa State Register* received an advance copy, and made the comment that the General had become "saturated with Victor Hugo's didactic style, as witness:

"All hail, glorious army!

"Champions of equal rights, freedom and brotherhood, I salute you!

"Around the altar of universal justice, I in

13

my heart clasp hands with each of you, while
we renew before the whole country our covenant never to cease our labors until we are
victorious." The further comment was added
that he did not say anything about the loss of
15,000 votes in Iowa in one year. "Such small
matters do not interest the undismayed and
hopeful General."[140]

X

CLOSE OF THE FIRST TERM IN CONGRESS

1880–1881

THE last session of General Weaver's first term in Congress lasted from December 6, 1880, to March 3, 1881. Legislation in which he took the greatest interest and the passage of which he opposed most vigorously was the bill for the refunding of the national debt. This bill had been left over from the preceding session, and was debated in the House intermittently from December 14, 1880, to its passage on January 19, 1881. At the very close of the session it was finally vetoed by President Hayes because of a provision in it which seemed to him to threaten the permanence of the national banking system.[141]

On December 21, 1880, the chairman of the committee on ways and means tried to dispose of the funding bill before the holidays by limiting debate upon it to two or three hours. There was considerable opposition to this proposal both because of the shortness of time before adjournment for the holidays and because of the presence of barely a quorum of members.

Among others Weaver opposed the proposition, saying that it was one of the most important bills then pending and that he protested most heartily against such haste. He protested in the name of his "constituents, and in the name of the people of the United States; and if there are sufficient members upon this floor who will stand by me — if there are twenty-five men who will sustain me in my efforts — I will see that it does not pass, and that it is not to be considered now."

The motion to limit debate was not agreed to by the House and consideration of the bill in Committee of the Whole proceeded. Congressman Gillette obtained the floor for one hour, and after speaking twenty-five minutes yielded the remainder of his time to Mr. Weaver who, as he was not fully prepared to speak, asked the privilege of retaining the time until some other occasion. The request was granted by unanimous consent. No member wishing to speak, it was moved that the committee rise. The question was then raised whether the committee could control its action in the future, and to obviate the difficulty it was proposed to give Weaver leave to print his remarks.

At this point the chairman of the ways and means committee, Fernando Wood of New York, who had been temporarily absent, returned and moved to proceed to consider the bill by sections. He declared that he was quite willing to allow the House to dispose of the bill, but that he did not propose to permit "a few members . . . . less than one-twentieth of its members, to force the House, and control this bill." He pointed out that there were two ways of defeating a measure. One way is to vote it down; "another is when those who desire to defeat a measure are not ready, and ask the House to delay action until they are ready. The gentleman from Iowa who held the floor obtained it for one hour. If he is not prepared to occupy his hour, any other gentleman who desires to speak is entitled to the floor, if the Chair recognizes him. But if nobody is ready to continue the general debate, it is my right and my duty to move that we now proceed to the consideration of the bill by sections."

Congressman Mills of Texas, who had already opposed the hurried consideration of the bill before the holidays, replied that the gentleman from New York [Mr. Fernando Wood, chairman of the ways and means committee] need not lecture him about his rights as a member of the House and that "he ought not to permit his zeal to serve the syndicates and bankers in Wall street" to lead him "to insult a member . . . . who is asking this House to give a grave and deliberate consideration to a great question, the passage of a bill which amounts to no less than to condemning the generations that are to come after us to the slavery of a perpetual debt to satisfy the godless greed of the men in Wall street, whom the gentleman represents." He notified Mr. Wood that he would resist his efforts to force the measure through by the use of every parliamentary means known to the rules of the House; he resented Mr. Wood's reference to the opposition of a few members. He then moved to strike out the enacting clause of the bill.

Mr. Wood protested that his remarks had not referred to the gentleman from Texas. He had had notice served on him "by the leader of a very small party in this House that every parliamentary stratagem and right they could possibly command they would make use of to prevent the passage of any funding bill." General Weaver interrupted the speaker with the statement: "and I now renew that declaration in the presence of the whole House".

Continuing Mr. Wood denied that he was connected "directly or indirectly in the remotest degree with any Wall street brokers or with any selfish interests." He was controlled by a majority of the committee on ways and means, and he regarded it as his duty to press for the passage of a bill that would enable the government to maintain its honor and its credit. He was not wedded to the details of the bill, but provision must be made for the redemption of the bonds maturing the coming summer.

A number of members, including Mr. Bland of Missouri and the Speaker, Mr. Randall of Pennsylvania, then took part in the discussion. General Weaver asked the latter a question in regard to the effect of granting discretion to the Secretary of the Treasury as to the issue of long or short time bonds, expressing the opinion that the capitalists would compel him to issue long time bonds. Mr. Randall replied that he was opposed to giving too much discretion to the Secretary, but that "the difficulty about the position of the gentleman from Iowa" was that he was not willing "to do anything that looks to a permanent debt, or the further exchange of any bond which continues even the present aggregate of the public debt. The truth is we have this debt on our hands, and if we have not the money to pay it off absolutely now, we have to provide for it by new loans in some way. Therefore the gentleman's position is not a practical one, nor does he present a business-like argument that would be applicable to the business either of an individual, a firm, a corporation, or a government."

In answer to the Speaker's criticism of his position, Congressman Weaver stated that he was opposed to any permanent debt, and that

Mr. Randall would be "if he was following in the footsteps of Thomas Jefferson." He himself was opposed to "the funding of any portion of the public debt beyond the power of the Government to pay it when it pleases." The Speaker pointed out that General Weaver would increase "the aggregate of the circulation of the country to meet these bonds", and would consequently "produce inflation and depreciate values of every description." Weaver's reply was that the gentleman did not understand the doctrines of the Greenback party, and to this statement the Speaker made the rejoinder that he was in favor of greenbacks before Weaver was.

To this sally from the Speaker Weaver answered that he was "like Saul of Tarsus, persecuting the saints at the time the gentleman was, like Judas, serving with the Apostles. I am not now in that condition. The resolution which I had so hard a time to get before the House at the last session proposed to pay the public debt according to the contract, and in no other way." In reply to another question about paying the debt in silver, Weaver remarked that no one had referred to the hoard of silver on hand in the Treasury which could be used for the purpose without endangering resumption. He declared that he would not support any measure that took from the government the right to pay the bonds in standard silver coin. "It is very marvelous that the leading democrats of the East are found to be in full accord with the republican party of this country when it comes to the consideration of the question of finance and other great economic questions."

Reference having been made to the recent political campaign, General Weaver declared that the success of his party in his section of the country was "very marked". The district which he represented was carried by the Republicans "by seven majority, and they had to put in one hundred and fifty illegal votes to count it that way. There was a republican majority of four thousand . . . . two years ago, and the district remains reliably anti-republican to-day." The Greenback party throughout the country polled "nearly 400 per cent. of an increase over the vote polled in 1876."

In answer to a question as to what length of time would be required to meet the debt falling due in 1881 if no refunding act should be passed, the Speaker replied that in his opinion the government could pay in ready cash $72,000,000, and of the remaining $600,000,000 that $400,000,000 certainly could be placed in 2–10 year bonds, and the balance only need be put into a permanent loan at 3%. To another question as to how long it would require to retire all the bonds falling due in 1881 at the existing rate of income, Mr. Randall estimated the surplus revenue to be $90,000,000 a year, and the number of years could be ascertained by dividing the amount of the bonds by the amount of surplus revenue.

Discussion then turned to the platform of the Democratic party in 1868 which demanded the payment of the bonds in greenbacks and to the fact that at that time General Weaver was a Republican. Weaver replied by saying that about the time he got converted to the Democratic theory, the Democratic party went back on it. Furthermore he declared that "the democratic party in its whole history has simply camped every four years exactly where the republican party camped four years before, and during the late campaign they were neck and neck with the republican party in their doctrine."

General Weaver pointed out that in 1876 the Democrats complained because the Republicans had not hastened resumption and urged the repeal of the resumption act that action might be taken immediately, he supposed, but they were beaten again. To the suggestion that they were cheated out of the election, he replied that they were "beaten out of it some way". Asked as to who was elected in 1876, he answered: "I do not believe anybody was elected." Again, in reply to a question for whom he voted in 1876, he said: "for Rutherford B. Hayes . . . . and I am sorry for it."

In 1878 the Democratic party in all sections of the country favored "the substitution of greenbacks for national-bank currency, and the abolition of national banks, one currency of equal legal-tender value with coin, and the abolition of national bank-notes."

But in 1880 the time came again as in 1860 when the Democratic party had to choose which set of ideas should dominate in the management of its affairs. In 1860 it had to decide between Stephen A. Douglas and Jefferson Davis; no agreement was made and the party was divided and defeated. In 1880 "it had to be determined whether August Belmont and the Bayards, the eastern wing . . . . should dominate on all these questions, or whether leaders like Hendricks of Indiana, Ewing of Ohio, Voorhees of Indiana, Trimble of Iowa, and Beck of Kentucky, should dominate in the councils of the party, and whether the policy of the South and West should be adhered to. The result was that the Bayards and the August Belmonts dominated, and the sequel was the overthrow of the democracy — a just retribution for forsaking the principles they had enunciated to the people.

"There is but one party in the country",

declared General Weaver, "that does adhere
strictly to the principles it has enunciated before the public — save and except the republican party, which is open and bold in its piracy
upon the rights of the people of the United
States. The party I refer to does adhere to its
maintenance of the rights of the people, and is
above-board in the declaration of its principles,
and will be till it sweeps this country. And let
me say to those who laugh at the diminutive
size of the greenback party that that comes with
an ill grace from the republican side of the
House, when in my own short memory I can
recall the time when the republican party did
not poll so many votes as did the national greenback party in the last campaign."

Another question from a Democratic member led Weaver to add that the platform of 1880
was "a slap in the face of every southern and
western democrat, and of every democrat who
formerly adhered to the declarations of 1868
and . . . . of 1878. It was the repudiation
of a Voorhees, a Hendricks, a Ewing, a Thur-
man, the wisest and most fearless and talented
leaders that the democratic party has produced
in modern times. It was an indorsement, and a
cowardly indorsement, of the republican theory
of finance and of funding. And the result was
that the people of the United States said, if that
is to be the settled policy of the Government,

we prefer to trust the party that has shown
itself the time-honored friend of the bondholder
and of the syndicates of the country; we will
not swap horses while crossing the stream.''

These remarks of General Weaver led to
angry retorts from Democratic members, in
which the charge made during the recent campaign that he used his influence in favor of the
Republican party was repeated. Congressman
Bland declared that he might deny it, but he
knew ''what is matter of public history, and
that men high in the caucus of his own party
charged him with this conduct in the canvass
. . . . his whole campaign . . . . cor-
responds with his speech here in the interest of
the party that has conducted this Government
and passed the laws he has complained of and
fixed them upon the people of this country, and
against the party that all this time has opposed
that policy.''

At this point Congressman William Sparks
of Illinois interjected a remark to the effect
that Weaver was then a Republican and supported those policies. Weaver understood him
to refer to the recent campaign and retorted:
''The gentleman is crazy''. To which Sparks
replied: ''The gentleman states a falsehood''.
Weaver rose to a question of privilege, but
Bland claimed he had the floor, and continued
his attack upon Weaver, whom he described as

"belonging to his pretended greenback party" while he "seems to be more hostile to the democratic party to-day than he was when holding to his old faith. That seems to be the whole purpose and object of these new parties, to supplant and cut down the democratic party . . . . My friend from Iowa seems to have the sympathy of gentlemen on the republican side of the House. They seem to be a sort of harmonious family, and therefore we may expect that when he makes another change it will be simply to go back to his old bed and lie down in the place that is mentioned in scripture where wallow and mire are named."

In reply to the insinuations of Congressman Bland, Weaver made answer that "the gentleman from Missouri has sought to create the impression that I have been a chronic office-seeker in the republican party, and that I left it because I was disappointed by not getting an office. That is not true. When I left the republican party it had sixty thousand majority in Iowa over all opposition combined. I left it because I believed, on investigation of its principles, that its policy was hostile to the interests of the people, and that there was no possible chance of reforming that party. That is why I left the republican party and have remained out of it ever since, and I am more at war this moment with that party than ever before; and no amount of abuse can drive me or inducements lure me into a party that is hostile to the principles which my party promulgates. I will organize with any man to fight the money power who will agree with me on the principles I advocate, without regard to the party to which he has formerly belonged.''

At this point Congressman Sparks asked Weaver to yield to him a moment and explained that his previous statement had not been intended in any way to reflect upon his conduct during the recent campaign, but had referred to his membership in the Republican party in 1868 to 1873 when the objectionable legislation was passed. General Weaver accepted the explanation, but refused to yield more time. He said that because of confusion in the House he had misunderstood the gentleman from Illinois and had replied in the way he did. ''The gentleman replied very offensively that that was a falsehood. Now, having been compelled once to apologize . . . . the gentleman should be very careful about using language of that kind. I did not take it as a personal insult; I did not take it as applying to me. · If the gentleman ever does apply such language to me, and does it within the reach of my arm, I certainly shall personally chastise him.'' Here Sparks again interrupted to say that ''the gentleman talks about what he will do within the reach of his arm. Sir, that gentleman could not do anything 'within the reach of his arm'. I spurn with contempt the reach of his arm. The reach of his arm would affect me about as little as it affected the last presidential election.''

Weaver replied by cautioning the member from Illinois not to talk when he was excited and said that he was perfectly safe so far as he was concerned. His apology was ample and he accepted it, but he warned him against the use of such expressions which he believed in Kentucky were ''regarded as the first blow . . . . And the gentleman is mistaken about my fighting weight; it is one hundred and eighty-five pounds.'' Mr. Sparks quite naturally replied by saying that his weight was two hundred and fifteen pounds. A further interchange of personalities led Weaver to denounce Sparks as a liar, to which Sparks responded by calling Weaver ''a scoundrel and a villain and a liar''. Mr. Weaver then advanced toward Sparks ''in a menacing attitude'', and said, ''If you get within my reach I will hit you.''

Members of the House interposed, the Speaker resumed the chair, and the Sergeant-at-Arms with his mace of office, moved about the floor of the House, and order was restored. After the committee of the whole had risen in due form, the House adjourned.[142]

The next day before the completion of the

reading of the Journal, "the disgraceful proceedings of yesterday" were considered. A
Republican Congressman from Massachusetts,
S. Z. Bowman, rose to make a parliamentary
inquiry preliminary to the proper punishment
by the House of the offenders; R. M. McLane, a
Democratic member from Maryland, proposed
that the offending members be allowed an
opportunity to apologize, as he felt sure they
would both be ready to do so. Objecting to
such mild treatment, Mr. Bowman introduced
a resolution for the expulsion of Weaver and
Sparks "for gross breach of the privileges,
rules and decorum" of the House. A third
suggestion came from Thomas M. Browne, a
Republican from Indiana, for the appointment
of a committee of three to investigate the conduct of the two offenders and report to the
House without delay "what proceedings should
be taken, if any, to vindicate its dignity."

After considerable discussion and controversy the last proposal, that of Mr. Browne,
was adopted by a vote of ninety to forty-three.
At this point Congressman O. D. Conger, a
Republican from Michigan, urged that the persons implicated should be given an opportunity
to speak if they desired to do so; by unanimous
consent such leave was granted.

General Weaver spoke first, expressed regret
at his part in the incident, and said that there

14

could not be "two opinions as to the propriety and necessity of an apology to the House for what took place yesterday. No one regrets the occurrence more deeply than I do myself. I know that I very rarely lose my temper at all either in public debate or in private life; and I had not intended to do so yesterday. I can only say to the House what is understood by every member and by the country at large, that the language used by myself was wholly unjustifiable under the rules of this House and the proprieties of debate, and was entirely out of order. I am not only willing, but I am anxious, to say so to this House; I am sorry I used such language in the presence of the House; and I make my apology. Such conduct is wholly unjustifiable. I certainly feel this as deeply as any other member.

"I wish to say further that I had borne myself through a long running debate, as I thought, with good nature; and the offensive language was used just before the close of my last remarks in reply to the gentleman from Missouri [Mr. Bland]. The occurrence was wholly unexpected at the time. I thought the whole difficulty was settled.

"I do not wish to raise at all any question as to who was to blame. I say that, whether I was to blame or some one else, or both to blame, our conduct was wholly unjustifiable as members of this body. I apologize to the House for my part of it, and ask to be excused.''

Mr. Sparks then apologized in the same ample way. Mr. McLane tried to withdraw his proposition, but was not allowed to do so; Mr. Conger urged a vote on the amended resolution of Mr. Bowman; and Mr. Singleton of Illinois moved that the whole subject be laid upon the table. By a vote of 105 to 44, with 142 not voting the last proposal was adopted.[143]

Referring to this episode in Congress, *The Iowa State Register* expressed itself editorially as follows: ''Gen. Weaver caught the eye and ear of the country again on Wednesday week. The Democrats were after him a long while before the General's patience gave out. But finally, after long badgering, and after one fellow had called him a liar, he became virtuously mad, told the fellow he was another, and pulled off his coat and descended upon him in a regular cavalry kind of charge. Mr. Sparks, who was the other fellow, seeing that there were several gentlemen ready to stop him, also advanced on the General. But the non-combatants finally persuaded the hot bloods not to do it, and they didn't. But we warn them not to presume on Gen. Weaver. He is a good Methodist, and likes peace as well as anybody, but then he was one of the Second Iowa men and so has the muscle and grit to take care of himself.

We hope, though, the General will oblige his own State so much as not to do his fist-fighting in the halls of Congress. However, if he cannot avoid it without appearing cowardly, we want him to take care of himself. If it does come to that and he don't whip the other fellow, he need never come back to this State."[144]

The funding bill was debated in the House at various times after the holidays until its passage on January 19, 1881. General Weaver took part in the discussion frequently, repeating his demands for the use of silver to pay the bondholders, opposing the refunding of the debt for a long period of years, and persisting in his hostility to the national banking system as fostering the money power. With great skill and the use of many parliamentary devices, he undertook to delay the passage of the bill, although he probably realized that eventually it would be put through in some form. It finally passed the House by a vote of 135 to 125, with 32 not voting. Later the House concurred in the Senate amendments, and the bill went to the President only to be vetoed by him.[145]

During this last session of his first term in Congress, General Weaver introduced only two bills — one for a pension, and the other "to authorize the construction and equipment of a double-track steel railway from the city of New York, in the State of New York, to the city of

Council Bluffs, in the State of Iowa." The pension bill was considered and passed by the House, but was lost in the Senate committee on pensions; the railroad bill was referred to the committee on railways and canals where of course it remained.

Of the two resolutions introduced by General Weaver during the same session, one was a minority report from the committee on elections, and the other was a proposed amendment to the Federal Constitution "providing for the election of Senators by vote of the people." Here, also, the only probable action was taken — namely, reference to the proper committee.[146]

General Weaver's interest and reputation were also shown by the nature of the petitions presented by him. By far the largest number of them opposed the refunding of the public debt, and urged the payment of the same, if necessary, by an issue of legal-tender notes. A few asked for the passage of the Weaver Soldier Bill; and there were single petitions for legislation to regulate interstate commerce, to reserve the public lands exclusively for actual settlers, and to make the Commissioner of Agriculture a member of the President's Cabinet.[147]

Another indication of General Weaver's chief concern during his Congressional service is found by following his incidental remarks from time to time. He opposed the repeal of the bill providing for the use of stamps on bank-checks for it would reduce revenue and facilitate the funding of the debt, and the tax was levied upon persons who were as able to bear it as any others.[148]

He objected to an appropriation for negotiations with foreign governments with a view to the international remonetization of silver for he regarded the proposal as "simply an attempt to bring about some kind of international agreement or quasi-legislation to be followed finally by an act of Congress by which the silver product of this country will be so manipulated that it will be impossible to pay it out for the public debt. For the purpose of placing this country, the greatest silver-producing country of the world, within the power of France, it will limit the amount of silver we shall have in circulation."[149]

In a discussion in regard to the appointment of managers for the national Home for Disabled Volunteer Soldiers, it appears that General Weaver proposed the name of General Benjamin F. Butler upon whom he said that it was unnecessary for him to pronounce any eulogy. "The country knows him; history will embalm his name and fame. Not only that, but the disabled soldiers in the very institutions named . . . . have felt the beneficial effect of his great executive and administrative abil-

ity. As to being non-partisan, there is not a
man in America who can show such a non-
partisan record as General Butler.''[150]

In a parliamentary tangle in the House over
the re-apportionment of Representatives in
Congress, General Weaver proposed that ''the
right and the left submit this matter to the arbitration of the center, and agree to abide by our
action. We will act impartially.'' A member
remarked that ''that would be a fiat decision'',
to which Weaver replied that ''it would be better than the House seems able to make.''[151]

During this session Congress showed the
effect of the results of the election of 1880. Before that election both Republicans and Democrats had feared the possible strength of the
Greenback party, and Weaver as one of the
ablest of its leaders was treated with a considerable amount of respect. Afterwards the
older party leaders felt their fears had been
exaggerated and that there was no immediate
danger of the formation of a strong third party.
Consequently they treated Weaver with less
respect.

The controversies of the campaign were also
reflected in Congress, especially the bitterness
of the Democrats against Weaver because of
his opposition to fusion with them. They regarded him as ungrateful for their assistance
in his election to Congress. Hence their treat-

ment of him and the charges and insinuations
that finally led him to lose his temper after a
long and trying debate.[152]

His leadership in a national way seems to
have been pretty thoroughly established by the
end of his first term in Congress. His nomination to the Presidency in 1880 would suggest
such a conclusion; but in numerous less striking
ways it was plainly evident. His membership
and service in Congress gave him national
leadership, and from 1881 he was constantly in
demand all over the country as a speaker and
advocate of economic and social policies.

XI

Political Activity

1881–1885

GENERAL WEAVER'S term in Congress and his candidacy for the Presidency in 1880 made him the leading exponent of Greenback principles in the United States. His well-known ability as a speaker and campaigner resulted in frequent demands for his services in different parts of the country. The months immediately following his retirement from Congress in 1881 were devoted to a campaign of education in the interests of the Greenback party. Late in September he declared that since April he had spoken nightly to audiences of from two to ten thousand; and a month later he stated that since March he had delivered one hundred forty-nine speeches in thirteen States from Massachusetts to Kansas.[153]

In June he spent over a week in Massachusetts, speaking in Boston, Reading, Lawrence, Newburyport, Danvers, Marblehead, Lynn, and Springfield. The tour was arranged by the State central committee of the National party, which tendered General Weaver a reception and a banquet at the Revere House, Boston, on Saturday afternoon, June 18th. Nearly one hundred persons from different parts of the State were present.

General Weaver declared in his Boston address that the Greenback party was peculiar as an organization because it believed in "something"— a statement that could not be made of either of the old organizations. In his opinion "the great task" before the new party was "that of preserving and perpetuating free government" in the United States. He pointed out how "the agents of commerce — money, transportation and the transmission of intelligence — necessary to the welfare and prosperity of the republic had been wrenched from the hands of the people and given into the hands of soulless corporations . . . . the old parties did not dare to champion the cause of the people. Only a party organized for the specific purpose of controlling corporations could ever accomplish the task . . . . Any party kept in power for twenty-five years will become corrupt. You might just as well keep a president in for twenty-five years as to keep a party in for that time. It is the same men that are controlling the party to-day that controlled it in 1860, the same old rings, and that is the tendency everywhere now." He described the Greenback party as being in the period of toleration, after passing through the periods of ridicule and abuse. "The greatest calamity that could have happened to the party would have been the election of your candidate last year".

During the week he met Wendell Phillips by appointment at his home on Essex Street, Boston. "The conversation covered a wide range of topics and embraced many pleasant reminiscences of the days when he and Garrison and Sumner stood side by side in the grand struggle for human liberty." Comparing the conditions in 1880 with those of forty years before, Phillips pointed out that the persons engaged in reform had taken their stand as a result of "calm deliberation and firm conviction", while in "the anti-slavery fight" they were "pitched into the fight and hardly knew it until they were in the thickest of it." He was at that time busy with the address delivered a few days later at Harvard College upon the "Scholar in a Republic". The visit of General Weaver to Wendell Phillips is an indication that he sincerely believed that the reform movement in which he was engaged was similar to the movement in which the great abolitionist had had so important a part.

Evidently General Weaver made a good impression during this week in Massachusetts for he was invited to return in October for two

weeks. One paper described him as "a hand-
some man and an orator of the true Western
flavor". He was in "good voice, full of his
favorite topic, and said his say with an emphasis indicating his heart to be in the work. His
remarks were listened to with rapt attention.
The good points, clinched with apposite anec-
dote or burst of eloquence or sarcasm, had the
seal of applause evidently born of conviction.
As a whole the lecture was instructive, eloquent
and convincing. The expose of the inner work-
ings of the national bank system was probably
the clearest and best ever given by any orator
of this persuasion, in this city. The brief reference to anti-monopoly was timely, and indicates the position of this party in reference to
the more than Trojan struggle involved, which
impends in the near future in this country. The
address was well calculated to confirm the
faithful and to make converts."[154]

During the months of July and August it
appears that General Weaver delivered twenty-
six speeches in Kansas "in the midst of
drought and hot winds, with the mercury from
104 to 110 in the shade." The meetings were
usually attended by from three to five thousand
people; and the addresses dwelt upon the duty
and prospects of the Greenback party, the hope-
less condition of the two major parties, and the
injustice of the national debt. The speaker

summarized Greenback policies as follows:
"We want three kinds of money. Gold, silver
and paper, and all issued by the Government,
and not by the national banks. We want bank
notes taken up and greenbacks in place of them.
We want to put gags in the mouths of the railroad monopolies, and compel them by law to
carry you and your products for a fair re-
muneration . . . . We want every man to
have the fruits of his labor. How are you going
at it? 1. Let the Government call in all national-bank notes, and issue greenbacks in their
place. 2. Pay off the bonds in legal tender
Government notes. And if they won't have
them, God Almighty has hid away in the bowels
of the earth silver enough to pay the balance in
coin, if they want it. If they insist upon coin,
let them back up their cart and take it. No
Greenbackers want to issue greenbacks in unlimited amount. It is an old, revamped lie to
say we do, but we do say that the Executive
and the representatives of the people know
their wants better than a few favored individuals working for their own interests."[155]

During 1882 General Weaver campaigned
less extensively throughout the country since
he was personally engaged in the canvass in
Iowa as a candidate for Congress in the sixth
district. He was the leader of his party in the
State, but there was considerable opposition to

him among the more extreme Greenbackers, who resented his willingness to fuse with the old parties and who were jealous of his wide influence and popularity. One of them declared "that he was tired of Weaverism, into which the remnant of the Greenback party in Iowa had changed, and that he should vote the Republican ticket". The Democrats, too, charged him with the defeat of Hancock in 1880, and accused him of being the active ally of the Republicans. They described him as having "deserted distinct Greenback ground", and passing "as an anti-monopolist . . . . a sham reformer, a sort of $25 a day reformer, who sticks his finger into the spigot but refuses to investigate the bung."

Under the circumstances, therefore, it proved impossible to arrange for fusion as in 1878. The Republicans, the Democrats, and the Greenbackers each nominated a candidate in the sixth district; and the same situation existed in the seventh and eighth districts. In the only district in Iowa — the fourth — where fusion was adopted, the Greenback candidate, L. H. Weller, was elected. The Greenback candidates took second place in the sixth and eighth districts, while Gillette, with such a strong competitor as Kasson in the seventh, ran only about nine hundred votes behind the Democratic candidate. It seems reasonable to infer that Weaver would have carried his district easily, had it been possible to arrange for fusion. The official returns gave him 8,569 votes as compared with 11,250 votes for the Republican candidate and 8,040 votes for the Democratic candidate. A fusion of Democrats and Greenbackers would have given Weaver 16,609 votes, two hundred forty-three more than he received in 1878. The Republican candidate in 1882 actually received over 3000 votes less than the same party candidate received in 1878.

The same methods of campaigning were used in 1882 that had brought success in 1878. According to *The Iowa State Register* the work began in March in the sixth and seventh districts. Reference was made to the statement of General Weaver that he had already raised $10,000, and that he was going to increase it to $50,000. Evidently the Republicans feared General Weaver as a campaigner, and tried by every means to weaken him in the estimation of the voters.[156]

In the election of 1882 Congressman Marcellus E. Cutts, the Republican candidate who had been Weaver's antagonist in the joint debates in 1877, was successful. But Cutts died soon after his reëlection — before, indeed, he had actually taken his seat in Congress. The Republican district committee sent a "distin-

guished ex-congressman'' to Weaver with the
proposition that, if he would announce himself
as an independent candidate for the vacancy
upon his own platform, they would not nominate a candidate against him. He might advocate on the stump and in Congress just what he
had been advocating as an independent. The
only promise they required of him was that
when elected he should enter the Republican
Congressional caucus. This proposal was made
to Weaver at the Savery Hotel in Des Moines:
it was promptly declined with the statement
that if it ever seemed his duty to return to the
Republican party he would do it without
reward.

The same offer was again made to Weaver by
a ''distinguished army comrade and was again
declined. The whole conversation between myself and these gentlemen would be illuminating.
. . . . The republican party . . . had
adopted a prohibition platform and the leaders
were fearful of defeat. I received a telegram
on Saturday to 'Come to Mount Pleasant, important'. I replied that I could not as I had an
appointment to speak in Missouri the next day
but would be at home at Bloomfield on Sabbath
and that the party could either see me there or
write. When I reached home I received a letter
requesting me to meet a very dear friend, an
ex-United States Senator at Albia at midnight

the Monday following; that he would be in the Pullman car on the Chicago, Burlington & Quincy railroad. I met him in obedience to that telegram and rode with him to Chariton. This gentleman stated that the republican state committee had requested him to come and make to me the following proposition: If I would come back into the republican party I could have any position I might desire and at the first opportunity that offered. That I could have his old place in the United States senate or any place I might want. I replied that I could not, with the convictions that I then entertained concerning public policy, accept the proposition and maintain my self-respect and hence was compelled to decline absolutely. He said he had told them there was no use making the effort but they had insisted so hard that he yielded to their importunity. Let it be remembered that the republican machine in those days could deliver the goods and set up one man and pull down another, just when they pleased."[157]

These offers made in 1883 indicate very plainly how Weaver was regarded by his former party associates, and how anxious they were to induce him to return to the Republican fold six years after his departure therefrom.

In August, 1882, General Weaver wrote Governor H. M. Plaisted of Maine that "the extreme urgency of the work" in Iowa made it impossible for him to visit Maine as he had been invited to do and as he had intended. He expressed his hearty endorsement of Governor Plaisted and saw no reason why, because of his nomination by the Democrats, any member of the national Greenback Labor party should hesitate to give him unqualified support. "When monopolies combine to crush out liberty and rob the people, shall not good men associate in self defence? Fusion between organizations whose creeds are contrary is hateful. It smacks of spoils. Honest men will shun it. But co-operation on the part of patriotic people who believe alike is commendable when resorted to to avert a common danger. In Maine, however, both our ticket and our principles have been alike accepted by the Democrats. What more can be asked?"[158]

Although giving close attention to the Greenback campaign in Iowa in 1882, General Weaver also kept in view the prospects of the party in the nation. Early in the year he had written ten letters to leading Democrats in the South and West, proposing a coalition between the Greenbackers and the Democrats. Among the Democrats written to was Daniel W. Voorhees of Ohio. If the Democrats would endorse the principles of the Greenback party, arrangements might be easily made about offices. Predictions of Republican defeat in the next presidential election were freely made, based upon this combination.[159] The result of the election of 1884 proved that General Weaver's political judgment as to the possibilities of a combination of the Democrats and Greenbackers was not unfounded. The opposition of a group of Independents to the Republican candidate and their support of Cleveland caused the election of the Democratic candidate. How much more decisive might have been the victory if the wide-spread sentiment represented by the Greenback party could have been definitely allied with the Democratic party!

General Weaver's political insight apprehended the opportunity for a coalition which would have anticipated by many years the later developments in American social politics. The elections of 1896, 1912, and 1916 might have been preceded by one in 1884 which would have made the later struggles unnecessary. A more sympathetic and discerning candidate than Cleveland might have made the work of Bryan and Roosevelt and Wilson easier, and our politics might be free from much of the confusion that now exists. Probably the situation was not ripe for such developments: possibly General Weaver was too far in advance of his contemporaries to get concrete results.

The campaign of 1883 was "one of the most hotly contested ever known in the State": it illustrated "what a genuine brand of Hawkeye politics looks like".[160]   General Weaver took an active part in this contest as the candidate of the Greenbackers for Governor. The unusual feature of the canvass was a series of joint debates between the Republican and Democratic candidates for Governor; eleven meetings were held, beginning August 29th and ending October 3rd. The request of the Greenback party to have its candidate included was refused by the Republican party because of the undue length of the meetings that would result, and also because there was no wide variance between the two parties comparable to that between the Republican and Democratic parties.

General Weaver, however, was not entirely left out of the joint discussions, since a series of appointments was made for him "in the evenings of the same days and at the same places" where the two other candidates were to speak in the afternoon. This gave him the advantages of large audiences without the disadvantages of limited time to which the other speakers were held. Probably a large proportion of the seventy-five thousand persons, who heard the speeches of the two leading candidates, remained to hear General Weaver. Unusually full reports of these meetings were published by the newspapers, and it was estimated that they were "read by over a million readers". Such a campaign marks a real gain in democratic discussion of public questions.

At the first meeting, which was held at Independence, General Weaver occupied a seat on the grand stand and was "greeted by a pleasant cheer". At the close of the joint debate, he asked the privilege of making a statement to the audience, in regard to a personal matter, which was granted by the Democratic candidate, Mr. Kinne; but the chairman of the Republican State committee said: "Weaver sit down, this is *our* meeting." The Republicans tried to get up a joint debate between General Weaver and Colonel W. P. Hepburn, but failed because Weaver refused to debate with any candidate not of equal rank. Then the Republicans announced that Hepburn would speak after Weaver. In the evening the crowd again assembled in the same place in which the meeting in the afternoon had been held. Weaver there announced that "this is *my* meeting and no Republican shall speak from this platform this evening, and there are a thousand men in this audience who will see that he don't." There was intense excitement for a few minutes, but that soon passed away, and Weaver spoke three hours and closed in spite of requests to continue.

The Republicans continued to urge a joint debate between Colonel Hepburn and General

Weaver at the second meeting, but it was declined for the same reasons. At several places Colonel Hepburn held opposition meetings in the evening, but after the fifth meeting at Atlantic they were given up: they were never very satisfactory or successful. General Weaver's meetings were all largely attended, and frequently the quarters proved entirely inadequate to accommodate all who wished to hear him. General Weaver was characterized in the reports of these meetings as ''prominent for his dramatic powers, his fine presence, his ability to work on the sympathy of his audience, and his wit.''[161]

But of a total of 327,233 votes, General Weaver received 23,089 — a loss of over 5000 from the Greenback vote of 1881. The combined Democratic and Greenback vote was 163,121, less by 974 than that for the Republican candidate. Governor Sherman received 164,095 votes in 1883 as compared with 133,328 Republican votes in 1881. The Democratic vote increased from 73,344 in 1881 to 140,032 in 1883. The total vote cast in 1883 exceeded that of 1881 by 92,181.[162] Both old parties showed decided gains, which indicated that the Greenbackers were resuming their old party relations. Under such circumstances even such an effective campaigner as General Weaver could not hope to stem the tide. The Democrats were destined to reap the first political results of the protests of the Greenbackers.

The principal topic of discussion among the Greenbackers of Iowa in 1884 was in regard to fusion with the Democrats, since it was becoming apparent to all but the extremists that practical results could be obtained in no other way. General Weaver advocated fusion strongly, and it was adopted by the State convention by a vote of two hundred twenty-five to eighty-eight. Fusion arrangements covered presidential electors as well as State officers. The majority for Blaine was less than 20,000 — the smallest vote for a Republican candidate since 1860. Politically the Congressional delegation stood seven Republicans and four fusion. Weaver was the only Greenbacker among the Congressmen elected, the others being Democrats.[163]

It was as one of the delegates at large from Iowa that General Weaver went to the National Greenback Convention which met at Chicago in May, 1884. His colleagues were L. H. Weller, E. H. Gillette, and W. S. Kenworthy. Indeed, Weaver was the permanent chairman of the convention which nominated Benjamin F. Butler for President upon the first ballot. It is probable that Weaver favored Butler because in 1880 he regarded him as the best man for the Greenbackers to nominate since there was good reason to hope that the election might be thrown into the House of Representatives, in which event the Democrats would vote for Butler in preference to a Republican. In his last service as Congressman in 1881 he had referred to Butler in eulogistic terms.[164]

Again in 1885 fusion with the Democrats was the main subject of discussion in the Greenback State convention. General Weaver favored fusion as he had in the preceding year, making the most effective speech in support of it. He described himself as tied to no party and favoring coöperation with the Democrats to overthrow the Republicans. He asked the minority opposed to fusion to give it a trial. Having followed the politics of the State for twenty-five years, he was confident that fusion would carry the State that year. He predicted that fusion would secure a Greenback Lieutenant Governor and State Superintendent, with an anti-monopoly Governor and Judge; and there was a possibility that they might secure a whole Greenback ticket. Weaver was made permanent chairman of the convention, and a motion to nominate only two candidates, unless the Democratic candidates proved unsatisfactory, was adopted by a vote of 370½ to 112½.[165]

The election resulted in the choice of the Republican candidate for Governor, William Larrabee, by a plurality of about 7000.[166]   The results of the elections of 1884 and 1885 showed that Weaver's expectations for the success of fusion were by no means unfounded. To reduce the Republican plurality from 50,000 to less than 10,000 in a State like Iowa was no mean achievement; but its significance was neglected because it did not lead to a successful issue. It was really a local manifestation of the same forces that brought about the Republican defeat in the nation in 1884. Weaver's advocacy of fusion in these years was a proof of his political insight and judgment: he had a keen eye for practical results — a power not usually combined with the qualities that make up a pioneer and reformer.

In these near victories of 1884 and 1885 General Weaver's part was fully appreciated by some of his Democratic allies. *The Des Moines Leader* described him as "not only the most effective speaker" but "one of the best organizers in the state . . . . with the help of two more such men we should have carried the state by a nice majority. He has the gratitude and the warm esteem of every democrat in the state."[167]

XII

RETURN TO CONGRESS

1885–1887

THE Forty-ninth Congress in which Weaver took his seat on December 7, 1885, was composed of one hundred eighty-three Democrats, one hundred forty Republicans, and two Nationalists. The candidates for Speaker were John G. Carlisle of Kentucky and Thomas B. Reed of Maine. Weaver voted for the majority candidate, and received committee appointments as a member of the committe on labor, and as chairman of the committee on expenditures in the Interior Department. The first session of this Congress lasted from December 7, 1885, to August 5, 1886.[168]

In the sixth district the opposing Republican candidate, Frank T. Campbell, contested the election of Weaver on the ground ''that 81 illegal votes were cast for the contestee by persons incompetent as electors, and that there were some errors in the count, amounting to perhaps half a dozen more''. It was also claimed that in one township in Mahaska County, there were one hundred fifty ballots

received from electors in violation of the registry law of Iowa, and that sixty other votes were
cast in another township in the same county in
violation of the same law.   General Weaver
denied all these allegations, and charged that
there were "some 50 illegal votes cast for the
contestant; that some of the persons casting
these votes were bribed and others were colon-
ized from adjacent regions of the country".
Since the majority for Weaver was only sixty-
seven votes, these charges, if sustained, would
have deprived him of his seat.

The committee of the House of Representatives reported that, after careful examination
of the evidence, they had excluded from the
vote of the contestee sixteen ballots as illegal,
and from the vote of the contestant "some 35
ballots" for the same reason.   According to
the opinion of the committee "the sole question
involved in the contest" related "to the affidavits upon which more than 200 voters were
allowed to vote."   The question was "purely a
legal one", and depended upon "the proper
construction of the registry law of the State of
Iowa."

In one of the townships where the registry
board was Republican, the evidence disclosed
"clearly that there was an attempt to manipu-
late improperly the registry-list for the purpose of depriving Democratic electors" of their

right to vote. The evidence was "uncontra-
dicted that out of a voting population of 800,
25 per cent., nearly all of them Democrats, were
purposely left off the registry-list. Men who
had voted there for years, old and reputable
citizens, were omitted, and on the day of the
election were so indignant and humiliated at
the neglect and impropriety involved in their
being left off the list that they absolutely abstained from voting." About one hundred fifty
of those left off the list prepared affidavits;
one hundred and three gave as reasons for their
names not appearing "neglect" and "left off
the registry-list"; while thirty-one others left
blank the space where the reason should have
been inserted. It was upon these affidavits that
the contestant based his claims to the seat.

The majority of the committee concluded that
the statute of Iowa left the matter to the discretion of the judges of election, and that after
the vote had been received there was no power
that could review or reconsider the action. The
only basis for a contest, thereafter, would be
whether the voters were legally qualified and
competent electors. There was no question but
that these citizens were, and it was "the barest
and most complete technicality . . . . that
was ever made the basis of such a claim either
in a court or a legislative body".[169]

The majority of the committee reported —

only three of the six Republican members dissenting — that Weaver was entitled to his seat, and when the vote was taken there were not exceeding six men who voted in the negative. Among those who voted in favor of Weaver "were the leaders on the Republican side of the House. They did not feel there was anything in the legal points or the facts sought to be made against" him.[170]

As in his first term of service in Congress, Weaver's chief interest was in money and finance, which he regarded as the "one great question of the world".[171] His longest speech was delivered in February, 1886, under the title of *The Conspiracy and the Re-action,* in which he reviewed the history of the monetary system during and since the Civil War.

He declared that "the present great duty" of Congress was "to establish once for all an adequate, permanent financial system" that should "serve as a basis for economic prosperity . . . . a system under which there shall be no privileged classes, and under which the rights of the humble laborer and the capitalist shall be alike secure. It will not be pretended that we even approximate to this condition at present."

In his opinion there were "two ever-present disturbing forces connected with our monetary system — the public debt and the national banks. They are the evil outgrowths of the Civil War, and the nation will ever be in peril until they are swept out of existence. The hostility of the national banks to silver coinage is only one phase of a conspiracy which had its origin in the early stages of the Civil War, and which has never yet been overthrown. The rebellion was overthrown, but this conspiracy never has been; and it will require all the power of the country, now happily reunited, to uproot it. It has grown with our growth and strengthened with our strength until to-day it defies the law and the power of the Government. I propose to trace some of the features of this conspiracy and of the reaction in public sentiment which is now in progress."

Weaver explained how gradually the conspiracy developed which gave control of the currency to the banks. The main objects were "to place the public debt beyond the possibility of payment, to increase its amount, and to secure for all time the right and power to control the volume of money." The conspiracy to prevent Congress from paying the debt in the "currency of the contract" began in 1867, and was the purpose of the war against silver. Silver was demonetized "by stealth" in 1873, and the act for the resumption of specie payments, passed in 1875, also provided for the destruction of the greenback currency. "It was to be redeemed in gold coin, and the coin was to be obtained by a new issue of interest-bearing long-time bonds, thus destroying our non-interest-bearing currency by converting it into interest-bearing debt." The result was to fill the country "on the one hand with wrecked fortunes, suicides, helpless poverty, and broken hearts, and on the other with exceptional individual fortunes, some of them so monstrous in magnitude as to be quite beyond the grasp of the human intellect."

Continuing Weaver declared that "the history of this struggle between the people and the confederated monopolies, like every other similar struggle through which we have been called to pass, proves that the confidence reposed in the people by the framers of our Government was not misplaced. The waves first arose, so to speak, on this vast ocean of human sufferers, and God is still lashing it into fury for the purpose of purifying the waters. The year 1876 witnessed the organization of a small body of earnest and patriotic men under the leadership of the venerable Peter Cooper."

The Bland Act of 1878 was "first blood for the people". It was followed in the same year by the law that stopped further destruction of the greenbacks, and this legislation in turn was followed by resolutions which declared it to be the right of the Government to pay all its obligations in standard silver dollars. These gains were only partial, because the Bland Act provided for the issue of only $2,000,000 worth of silver per month, and the Treasury department had been in the hands of the conspirators, and had defied the efforts of the people in favor of silver. The greenback, however, had become permanently incorporated into the financial system and its constitutional status had been fixed by the Supreme Court. "This was the second victory for the people in this protracted struggle."

"The year 1884 brought about a great change. To use a homely illustration, in November of that year the people took hold of Uncle Sam's wagon, lifted it out of its old ruts and out of the mire, unhitched the old team, hooked on a fresh one, and changed drivers. Now why not move out on the high lands? Why return to the miserable old ruts from which, with great difficulty, we have been extricated?"

Weaver's conclusions, based upon this survey of events, were that in the matter of finance four things must be done by Congress in order to relieve the conditions of trade, labor, and commerce.

"Congress must provide for the unrestricted coinage of American silver into standard silver dollars on private account.

"A law must be passed to issue Treasury

notes to take the place of bank notes as fast as they are retired. The banks are now retiring their circulation, as is well known, with great rapidity. This vacuum must be filled or business, now sorely languishing, will absolutely perish.

"The larger portion of the surplus now in the Treasury must be paid out in liquidation of interest-bearing public debt now subject to call.

"We must forbid by law any further discriminations against our silver coin."

In Weaver's judgment these propositions were reasonable. They did not involve the inflation of paper currency — the thing that frightened so many people. The only increase would be an increase of specie. He predicted that a refusal to adopt these proposals would meet "with condign and wrathful retribution from the country."

Toward the close of his speech he referred briefly to some other measures that he believed Congress ought to adopt as promptly as possible. He would guard every acre of the public domain as the apple of the eye, and forfeit every land grant where the equities are not clearly with the grantee. He would organize unoccupied territory, and let the homeless families have where to lay their heads. He would place the remnant of the Indian tribes upon a reasonable area, and open "the remainder to civilized men, to law, to the church, and to the school-house, instead of to the cattle syndicates and corporations, either foreign or domestic". He would give to the people fair rates of transportation, and fair facilities for getting their surplus to market.

In conclusion Weaver declared that the reason why so little progress had been made is seen in the fact that for twenty years every branch of the government had been in the grasp of monopoly. "When the people ask for an adequate system of finance commensurate with the wonderful energies of the nation, the banking corporations forbid it. When they ask for a postal telegraph, another powerful corporation forbids that. When they ask that the cost of transportation may be cheapened, another hydra-headed being, more terrible than the apocalyptic beast, rises up out of the land instead of out of the sea. When the people want cheap fuel and light, a confederation of monopolists show their teeth. When they ask that their burdens of taxation may be lightened by transferring a portion to the wealthy classes through a graduated income tax, why then those who have been shirking their share of the public burdens rise up and declare with one voice that such taxes are odious. When the whole country cries out for silver, up jumps a triple power, composed of the national banks, gold speculators, and holders of Government bonds, backed by all the aristocracies of Europe, and they cry out with united voice, 'Oh, the silver dollar is a dishonest dollar, it is only worth eighty cents!'"[172]

In July it appears that Congressman Weaver spoke for ten minutes upon a resolution, requiring the Secretary of the Treasury to disburse monthly in payment of the public debt all surplus money in excess of $100,000,000 — a disbursement that must be in sums of not less than $10,000,000 per month.[173] In opening his remarks he referred humorously to the presumption of a man who did not live in New York having any opinion upon the subject. Perhaps the common people ought to defer to the judgment of New York, he said, but "we shall have to discuss it for a few minutes anyhow."

In his opinion the resolution was mild and conservative, for he believed that the government could safely pay out twice as much as would be paid out and then have money to spare. Nevertheless he favored it because it directed the payment of the public debt and established that as a policy. "This, of course, will undermine the national banks and direct public opinion to the great question of what shall be the permanent currency of the Republic.

"The payment of these 3 per cent. bonds will be followed by contraction of national-bank circulation, but not to an extent greater than the amount paid out on the bonds. There will be a saving of the interest which we are now paying on the 3 per cents. I shall vote for the resolution, but I wish to amend it so as to define what is meant by 'surplus or balance', and also so as to require the disbursement of all surplus money in the Treasury in excess of $50,000,000. I think this is enough and more than is needed as a working balance and to satisfy the hallucination that possibly some one may want at some future time to present a few greenbacks to be exchanged for coin."[174]

Later when the resolution came before the House again as a conference report and in a still more conservative form General Weaver announced his intention of voting against it. The original resolution having passed the House by a three-fourths vote, he characterized the action of the House members of the conference committee as a "cowardly surrender". After its passage by the House he said that "Wall street issued its decree. A caucus was called of gentlemen belonging in the other House of Congress, at the home of a former Secretary of the Treasury, and in that caucus the House resolution as amended by the Senate and substantially as finally reported by the committee of conference was agreed upon".[175]

How Weaver would apply his financial principles concretely is shown by the bills he introduced and the amendments proposed by him to measures before the House. On December 21, 1885, he offered two bills and a resolution upon financial subjects: one bill provided for the free and unrestricted coinage of the silver dollar; the other bill provided for the issue of silver certificates on the deposit of standard silver dollars; while the resolution instructed the Secretary of the Treasury to apply the lawful money in the Treasury to the payment of an equal amount of the interest-bearing public debt.[176] On January 11, 1886, he offered a bill to retire bank-notes and to prevent fluctuations of the currency by substituting treasury notes in place of bank notes, and also a bill to provide for the issue of fractional paper currency.[177] Six months later, on July 21, 1886, he offered an amendment to the sundry civil appropriation bill to the effect that no portion of the appropriations should be expended for printing United States notes of large denomination in place of notes of a small denomination cancelled or retired.[178]

During July he took an active part in a debate as to the right of the Secretary of the Treasury to alter the denominations of the United States notes. He claimed that the law of 1878 forbade the changing of the denominations of notes that were outstanding at the time of its passage, while his opponents maintained that the matter was left to the discretion of the Secretary of the Treasury. In addition there arose a controversy between the advocates of greenbacks and silver. Congressman Bland of Missouri urged that the greenbacks were kept in circulation by law, while there was discrimination against silver. He favored a provision for the issue of one and two dollar coin certificates to force silver into circulation. He would not issue legal tender notes under twenty dollars, thus making room for one and two dollar coin notes issued upon silver.

General Weaver replied that Bland's position was not tenable. He discussed the question as if there were a sufficient amount of money in circulation, and as though the question was whether there should be greenbacks or silver. He gave the gentleman from Missouri notice that he was just as good a silver man as he was; but if the fight was between the greenback and silver, he was for greenbacks. A better way to get silver into circulation would be to pay it out on the public debt. He favored the greenback because it was far more convenient. There was no need of conflict. There was ample room "for the circulation of all the gold we can get, and all the silver that will come to us, and of all the greenbacks now authorized by law, and a great deal more.'' He knew that he had been considered by some people as rather extreme in his notions of finance, but he had ''always been in favor of gold, silver, and paper money, all issued by the Government and all full legal tender and properly limited in amount.''[179]

At this session General Weaver again introduced a bill for the relief of soldiers and sailors such as he had urged during his first term in Congress — a bill that had come to be known as the Weaver Soldier Bill. The measure proposed to restore to those who had fought in the Civil War equal rights with the holders of government bonds, which meant that the soldiers should be paid the difference in value between the depreciated paper in which they had been paid and gold as had been done in the case of bond-holders. It embodied two great interests of its author — the soldiers and their claims and the monetary problems of the time. The bill, of course, never had any prospect even of consideration by Congress, although it represented a demand that had a good deal of support throughout the country. The obligations of the nation to the soldiers have been met by pensions rather than along the lines suggested by Weaver. He was the channel through which a good many petitions urging the passage of such a measure and of kindred legislation for the relief of the soldiers and the common people reached Congress.[180]

The other subject to which Congressman Weaver gave extended consideration during his second term of service from 1885–1889 was that of the Indian policy — especially in connection with the opening of Oklahoma to settlement. On December 21, 1885, he offered a bill "to provide for the organization of that part of the territory of the United States now known as 'The Indian Territory' and the 'Public Land Strip' into a Territory to be known as the Territory of Oklahoma, and to provide a temporary government for the same, for allotment of homesteads to the Indians in severalty, and to open unoccupied lands to actual settlers."[181]

Weaver's general position as to Indian policy was stated on the floor of the House in January. He hoped the time was not far distant when the government would adopt a sensible policy toward the Indians. The uncivilized Indians were not self-supporting and never would be. They were chiefly found lying around agencies, dependent on the government for their support. They were allowed to occupy 134,000,000 acres of land, very little of which they cultivated, and there were but 260,000 Indians under the jurisdiction of the United States. Gratuity appropriations could only be justified on the ground that the Indians were the wards of the government. Let a policy be adopted that will make them citizens under such safeguards as will insure their proper protection and bring them in proper relations to the government and their white neighbors.[182]

A substitute for Weaver's bill was reported by the committee on Territories late in March, recommitted and reported back in April, and debated on May 1st and June 3, 1886. Final action was not taken by the House during this session, and in the debate Weaver took part only occasionally by brief remark or question. His deep interest in the problem is further evidenced by his participation in the discussion of an Indian policy in connection with other measures, his most extended remarks being recorded on March 11, 1886, during the debate upon the Indian Appropriation Bill.[183]

General Weaver prefaced his discussion by the declaration that "the group of questions" involved in the bill before the House was of the greatest importance because the relation which the various tribes of Indians sustained to the government of the United States had assumed in the past few years a new phase. When the government treated with the Indian tribes as separate and distinct peoples or nations, a different rule obtained from that which must now be observed. Since 1871 the government had been in the relation of trustee of the estate of the Indian. It must manage the estate of its wards "with reference to two things: First, the interest of the ward; second, the general interest of the people."

With these statements as a basis for action, Weaver turned to a consideration of the situation in the Indian Territory, a map of which he had prepared and placed upon an easel in the House. He then pointed out the country occupied by what were known as the five civilized tribes; next the "Oklahoma country, ceded to the United States by Creeks and Seminoles by the treaties of 1866"; what was known as "the Cherokee outlet, or Cherokee strip", west of the territory of the five civilized tribes; and the Public Land Strip, or No Man's Land, ceded by Texas in 1850, west of the Cherokee strip. West of Oklahoma and southwest were the reservations of the Cheyennes, the Arapahoes, the Wichitas, the Kiowas, the Comanches, and the Apaches. The territory contained 44,154,240 acres of land, "an area as great as that of the States of Iowa, Massachusetts, Rhode Island, and New Jersey combined, larger by 266,600 acres than the seven states of Maine, New Hampshire, Massachusetts, Rhode Island, Connecticut, New Jersey and Delaware."

This vast territory possessed a delightful climate, unlimited resources, and a soil suited for the raising of all the cereals. In some portions cotton could be cultivated with profit, and its grazing and stock-raising resources were unexcelled. And yet this beautiful country was "a block in the pathway of civilization". It was preserved "to perpetuate a mongrel race far removed from the influence of civilized people — a refuge for the outlaws and indolent of whites, blacks, and Mexicans". It cost the government hundreds of thousands of dollars to peaceably maintain from sixty to eighty thousand Indians when the Territory was capable of supporting many millions of enlightened people. Prompt legislation by Congress was necessary to remove these conditions.

Weaver then turned "to a different branch of the question, the unoccupied portion" of the Territory. He used the word "unoccupied" in the legal sense, meaning that the country was not occupied by any person having a legal right to be there, but he did not deny that there were trespassers in the Territory. If the Indians on reservations were given reasonable amounts of land per person or family and their holdings consolidated, there would remain in the Indian Territory "over 20,000,000 acres of unoccupied land, all available for settlement — an area nearly as large as the State of Indiana". This would not be an injustice to the Indians, for over a thousand acres could be given to each family, and still leave the 20,000,000 acres for settlement. Furthermore, he would not take these lands from the Indians without their consent, nor without compensation. "Be just to the Indian, be humane to him, but at the same time be humane and just to our own constituents."

In the next place Weaver called attention to what he described as "one of the most disgraceful chapters in the history of this whole controversy over the Indian Territory." He exhibited a map prepared by a cattle syndicate in 1883, showing the existing condition of the Cherokee strip. The syndicate that had this map prepared leased from the Cherokee tribe the entire strip containing over 6,000,000 acres. They agreed to pay $100,000 for the privilege of occupying that country with their herds; and then they sub-leased it for about $500,000 per annum to different cattle companies —"a net profit of $400,000 yearly to this syndicate which holds possession of the strip to the exclusion of white settlers, and in plain violation" of the laws of the United States. The names of the sublessees were significant; among them were the Dominion Cattle Company of Canada, the New York Cattle Company, and the Standard Oil Company. "These lessees are all pooled and it only costs about 28 cents to raise a steer until he is three years old. How can an honest farmer compete with that kind of thing?

"Now, I submit that the question is no longer whether the red man or the white man shall occupy this Cherokee strip. The white man already occupies it. He has been placed there by the Indian himself in violation of the law. The real battle is whether the poor man seeking a home, who has but a single yoke of oxen perhaps to draw his family to the Territory, shall have a right to go there taking with him his family, the church, and the school-house, or whether he shall be excluded by the rich foreign and domestic cattle syndicates that are there in violation of law."

In reply to questions Weaver stated that in the campaign in Iowa in 1885 he had believed that the administration had issued orders for the removal of the cattle syndicates, and that the orders were being honestly enforced, and he had so declared during his canvass. Later he learned with great regret that he was mistaken in his belief. He had come to Washington immediately after the inauguration of President Cleveland and had placed the whole matter before him, using the very map he had just shown to the House. The same facts and the same map had been placed before the Secretary of the Interior, to whom the occupancy of the territory by cattle syndicates was very objectionable and who signified his intention of expelling them as soon as possible. As soon as it was telegraphed west that Weaver and his companion, Hon. Sidney Clarke of Kansas, were in Washington asking justice for the settlers and opposing the rings and syndicates, "the city swarmed with the paid attorneys and representatives of the cattle-men as it swarms now, and I met Senators who I believe to be interested in the cattle syndicates, and who stepped into the Department as I was retiring, and they spoke to me, introducing the subject in an offensive manner — at least one of them did so."

Finally, Weaver protested against the opinion expressed in the House to the effect "that the poor men who assembled on the border of the Indian Territory, with a view of locating their families on lands in that Territory, were lawless men. They were from the States of Kansas, Missouri, Arkansas, and Iowa, and to my personal knowledge a large majority of them were just as law-abiding men as this country affords. When the President of the United States ordered them to leave the Territory they left. Not only that, but I protest against this assault upon those poor people when it is known that the cattle syndicates of this country are occupying that Territory in violation of law."[184]

In the debate upon the Indian Appropriation Bill a week later Weaver took part occasionally; and early in April he opposed the appointment of an Indian commission "to inspect from time to time", as the Secretary of the Interior might require, "the condition of the Indians of the various tribes and bands on the different reservations under the care, control, or jurisdiction of the United States." He thought the desired information could be obtained by the existing machinery of the Indian bureau. Still later, in May, he opposed the proposed commission because of the great difficulty of finding suitable members to place upon it without taking persons already engaged in the Indian service. He opposed the commission plan also because it would have power to remove Indians from the West, beyond the rain-belt, to the fertile portions of Oklahoma — what he called "blanket Indians", who would have no use for tillable land and would keep out white settlers who would make good use of the land. He moved to strike out the section describing the powers and duties of the commission, but his motion was not agreed to.

The bill was debated from time to time, but final action was not taken during the session. Evidently Weaver regarded this bill as antagonistic to the bill for the organization of the Territory of Oklahoma, because when an effort was made the last day of the session to obtain unanimous consent to have it made a special order for the second day of the next session he said that he had no objection if the Oklahoma bill was made a special order for the first Thursday of the next session, and from day to day until disposed of. Adjournment was taken without action upon either of these requests.[185]

Ideas on Indian policy and the organization of Oklahoma as a Territory entertained by General Weaver were closely allied with his opinions concerning the administration of the land laws — in fact all three subjects were viewed from the angle of the needs of the people. The key to his position upon public policies is to be found in his persistent spirit of democracy and its application to the concrete demands of the people. Money, banking, finance, Indian policy, and land laws were to be framed, passed, and administered in the interest of the rank and file. In his day and generation Weaver was the exponent of the fundamental democracy of the West.

During June he took a brief part in the debate upon the repeal of the preëmption laws. He supported the repeal "because the idea of giving to the homeless citizen a homestead is a humane one; but our public-land policy ought to be confined to that, and no one should be allowed to speculate in the common inheritance of all. This bill, as I understand, simply cuts out of our public-land system the idea of specu-

lation; and that is right. The present law is
the law of the speculator and not of the honest
home-seeker. . . . The policy of this bill
should have been adopted at the very cradle of
the Republic, and not one-quarter section of the
public lands should ever have been disposed of
to corporations or speculators. It should have
been sacredly held for homesteads. If this
policy had obtained labor troubles would now
be unknown and the scandalous legislation of
the last few years would have been avoided.''[186]

Again, later in the same month he referred
to the dishonest raids made upon the public
domain by the cattle syndicates and land speculators. He protested against a land policy
which enabled ''the speculators to get hold of
the virgin lands of the West to the exclusion of
the poor settler who seeks to secure a home''.
He declared himself the friend of the ''Oklahoma boomer'' because he believed him to be
''a poor man honestly seeking a home upon the
public domain''. The action of these honest
home-seekers who obeyed the President's proclamation was very different from that of the
cattle syndicates who had taken possession in
violation of law. In answer to a question as to
whether he was not the paid attorney of the
''Oklahoma boomers'', he replied that he was
not, but that ''on the contrary, without hope,
expectation, or desire of any reward whatever''

17

he had contributed, and would again contribute if necessary, money out of his own pocket to pay the expenses of those defenseless men who were on that border seeking to obtain homes.[187]

Early in July in another debate upon the repeal of the preëmption laws, he described two theories of public land policy as struggling for supremacy. One was presented by the bill under discussion as it passed the House, and the other by the Senate amendments to it. ''The House bill proceeds on the theory that all the remaining public domain should be held for settlement under the homestead laws in parcels not greater than 160 acres. Following and in harmony with that theory is the other bill, passed by the House, which appropriates money to enable the Land Department to discover and unearth the frauds that have been heretofore perpetrated in relation to the public domain. And following along third in order is the bill . . . . making appropriations for digging irrigating ditches in what are known as the arid regions of the public domain.

''Now, these three measures are in harmony, and constitute a well-defined theory . . . . First, preserve the public domain to actual settlers; next, unearth the frauds that have been perpetrated and appropriate money for that purpose; third, when you reach the arid region appropriate money for irrigating ditches, so that when our population becomes crowded and there is no longer arable land within the rain belt you may enable the settler to go upon the arid region and raise crops by means of irrigation. This is the true and wise theory.

"Now, what is the theory represented by the Senate amendment? It is this: Validate the frauds that have been perpetrated upon the public domain; allow what is known as the arid region to be taken up by cattle speculators and syndicates, and strike down the appropriation for the investigation of frauds, so the Land Office will be powerless to protect the inheritance of the people. Can this House hesitate which theory to adopt?"

Finally, in the discussion Weaver called attention to the tendency toward large holdings and tenant farming in the United States. He declared that the census report of 1880 showed that the tendency was in that direction, instead of toward the division of land into small holdings as his opponents claimed. The tendency of the population was away from the country, and toward the city. According to the census the number of tenant farmers had increased enormously of late years: tenant farmers outnumbered the free-holders of the country. The tendency was to "large holdings; whereas in a healthy condition of our land laws and of the Republic the tendency ought to lead from the city to the country, and the result should be small farms and high cultivation."[188]

The third subject to which General Weaver gave considerable attention during this session of Congress was that of labor. One of his two committee appointments was upon the committee of labor. On December 21, 1885, he introduced a bill "to establish at the seat of Government an Executive Department to be known as the Department of Labor, with a Secretary of Labor" at the head of it. This bill received no attention in the House during the session, simply being referred to the committee on labor, from which it was never reported. Many years later, in March, 1913, such a department as Weaver proposed was finally established.[189]

During 1886 there was a series of strikes upon the railroads of the country, culminating in the so-called Southwestern Railway Strike upon the Gould system in the Southwest. Beginning in February, this strike spread until six thousand miles of railway were tied up and resulted in considerable violence. As a consequence of the outbreak an investigation was made by Congress and several bills were introduced for the purpose of "creating boards of arbitration for the speedy settlement of controversies and differences between common carriers engaged in interstate and Territorial com-

merce or business and their employés''. President Cleveland called attention to the situation
in a special message to Congress on April 23rd
in which he recommended a commission on
labor of three members to be ''charged among
other duties with the consideration and settlement, when possible, of all controversies between labor and capital.'' He suggested that
this commission ''could easily be ingrafted
upon'' the Bureau of Labor by the addition of
two more commissioners and by the necessary
extension of the powers of the commissioners.[190]

Weaver's most extensive discussion of the
questions involved in these measures occurred
on March 31, 1886, when he submitted his
views upon the merits of the bills, and upon the
situation to which they were intended to apply.
He stated frankly that he was opposed to all
legislation with regard to existing strikes because it would not be effective. Incidentally he
remarked that compulsory arbitration, which
he described as ''a misnomer'', could not settle
such difficulties. He declared that he was ''not
a believer in the power of legislation to cure
the evils to which society is heir — I mean
direct legislation.'' He was a believer in the
kind of legislation that would create conditions
out of which prosperity might be evolved, and
under which evils might die away. He declared

that the primary causes for the present discontent were the result of the neglect by Congress "to make suitable provision to preserve the prosperity of the Republic".

In pointing out the necessary measures that should be taken by Congress, he declared that there should be a law to regulate interstate commerce, and that provision should be made for a sufficient volume of currency. "This labor controversy the world over is purely a question of money, and nothing else. There is just enough money in this country to-day to enable the corporations to corner it. Just enough to enable the banks and the usurers to extort usury . . . . there are three classes of vampires who are sucking up the last drop of the blood of honest toil — the land monopolies, the railroad monopolies, and the money monopolies. And if my voice can reach beyond the walls of this House to the humble abodes of suffering labor throughout the land, I say to the toiling millions of this country, you must overthrow these three great confederated monopolies, and this can only be done by proper legislation. Hence, you must strike at the ballot-box, and strike against every man who is full of promises when he is a candidate, but who disappoints you after he reaches his seat in this House.

"The only proper remedy in a republic for

popular evils is through the exercise of the
ballot. Strikes are only justifiable as a *dernier
ressort*. If this Congress will not protect labor
it must protect itself."[191]

In this discussion of labor Weaver showed
how fundamental he regarded the money and
monopoly problems. As has already been suggested, no matter what the subject under consideration might be, he usually connected it
with some phase of the money or monopoly
problem. Interstate commerce, the administration of the public lands and the land laws, as
well as labor troubles and social unrest, all
seemed to him to be the result of the lack of a
sufficient volume of the currency. In a broad
sense there was a large measure of truth in his
contention, although in details and the concrete
administration of financial affairs he was often
mistaken and visionary. He was a pioneer and
a prophet, with the strength and the weakness
of such a personality. Many of his ideas have
been incorporated into our laws and conduct of
government, while others were impossible of
application and have been forgotten.

In December, 1885, Weaver re-introduced his
joint resolution proposing an amendment to the
Constitution of the United States to provide
for the election of United States Senators by a
vote of the people in each State. He first introduced such a resolution in January, 1881, dur-

ing his first term in Congress. The bill was
referred in both instances to the committee on
the judiciary, and no further action was taken.
The country has finally adopted the plan which
was proposed by Weaver first in 1881 and again
in 1885.[192]

Among other matters to which General
Weaver always gave a good deal of attention
was that of pensions or claims for relief of
persons who had served in the army during the
Civil War or of their dependent relatives. Of
the bills he introduced during this session of
Congress sixteen were for pensions or the relief
of individuals.[193]

Other subjects in which he showed his interest by the introduction of bills, or by participation in debate, were the enlargement of the
powers of the department of agriculture, the
institution of a tax on oleomargarine, the establishment of a postal telegraph, and the indebtedness of the Pacific railroads.[194]

Altogether he introduced thirty-three bills
and resolutions, of which nineteen were of a
private character, while fourteen were of a
public nature.[195] He remained the leader of
the Greenbackers, although as a party the
group was rapidly waning in strength — there
being only two who were listed as Greenbackers
in the Forty-ninth Congress. By his ability as
a debater and parliamentarian he had earned

the respect of the leaders of the two old parties. Among the Republicans who served with him were Thomas B. Reed and Nelson Dingley of Maine, William McKinley of Ohio, Joseph G. Cannon of Illinois, and Robert M. La Follette of Wisconsin; while among his Democratic colleagues were Samuel J. Randall of Pennsylvania, Charles F. Crisp of Georgia, Abram S. Hewitt of New York, Roger Q. Mills of Texas, and William R. Morrison of Illinois.

During the second session of the Forty-ninth Congress, which lasted from December 6, 1886, to March 3, 1887, General Weaver's chief activity was in connection with the Interstate Commerce Act, which was finally passed during that session after having been under discussion for a number of years. On January 19, 1887, he gave his reasons for opposing the bill as finally reported by the conference committee.

"For eight years", said Weaver, "ever since I became acquainted with the provisions of what is so widely known as the Reagan bill, I have given it my unqualified support. I voted for its consideration in the Forty-sixth Congress. Under the leadership of the gentleman from Texas [Mr. Reagan] I voted with the majority of this House at the last session to strike out all after the enacting clause of the Cullom bill, and to substitute in its stead the Reagan bill. . . . In common with my constituents, I considered the Reagan bill a wise and well-guarded measure for the regulation of commerce among the States. I considered it both safe and conservative, and free from dangerous experimental provisions.''

But the sections on rebates, preferences, and advantages, the long and short haul, and pools in the bill then before the House he criticized as vague and doubtful in their meaning. "Now, these are the controlling provisions . . . . except the provisions which relate to the commission and that portion which relates to the courts that shall have jurisdiction to hear complaints. . . . Neither the commission clause nor the court clause that you have in this bill were in the Reagan bill. Neither were your rebate section, your preference section, your long and short haul section — none of those were in the Reagan bill, and they are the controlling and important sections of the bill.

"It seems to be the theory of the pending bill to do as little for the people as possible; and in making that remark I wish to say I am entirely impersonal in everything I say here, and desire to be so. It seems to be the theory of the pending bill, I repeat, to do as little for the people as possible and to render those sections of the bill relating to the rights of the people as obscure and unintelligible as human ingenuity can make them. To use the language of a distinguished member of this House, 'If the hand of a Talleyrand was not present in the construction of this bill then all appearances are deceptive.'

"Suppose the great Lawgiver had constructed the Ten Commandments with the same uncertainty. Suppose he had said: 'Thou shalt not steal; thou shalt not bear false witness; thou shalt not covet — contemporaneously or under substantially similar circumstances and conditions'; or suppose, at the conclusion of the decalogue the following provision had been added: 'Provided, however, that upon application to the high priest or ecclesiastical commissioner appointed under the provisions of this act persons so designated may be authorized to cheat, steal, bear false witness, or covet, and said commission may from time to time prescribe the extent to which said persons may be relieved from any or all of said commandments.' Under such circumstances would not the world have been without moral law from Moses to Cullom and from Mount Sinai to Pike's Peak?"

The bill before the House was finally described as one "to more completely give over the control of the business and political interests of the people into the hands of the confederated monopolies."

"Where did this movement originate but with

the Democratic party? The author of the Reagan bill has been the champion of this controversy with the railroads for more than ten years; and the Democratic party, the Nationals, and the Anti-Monopolists have stood behind him, while the Senate has stood like a wall of iron against the passage of that measure. Finally, seeing they had to let us have something, they licked their bill into a shape satisfactory to themselves, but most dangerous to the people.''[196]

As to other matters considered in the session Weaver's part was of incidental or occasional character. On December 13, 1886, he offered a resolution of inquiry relative to the issue of legal-tender notes. He aimed his inquiry particularly at the substitution of notes of large denominations for those of smaller amount, which he claimed was illegal under the law of 1878 prohibiting the further retirement of greenbacks. He called attention to the fact that a distinct provision had been inserted in the sundry civil appropriation act, passed at the last session, forbidding the use of any funds obtained through that act for the printing of United States notes of large denominations to take the place of those of small denominations cancelled or retired. The notes with which he was especially concerned were the one and two dollar bills, for the issue of which the same act had made a special appropriation. He asked for answers to three questions. Of the funds appropriated, had any been used for the issue of notes of large denominations? How many, if any, one and two dollar notes had been cancelled and retired since the passage of the appropriation bill referred to above? Had notes of like denomination been issued in their places?[197]

A few days later he took part in a debate upon a bill for the allotment of lands in severalty to Indians, urging that the amount assigned should not be too large because "the Indian never will cease to become a herder until he becomes an agriculturist. He is a natural herder. The white man must be considered in this matter as well as the Indian. Under the bill, if the amendments be adopted, a family of four persons, supposing the children to be over eighteen years of age, will be allotted 360 acres of arable land and 360 acres of grazing land, or 720 acres in all. In my judgment that is too much, but on the contrary you will sooner civilize them if you will confine them to a less area."[198]

About the middle of January, 1887, General Weaver engaged in a debate upon the question of the recovery of an income tax paid by the warden of the Kentucky penitentiary during the years 1863 to 1867. The amount involved was $35,000, and the claim was based upon the fact that the warden was paid no salary, was required by law to keep the convicts at work, and made a profit by the employment of convict labor. Weaver opposed the refund, and gave as his reasons that "the correct policy" was "to tax incomes. All ought to be taxed over a given amount. In this case the amount was paid long years ago, and paid by an individual who was receiving enormous profits as compared with those employing free labor. I am opposed to the whole convict-labor system, particularly to rewards for such labor; and this would be nothing but a reward to a person engaged in employing that class of labor over and above his brother who employs free labor."[199]

In February he undertook to have the bill for the organization of Oklahoma made a special order and to have continuous consideration of the measure from day to day until it was finally disposed of. But in this effort he did not succeed, no further action being taken during the session.[200]

On the last day of the short session he opposed the acceptance of a donation of about six hundred acres of land near Chicago for military purposes. His reasons for opposition were that "the original democratic features" of American society seemed to be rapidly passing away. "We are approaching that condition of things in which, unless we adhere to the old landmarks, you will have to adopt in this country the repressive policy resorted to by the monarchies of the Old World in order to keep the people in subjection. This measure is but an unmistakable indication of the tendency of things in this Republic to-day."

He pointed out that there were bills before Congress that had been under consideration for a number of years, "bills to compel wealthy corporations to release their clutch upon fifty-odd million acres of land which ought to be consecrated forever and reserved for homeless people who are now, under our land policy, excluded from occupancy of this land and compelled to congregate in the large cities.

"The tendency is away from the farm and away from the rural districts; the trend is toward the city, where the needy congregate and where crime becomes organized and where the Republic is stabbed . . . . if you want to prevent communism in this country, if you want to do away with labor troubles, pass laws here which shall be equal in their bearing upon all classes. Repeal your class laws, take the burdens off the people, unlock your Treasury, pay your debts, and relieve the distress of the country. In this way you will have less communism and fewer strikes than you have to-day."

He declared that if the government wanted a military site near Chicago it was able to buy and pay for it; if the gentlemen donating the land had more land than they needed "let them build homes upon it and donate it to the poor wretches around the streets of Chicago. If they will do this they will have less use for a military encampment there. And after doing this if they still have a superabundance of land, they can donate a part of that magnificent tract numbering millions of acres granted to one of these gentlemen by the State of Texas. . . .

"It is an idle slander to say that every man about Chicago belonging to labor organizations is a communist. No man in this House has less sympathy with that class of people than I have. Let us show ourselves just, and then we can reasonably demand obedience among the people. Our legislation must be pure and honest before we can reasonably expect it to be peaceable.

"And I warn this House, in the name of the laboring men of this country, not to pass legislation which looks to overawing the people by military establishments, but to go to work and undo the legislation which has brought about our present discontent. It is the greed of the rich and not the dissensions of the poor that we should dread the world over."

For these reasons Weaver expressed himself

as opposed to the proposed measure. He regarded it as a plan intended "to build up a grand military establishment in the neighborhood of Chicago and to override and overawe the people." In reply to a remark containing the words "and to overawe anarchists", he answered, "not to 'overawe anarchists'. The anarchists are now in the clutch of the law, and ought to be there."[201]

18

XIII

LAST TERM IN CONGRESS

1887–1889

By a fusion of Democrats and Greenbackers, General Weaver was reëlected to Congress in 1886. John A. Donnell was his opponent, and the vote was 16,572 to 15,954. In the State at large there was fusion of the Democrats and Greenbackers, although the opponents of Weaver and fusion held a convention at Cedar Rapids in May and nominated an independent ticket — which apparently received no votes at the election. Besides Weaver the Congressional delegation from Iowa consisted of seven Republicans, one Independent Republican, and two Democrats.[202]

The Fiftieth Congress was composed of one hundred sixty-nine Democrats, one hundred fifty-two Republicans, two Labor representatives, and two Independents. John G. Carlisle was reëlected speaker by a vote of one hundred sixty-three to one hundred forty-seven for Thomas B. Reed. Weaver voted for Carlisle, and he received as his committee appointments the chairmanship of the committee on patents, and membership on the committee on private land claims. The first session of this Congress lasted from December 5, 1887, to October 20, 1888.[203]

President Cleveland's annual message was entirely devoted to the tariff, which became the chief topic for discussion during the session. The President's advocacy of a reduction committed his party to tariff revision. In the House where the Democrats were in control, the Mills Bill was the result of the President's recommendation — although his party was by no means united on this measure. A Republican Senate proceeded to substitute for the Mills Bill a measure of its own. No legislation resulted, the proposed measures merely serving to put concretely before the country the divergent views of the two parties. The campaign of 1888 ended with the defeat of Cleveland and the election of Harrison.[204]

The Mills Bill occupied the attention of the House of Representatives from April 17, 1888, till its passage on July 21, 1888. It was on May 16, 1888, that Congressman Weaver gave his reasons for supporting the bill. He had "listened to the oral discussion of this measure, with great interest, and after the publication of the speeches in the *Record* I have read many of them over with care in the quietude of my room. The result with me is an overwhelming convic-

tion that this is a fair and liberal bill, and that
it is my duty to support it. I believe it to be an
honest effort on the part of the majority of the
Committee on Ways and Means to relieve the
people. The framers of this bill have, as I shall
show, manifested a fairness and liberality towards the protected industries which those
industries and lines of business connected with
them utterly refuse to extend to the great body
of the people who use and consume their
wares.''

After this statement of his position in general terms, Weaver proceeded to discuss the
situation. He pointed out that it was conceded
that the national revenues were annually about
$60,000,000 in excess of necessary expenditures;
that the surplus now in the Treasury amounted
to $100,000,000, and was increasing ''rapidly
and constantly''. The situation, in his opinion,
was the result of unwise and improvident legislation. ''Instead of prudently reserving the
right to annually redeem at par an amount of
interest-bearing bonds equal to any surplus
money that might from time to time accumulate, instead of a wise reservation like this, you
in effect enacted that there should be a surplus
and then clothed the holder of public securities
with power to extort blood-money in the shape
of unconscionable premiums''.

After such a ''blunder — to use no harsher

term —'' the Republicans had no ground upon which to claim the exclusive privilege of dealing with the outcome. The majority of the committee had united in presenting a scheme of tax reduction, while the minority simply opposed the proposed plan. Although Republican platforms had pledged the party to revise and reduce the tariff, when the Democrats undertook to make the reduction, and prevent surplus accumulations in the Treasury, they were ''denounced as free-traders, and accused of trying to unsettle the business prosperity of the country.''

General Weaver then turned to a discussion of the record of the Republicans in Congress upon the reduction of the tariff; and he described the attitude of the Senators and of several Republican Representatives from Iowa. He noted certain inconsistencies in their records, and accused them of ignoring the real needs of the people. He thought that the reduction should be made on ''the necessaries of life; on the lumber that shelters our people, and out of which our houses and barns and granaries must be constructed.'' It should be made on ''the clothing our people wear, the food they eat, the salt that seasons their frugal meals, the implements they use in their daily toil, upon the blankets that keep us and our little ones warm when the mercury is below zero, and upon steel rails, the cost of which enters so materially into the cost of transporting our produce to market".

Next he showed that the protected industries were unwilling to treat their customers with the same liberality with which they were treated by the revenue laws. They had "ignored the equities of their contract", and had gone into the markets of the world and "bought their labor where they could buy it the cheapest". But they were not satisfied with this advantage. Secure from foreign competition, they resorted to "trusts" to do away with competition at home. He then named "a few of the protected industries and connected lines of business which are controlled by trusts: linseed-oil, watches and watchcases, rope and cordage, salt, nails, screws, envelopes, iron beams for houses, bridges, etc.; terra-cotta goods, wall-paper and paper hangings, candy, bagging, the manufacture of steel, barbed wire, plated wire, upholsterer's goods, galvanized sheet-iron, castor-oil, gutta-percha goods, tacks, wrenches and hinges, boiler-flues, glass, lumber, writing-paper, wrapping-paper, wooden-ware, oil cloth, carpets, silver plate. . . . I could extend this list almost indefinitely. There is scarcely a protected industry in America to-day — or unprotected, for that matter — that has not resorted to combination and to the trust; and for what purpose? For the purpose of destroying home competition."

In conclusion he declared that it was "a fraud and a pretense to claim that labor is getting the benefit of protection. Our tariff laws pour a golden stream into the pockets of the manufacturers, but it never returns to bless and enrich the children of toil." He called attention to the fact that recent strikes had failed, even where a strong labor organization, like the Brotherhood of Locomotive Engineers, was involved. Capital was master of the situation, and labor needed protection, not so much from foreign competition as from corporations, syndicates, and trusts. Labor possessed one thing which capital did not — the ballot. His advice to labor was to use the advantage, and to use it quickly. "If you wish capital to take its legitimate place as the servant of mankind, if you would avoid serfdom for yourselves and your posterity, you must immediately throw about the people such safeguards as will insure that result. You must erect anew the barriers which our fathers erected, but which have been trodden down."[205]

Again on May 31st and June 1st, 6th, and 7th, Weaver engaged in the tariff debate in favor of free lumber. He appealed for the removal of the duty "in behalf of the citizens who dwell in the prairie States, and who must have lumber to build their homes, their barns, their granaries''. Protesting against any action that would result in fastening a lumber trust upon the farmers of his district, he demanded in the name of his constituents that lumber should be on the free-list. He also declared that the trust controlled the local dealers and compelled them to sell at a schedule price. Through their combination with the transportation monopolies, no one could engage in the lumber business without the consent of the lumber trust and transportation companies, which together formed ''one of the most unconscionable trusts ever organized'', and which was organized to plunder the people who were ''far removed from the great centers of lumber manufacture''.[206]

In reply to a member of the House who denied the existence of a ''lumber trust'' and who said that his credulity had been imposed upon by ''some designing free-trader'', and who also suggested that he (Weaver) was the same man who some years before ''believed that money could be made by the use of the printing press and plenty of paper'', General Weaver declared that the gentleman's lack of knowledge concerning the lumber trust was only equaled by his lack of knowledge of finance. ''I saw this great Government, by an exercise of its sovereign power, create money and with it preserve the life of this nation. The gentleman twits me with believing that the Government can make money out of paper. It is not a matter of faith. I know it. The whole country knows it, and the Supreme Court have declared it lawful in war and constitutional in peace; and I am not only opposed to the lumber trust but to the national-bank trust, and to all other trusts as well.''[207]

On still another day Weaver had an amusing controversy with E. H. Funston of Kansas over the duties on lumber and barbed wire. Each tried to get the other to answer a definite question which would commit him upon the points at issue. Funston described himself as a protectionist, ''not merely for the things that we produce ourselves, not upon the ground that I want all things that we consume in my State to come in free and a duty to be laid upon all things we produce'', but upon ''the broad principles of Henry Clay, who so ably advocated the doctrines of the protective system.'' Weaver tried to make plain that the Republican legislature of Kansas had taken the position that he maintained, and that four of Funston's colleagues had voted for free lumber. Funston replied that Weaver misrepresented his own State. ''He came down into my district last fall and made a canvass there. The people of Kansas have learned by experience that whenever there is a drought in the Rocky Mountains we get grasshoppers, and whenever there is a failure of crops in Iowa we get the cranks.''[208]

During June it appears that Weaver took part several times in debates upon legislation in regard to the public lands. He was interested particularly in the active prosecution of fraudulent claims to prevent corporations from getting control to the exclusion of actual settlers. He urged ample appropriations for this purpose in order to preserve for settlement as much as possible of the public domain which was almost exhausted.

Challenging the statement, made by a member of the House, that all the parties had in times past favored the grants to railroads, he asserted that ''in the pure days of the Republican party, before they obtained power and were brought face to face with the temptations incident to power, they were not in favor of anything of that kind,'' and he quoted from the platform of the Free Soil Party of 1852, ''made by the grand old men who made the Republican party'', to support his position. After the Republican party ''got into power it turned around and granted the public domain to corporations and opened it to private speculators . . . . in violation of the principle announced in the platform'' of 1852. The ''land grants were a mistake, to draw it mildly—and we may as well all admit it now; it was a great wrong to grant a single acre of the public domain to corporations. . . . Every acre of the public lands should have been held for homes for the people, under a well-guarded homestead law. That was the proper way to deal with the public domain; but instead of that it was thrown open to ruthless speculators, who have speculated in it until the poor people of this country to-day have to fight for standing room."[209]

At another time Weaver urged the protection of mineral lands, especially of the coal deposits. He was not so insistent about the iron deposits, "because iron is not so much an article of daily necessity"; but he would retain the title to all coal lands, giving to the user of the soil the right to take so much as may be necessary for his private purposes, and guarding "the balance carefully for the use of the people, so as to protect them against paying tribute to monopoly." He would allow the government to lease the coal lands, and to prescribe "the maximum price beyond which the coal shall not be sold". Nor would he use government control as a source of revenue or of profit, as was done in European countries: he did not want the government to enter into mining operations, but to "retain sovereign control over the source of the fuel supply".[210]

Another matter in which he was interested was the reservation along all water courses, lake and sea shores for public use of alternate strips of land one hundred feet wide and one thousand feet long. His object was to keep people from being fenced off from water for stock and other necessary water supply. Such a provision was just as necessary as the one for highways to give access to land. Often in the West twenty or thirty men entered the whole front of a stream, and on the side of it, and thus cut off all others from access to it. The cattle men excluded other settlers from water, and then acquired all the adjoining land since no one else could use it under the circumstances.[211]

In September, 1888, Weaver argued for the reservation of land for reservoir sites and for irrigation ditches, and a "moderate" appropriation "for the purpose of obtaining the information necessary to a proper understanding of this great project." He had "for the past ten years" been doing what he could to attract the attention of the American people to the importance of the question of homes for the people. It had become apparent to the speculators that the great area, 1,000,000 square miles, of what was known as the arid or desert land would soon have to be occupied and that irrigation must be relied upon to make it fruitful and inhabitable. Consequently, they were investing in that part of the arid region which must be used for sites for reservoirs for the surplus water which falls in certain seasons of the year. Hence the immediate importance of the reservation of such lands.[212]

In the Fiftieth Congress it appears that Weaver again introduced his bill for the organization of Oklahoma as a Territory; and Congressman William M. Springer introduced two bills for the same purpose, the second of which, introduced on June 25, 1888, was debated on July 25th, August 6th, 28th, and 30th, and on September 12th and 13th. On August 30th Weaver made some brief remarks upon it with reference to a proposed amendment which he thought would prevent a man from selling a mortgaged farm and making a new start in Oklahoma. In his opinion it would exclude worthy men whose misfortune it was to be mortgaged beyond their power of redemption.[213]

Another related measure was a bill passed by the Senate which extended the laws of the United States to the unorganized territory, south of Kansas, west of the Indian Territory, and north of the Panhandle of Texas, known as No Man's Land or the Public Land Strip. The proposition was to create a land office there and allow lands to be acquired under the homestead laws, and also to extend the laws of the United States over the district. The advocates of this bill claimed that there were 15,000 people settled there without any form of government. On the other hand, the supporters of the Oklahoma Bill declared that it would be just as easy to pass their bill, and if it were passed there would be no need for the other measure. The Oklahoma Bill was a more satisfactory solution, since it would establish a local government; while the other bill would merely extend over the district the laws of the United States which do not furnish any protection under the criminal code nor any protection for property. Weaver, of course, opposed the Senate bill, which he described as "a rival project" that was "designed to disembowel the Oklahoma proposition." He declared that it had been denounced at a recent meeting by the people living in the district who favored the Oklahoma Bill, and that 600,000 laboring men had petitioned for the passage of the broader measure. Apparently, the opposition to the Public Land Strip Bill was successful as there was no further discussion of it during the session.[214]

General Weaver's remaining share in the work of the session was of a miscellaneous character. He took part in a debate in March upon a bill to make changes in the Department of Labor; he asked whether it would become an executive department, and whether its head would be a cabinet officer. Evidently he had in mind his bill of the previous Congress. The law to "create boards of arbitration for settling controversies and differences between railroad corporations and other common carriers engaged in interstate and Territorial transportation of property or passengers and their employés" was passed at this session, but Weaver seems not to have taken any part in the debate upon it. As he had stated in debate in the previous Congress, he was not a believer in such legislation: he would improve the fundamental conditions out of the maladjustment of which strikes and labor difficulties arose.[215]

When in the course of the debate over the Department of Labor the question of farm mortgages came up, Weaver declared that during the summer of 1887 he had travelled "from Western New York, through portions of Pennsylvania, Indiana, Illinois, Iowa, Missouri, Kansas, and Nebraska", and the very best testimony he could procure indicated that "two-thirds of all the farms in the United States and Territories" were under mortgages. He believed "this fearful state of affairs" was "the result of excessive interest charges, excessive transportation charges, and insufficient volume of money, excessive taxes, and improvident management" of the public domain.[216]

During the session Weaver introduced forty-four bills and resolutions — of which twenty-six were pension, relief, or other private bills; two were for public buildings, one at Oskaloosa and the other at Ottumwa; and sixteen were of a public character. Of the latter, four were currency or financial measures; five, including the

Oklahoma Bill, had reference to the public lands; while of the remaining seven, one was for the popular election of United States Senators, another was his Soldier Bill, and the others were to repeal the duty on lumber, to establish a postal telegraph, to amend the patent laws, to define the time when pensions should take effect, and to donate some condemned cannon to an Iowa town.[217]

General Weaver availed himself of every opportunity to attack the national banks. Especially did he oppose the then recent practice of depositing large amounts of government funds in the banks without interest — a practice widely extended at that time because of the large surplus that had accumulated. In a debate upon a bill to provide for the purchase of United States bonds by the Secretary of the Treasury it appears that Weaver followed McKinley and was in turn followed by Reed. Mills assigned thirty minutes to Weaver, who described the country as ''within the grasp of a gigantic, cold-blooded money trust, which limits the money output, prescribes the conditions on which it deigns to accept the currency at the hands of the Government, determines the channels through which it shall reach the people, and the terms upon which it shall be doled out. . . .

''For a quarter of a century this trust has

overawed Congress, and at this time is setting
at defiance laws which it does not approve. It
is a national organization, with ramifications
everywhere. It holds annual sessions, has an
executive council, which meets in secret, and is
clothed with power to collect large sums of
money and to disburse the same for purposes
which are not made public. It is the architect
of our present financial structure. They have
built it to suit the cupidity of the usurer and so
as to administer to the devouring appetite of
money ghouls, rather than to serve the legitimate wants of business and trade. They have
made it a snare, a delusion, and a rack of tor-
ture to those who are content to accumulate
wealth by production, and it has proved a bed
of quicksand to business energy and honest
thrift.''[218]

The second session of the Fiftieth Congress,
which was Weaver's last period of service at
Washington, lasted from December 3, 1888, to
March 2, 1889. Being the short session it was
devoted largely to the passage of appropriation
bills. Weaver again attracted the attention of
the country, as he had in 1880 by his fight for
the consideration of his resolution against the
refunding of the national debt. At this time he
led a filibuster in the House which resulted in
the passage of the Oklahoma Bill in the face of
strong opposition.

19

The filibuster began on Tuesday, January 8th, and continued until Saturday, January 12th, "preventing thereby totally the transaction of any public business, except a few conference reports." By a series of dilatory motions and by requiring votes thereon, the time of the House was consumed for four days. Saturday morning an arrangement was made between the Democratic leaders — Carlisle, Randall, and Mills — and General Weaver, according to which he was to cease to filibuster and the Speaker was "to recognize a motion to pass the Oklahoma bill under suspension of the rules on the next 'suspension day', and if the opponents of the bill filibuster to prevent a vote", the House was to be kept in continuous session from day to day until a vote should be taken on the passage of the bill. In accordance with this understanding Weaver ceased to make dilatory motions Saturday morning, and on Monday the necessary changes in the rules were made by a vote of one hundred fifty-six to eighty-five, eighty-two not voting. "All over the country", to use the words of one Congressman, "in every newspaper in this land, from the great metropolitan dailies down to the little country papers . . . . the gentleman from Iowa has a notoriety, not to say reputation, which has not been equaled by the performance of any other gentleman who has occupied a seat

on this floor since my public career began".[219]
As a result of Weaver's effort the Oklahoma
Bill was taken up on January 30th, debated on
that and the following day, and passed by the
House on February 1st by a vote of one hundred
forty-seven to one hundred and two, seventy-
two not voting. The bill then went to the Senate
where it failed to receive attention because of
the lateness of its passage in the House, and
because of the congestion of business incident
to the close of the session. A bill for the organization of the Territory of Oklahoma was
finally passed in 1890.[220]

Although the organization of a Territorial
government was delayed until the following
year, the opening of Oklahoma for settlement
was provided for at this session of Congress.
On January 19, 1889, delegates of the Creeks
agreed to cede to the United States the western
half of their domain in consideration of
$2,280,857.10, the agreement being ratified by
the Creek Council on January 31st and by Congress on March 1, 1889. A provision was inserted in the Indian Appropriation Bill for the
appointment of three commissioners by the
President to arrange with the Cherokee and
other Indians owning or claiming lands west of
the ninety-sixth degree of longitude to cede
their lands upon the same conditions as those
made with the Creeks. If these terms were

accepted, the President was authorized by proclamation to open the lands for settlement. No preparations for the government of the opened lands were made by Congress other than the establishment of a United States court for the whole Indian Territory. Land offices were established at Guthrie and one other place, and a military force was placed in the district to keep it free of intruders until the time set for its legal opening.

By these provisions for the purchase of the Indian lands one of the objections raised in the debates on the bill for the organization of a Territorial government for Oklahoma was removed. The argument that the government had not as yet secured title to these lands from the Indians could no longer be used; this action would therefore pave the way for the establishment of a regular form of government. General Weaver took only an incidental part in the debates on these cessions; but he was nevertheless keenly interested in the passage of these portions of the bill, and one of the incidents he delighted to recall was his "breakneck ride" down Pennsylvania Avenue with Senator Jones of Arkansas to get President Cleveland's signature in the last hours of his first administration. An agreement was made with the Seminoles for the release and conveyance of 5,439,865 acres of land, for which the sum of

$4,193,799.12 was paid, and these lands were opened to settlement by presidential proclamation on April 22, 1889.

From the date of the President's proclamation a steadily increasing number of home-seekers, with adventurers of all kinds, collected on the borders of the district. "Whole outfits for towns, including portable houses, were shipped by rail, and individual families in picturesque, primitive, white-covered wagons, journeying forward, stretched out for miles in an unbroken line." No person entering the district before the appointed time could ever acquire lands. The law forbidding the introduction of liquor into the Indian Territory was strictly enforced, and to this action was largely due the peaceful occupation in spite of the fact that most of the settlers were armed. "The blast of a bugle, at noon on a beautiful spring day, was the signal for a wild rush across all the borders. Men on horseback, on foot, in every conceivable vehicle, sought homes at the utmost speed, and before nightfall town sites were laid out for several thousand inhabitants each. Upward of 50,000 persons entered the Territory, and between 6,000 and 7,000 were conveyed from Arkansas City to Guthrie by rail in the afternoon of the first day."

This dramatic beginning of the present State of Oklahoma marked the end of a long struggle.

As early as 1879 an extensive scheme was planned to take forcible possession. Parties from Missouri, Kansas, and Texas entered the Territory, carrying household goods and farming implements with the intention of locating homes; but a proclamation of President Hayes forbade the movement, and ordered their removal by military force if necessary. A second proclamation to the same effect was issued early in 1880. David L. Payne, the leader of the "boomers" till 1884, was "repeatedly arrested by United States troops and expelled" from the region, "the number of his followers increasing with every successive expedition". After the death of Payne, raids were organized by W. L. Couch and others who had previously acted as his lieutenants. In December, 1884, Couch entered the Territory with a large body of armed men, encamped, and defied removal by the military. In January, 1885, he was obliged to surrender, he and his leading associates being arrested upon "a charge of unlawfully engaging in insurrection against the authority of the United States". The suits were subsequently dismissed. President Cleveland followed the same policy, and the removal of intruders several times a year continued until 1887. Meanwhile negotiations were opened with the Indians for the settlement of unoccupied lands.[221]

The great force opposing the opening of Oklahoma came from the rich cattle men, who herded hundreds of thousands of cattle on the ranges. There were three forces that opposed the cattle men: the "boomers" who desired to occupy the land; their friends throughout the country who contributed to the expense of the long campaign; and a few members of Congress headed by General Weaver of Iowa, Springer of Illinois, and Mansur of Missouri. "The cattle men were rich and powerful. Some members of Congress were supposed to be personally interested. Other members had friends who were interested. A powerful lobby was maintained in Congress by the cattle interests, and at one time a Congressional investigation of alleged corrupt use of money among Congressmen was threatened". Many meetings were held in Iowa and Kansas where ways and means were discussed and provided to wrest the Territory from the cattle men. A number of these meetings were held at the Weaver home; and one at Wichita, Kansas, was attended by 2000 persons, the speakers being Weaver, Couch, and Mansur.

After the opening of the country disorder became so prevalent that some sort of a local government became necessary; and so a meeting was called for a certain evening at Oklahoma City. The meeting was held on the open prairie, a large dry-goods box serving as a platform. Speeches were made by General Weaver, who presided, and by others. It was decided to call an election the following morning and elect a city ticket, although there was no legal basis for such procedure. Captain Couch, for years the leader of the boomers, was the nominee of the meeting for mayor; and he was elected on the following day. A Federal officer administered the oath of office and the officials immediately assumed office. Order was restored and government was administered in this way until Congress organized the Territory of Oklahoma in 1890.

Other Oklahoma communities met the situation in the same way; mass meetings were assembled, and within two weeks city governments were in full operation. "Though these governments had no legal basis, being founded solely on the consent of the citizens, they operated efficiently; the mayor's orders were obeyed, the ordinances passed by the city councils were complied with, and the jurisdiction assumed by the police courts was accepted, in both civil and criminal cases. No further governmental organization occurred until, after more than a year, a dilatory Congress took action." At the beginning the Territory embraced only about three thousand square miles, located in the west-central part of the original Indian Territory. It was rapidly expanded by subsequent "openings" until in 1901 its limits touched Kansas on the north and Texas on the south and its area increased ten times.[222]

In December General Weaver spoke briefly in favor of a bill to incorporate a company to build a canal on what was known as the Nicaragua route. He believed the bill was "one of the most important measures that have been before the American Congress for a decade. It bears the same relation to the trade of America that the discovery of the Cape of Good Hope bore to the commerce of the Old World. The discovery of the Cape of Good Hope turned the commerce of Asia away from the cities of the Mediterranean to the cities of London and Liverpool. The completion of this great canal will turn the commerce of the Orient away from the cities of Liverpool and London to our shores and to the cities of the United States. It will give us more than 3000 miles of advantage, and we can trust American pluck and enterprise to do the rest . . . . I venture to hope it may pass this body unanimously."[223]

Under date of February 6, 1889, General Weaver printed some brief remarks upon the same subject. He again expressed approval of the general purpose of the measure, although it did not contain "all the safeguards" that he deemed desirable in such an important piece of legislation. He found "the Pacific railroads present in great force, opposing the passage of this measure with all their power. The reason for this opposition is plain. The measure takes from them their monopoly of the transcontinental carrying trade . . . . This canal should be built by the Government of the United States, and the day will come when the wisdom of this suggestion will be appreciated; but it is impossible to secure such action at this time. Let me suggest also that the day for the construction of this great commercial enterprise has arrived. If we do not authorize its construction Germany or some other foreign power will do so at once. I trust the measure may pass, and that this great route, which shortens our pathway to the Orient between eight and ten thousand miles, may speedily be constructed."[224] The bill passed Congress and was approved by the President on February 20, 1889.[225]

No canal has ever been constructed along this route, and the present Panama Canal was not begun for many years. But Weaver's prediction that such a canal should be built by the government finally came true, and is an illustration of his keenness of vision, or rather of his ability to see intuitively in advance of his contemporaries: many times he somehow sensed things that public men and business men have only come to see much later than he did.

The surplus revenue which the government received, and which was one reason for the President's proposed reduction of the tariff, led to many schemes of lavish expenditure. One of the most striking of all the proposals was the measure for refunding the direct tax which had been levied in 1861. Naturally but little of this tax had been collected from the southern States. The northern States would receive back practically all of the $17,000,000 which they had paid, while the South would enjoy merely the remission of a tax which no one supposed would ever be collected. Southern representatives, with some help from the North, opposed the measure.[226]

Ten minutes were allowed to General Weaver during the debate upon the bill on December 12, 1888. He could not see his way clear to support it, and proceeded to give some of the reasons for his opposition. The direct tax was "lawfully levied for a patriotic purpose". The proposition to refund was simply one "to donate the money to the various States"; and he denied "the existence of any constitutional authority to make such a donation." It was claimed in Iowa during the campaign that the State was in debt, and that the $400,000 it would get in this way would enable it to pay its debt without taxing the people in the usual way. To this argument Weaver replied that however convenient it might be for any State, the plan lacked "constitutional validity."

Furthermore, Weaver maintained that it was "a proposition to pay Southern war claims". Virginia, North Carolina, South Carolina, Georgia, Kentucky, Missouri, and Texas paid about $4,500,000 out of the $17,000,000 actually collected; that amount was consequently paid by States that were "either in open rebellion", or "furnished troops to the Southern army." Such a proposal in direct form would never be tolerated, but that was really what the refund did, "relieved somewhat . . . . by the fact that the Northern States get a 'divy'."

Furthermore, "the Southern States did not pay their share in putting down the rebellion. They did not pay their share of the stamp tax, the whisky tax, the income tax, the tax upon the gross earnings of railroads, the tax upon manufactures, or of any other tax levied to suppress the rebellion; and if you are to pay back to the States of the North — the loyal States, if you please — their share of this tax, upon the theory that the South did not pay their fair share, why is it not proper to go into a regular examination of the respective shares paid by the Southern and Northern States, rip up the whole question and have a readjustment, and assess the whole country to pay back to the loyal States all that they paid out for the suppression of the rebellion? This proposition is not only unconstitutional, but highly unreasonable and absurd.

"The fact that we have a surplus in the Treasury does not give propriety or justice to this measure. If the Government of the United States owes the States — the States that paid this tax — the amount provided for in this bill, it owes it without regard to whether we have a surplus in the Treasury or not. We are the trustees of the money now in the Treasury. It was collected for certain purposes, and we are in honor bound to thwart all propositions to expend it unlawfully. If we must pay back the seventeen and a half millions collected through the direct tax, let us do so by levying another direct tax for that purpose. Let each State pay its proportion." The bill was passed by Congress, but vetoed by President Cleveland as a "sheer, bald gratuity."[227]

The last brief remarks of General Weaver in Congress were made on February 22, 1889, upon the bill to place General William S. Rosecrans upon the retired list of the army. He declared that he had had the honor to serve under General Grant and that he cherished his memory. He also had had the honor to serve under "the distinguished general whose name was under consideration", and he was his friend. "I care nothing about the controversy that existed between the two generals while they were both living. It would be unbecoming in me to do so. They were both patriotic, and I believe the cause of the Union would have fared badly had they not been in the service of the Government.

"I, too, had the honor to participate in the battle at Corinth in 1862, and I know, and the country knows, that but for the magnificent strategy of Rosecrans, his soldierly bearing, his wonderful grasp of and attention to the details of that battle, the Army of the Southwest would have been overthrown, and the consequences could not have been foretold. He decoyed the army of Price on to the spot where he designed to fight the battle, and the result was that he was victorious and captured parts of sixty-nine different commands serving under Price and Van Dorn and the other Confederate commanders. In that important battle he saved the cause of the Union in the Southwest. Rosecrans was a splendid soldier, a valuable officer, and he is now a most honorable citizen. Few are more distinguished. He is one of the heroes of this age, and his name will live forever. I am for this bill. It must be passed. We cannot dishonor him by voting no. I would like to see a unanimous vote."[228]

During his three terms in Congress the records show that General Weaver supported

many different measures, some of which have
long been upon the statute books, others are
still under discussion, while some have been
shown to be mistakes and have been wisely forgotten. His financial policy included the payment of the national debt incurred during the
Civil War as rapidly as possible instead of its
funding, the permanent use of greenbacks and
the retirement of the national bank notes, and
the free coinage of silver. His public land policy was based upon the preservation of the
public domain for the use of actual settlers, and
included the opening of Oklahoma, the forfeit-
ure of railroad land grants, the reservation of
coal deposits, the allotment of lands to Indians
in severalty, and the irrigation of the arid lands
to fit them for settlement. In addition he
favored the reduction of the tariff and free raw
materials such as lumber together with the use
of an income tax for revenue purposes. In the
main he seems to have supported the tariff
policy of President Cleveland in his message of
1887. He believed in the regulation of the railroads by the government, and he opposed the
Interstate Commerce Act because he did not
regard it as sufficiently definite and explicit in
its provisions. His judgment was justified by
the early history of its operation. He favored
a number of other measures, such as the popular election of United States Senators, the

establishment of a Department of Labor with
the secretary as a member of the cabinet, the
construction of the Nicaragua Canal by the
government, a postal telegraph, and the Oleomargarine Bill. He opposed trusts and monopolies in every form, and he anticipated the more
recent hostility to convict labor.

The *Kansas City Times* in 1889 described
him as "a man of mark in the councils of the
nation, and however much his greenback and
other political theories may be attacked or be-
littled, his adversaries regard him as a stub-
born, hard fighter, not easily taken at disadvantage, capable of maintaining himself with
credit either on the stump or in the halls of
legislation . . . . General Weaver is well up
in all matters of legislative history and prece-
dent. He is a fluent and forcible speaker, and
although gifted with superior oratorical powers, employs them with prudence and reserve.
He is strong in running debate, takes punishment well and repays with compound interest.
He is a punctual and faithful committeeman
. . . . His habits are industrious, and he is
always happier when busily employed . . . .
General Weaver has a pleasing presence, is
above the average height and compactly built.
He looks as if he could stand no end of physical
fatigue and his movements are quick and nervous. Socially considered, he fills the bill of

cleverness in the American sense. Anybody can see and talk to him, as he is a plain, unostentatious man in both dress and address. His personal habits are excellent, and, considered generally, he may be ranked among the superior men of the House. Independence of thought and action are his leading characteristics and he stands loyally by his friends."[229]

President Cleveland advised with him about appointments in Iowa and followed his advice. He is quoted as saying that "Weaver is one of the few men who come to talk with me about something else than politics — about legislation."[230]

XIV

FROM GREENBACKER TO POPULIST

1888–1892

THE immediate cause of General Weaver's defeat for reëlection in 1888 was the late adjournment of Congress in that year. It was late in October before the session closed; and since Weaver remained in attendance until almost the end of September, he had only a few weeks for his campaign. Furthermore, special efforts were made by the Republicans to accomplish his defeat: his three elections from the same district made the Republicans especially anxious to dislodge him. Major John F. Lacey was drafted for the purpose of making the contest, which it was felt "was desperate indeed."

There was also believed to be in the district a "secret oath bound organization . . . . under the personal supervision and management of one A. F. Mitchell, who carried with him autograph letters from Gen. Harrison commending Mitchell's plan of work, and urging the Republicans to adopt it." This organization had been at work in Weaver's home county for more than a month before his return.

Indeed, the same kind of work was vigorously pushed in all the counties. The charge was made that money was used among purchasable voters, who were instructed to keep on apparently in the Weaver ranks. A Bloomfield paper stated that there were men in that city with plenty of money after the election who were not known to have money before.[231]

The campaign was "one of the most notable . . . . ever made in Iowa." There were joint discussions in every county and people turned out in large numbers. The main issues were the Mills Bill and the question of free trade. "At Newton, Iowa, the speakers stood under the court-house portico with a vast throng in front of them. The Sackville-West affair had just occurred, in which the British minister had written a letter advising all naturalized Englishmen to vote the Democratic ticket. Mr. Lacey of course made good use of this incident. General Weaver closed the debate that day, and just as he was nearing the last part of his very eloquent and beautiful peroration two birds fluttered down in front of him from the portico above and hung balanced in the air a few feet in front of his breast. They fluttered playfully against each other and remained in the same position for perhaps thirty seconds. The General caught the inspiration of the situation and throwing up his hands to-

ward heaven, said in earnest tones, 'The very
birds in the air bring happy omens of our victory.' Quick as a flash Major Lacey spoiled all
this oratorical effect by rising and crying out,
'Beware of them, General! They are English
sparrows.'

"Here the General's time expired and the
crowd dispersed laughing and shouting. Until
the end of the campaign everyone talked of the
pestiferous English sparrows nestling in the
bosom of the eloquent general. General Weaver
in accounting for his defeat always gave considerable weight to this incident."

Weaver's reference to Lacey as the "dapper
little corporation attorney" suggests the contrast between the two men. Lacey was a successful lawyer who had been drawn into politics. He had no sympathy with any of Weaver's
ideas. He waged the campaign along the traditional lines so often and so successfully used
by the advocates of protection. He was a "Republican of the uncompromising conservative
order", who lost his seat in 1906 through the
rise of the "Progressive movement" with
which he had no patience.[232] Lacey and Weaver
represented most excellently the older and
newer types of politics: one was unconscious of
the newer forms of social politics; while the
other, equally unconscious, was pioneering the
way in that direction. The contest in the sixth

district of Iowa was a suggestive and significant one, both personally and from the point of view of social politics.

Although he received 609 more votes than in 1886, Weaver lost the election by a vote of 17,181 to 18,009. Lacey's vote was larger by 2,055 than that of the Republican candidate in 1886.[233] It was the year of Harrison's election when the Republicans were especially eager to redeem the defeat of 1884. Weaver ran four times as a fusion candidate in the district: he was elected three times. At each election he ran ahead of the vote of the parties that supported him. His victories were largely personal, and he probably represented the real views of a majority of his constituents. He never had a strong party organization behind him as did the Republican candidates.

The larger causes of Weaver's defeat are to be sought in the political conditions of the time. He entered Congress as a Greenbacker when the new party was at the height of its power; and when he was reëlected in 1884 and 1886, that party was still in existence, though rapidly declining. As already pointed out, the Democratic victory of 1884 represented in a certain sense the climax of the Greenback agitation. During the years from 1885 to 1889, while Weaver was serving in Congress, the Greenback party disappeared, and a temporary party,

known by the name of Union Labor, absorbed
its remnants. Other Greenbackers returned to
the Republican party from which they had
come, while some joined the Democratic party.
President Cleveland received the support of a
good many independents who were chiefly interested in good government and who had little
interest in social politics.

In 1886 Weaver referred to himself as a
Greenbacker in a discussion in Congress in regard to the lack of definite policies or tests of
membership in the two old parties. He told
the Democrats that "we Greenbackers in Iowa
affiliate with you and here in this House as far
as we can, but, reserving to ourselves all the
time the right to our own independence and the
independence of the organization . . . . If
the Democratic party will do anything for the
people of this country, we say, amen. We will
help you to do it."[234]

Two years later in July, 1888, in explanation
of charges of inconsistency in his public utterances, he described his party changes from before the Civil War to the time at which he was
speaking. He gave his reasons for leaving the
Republican party in 1877, declaring that the
events of the past ten years had justified his
action. He spoke of himself as a member of
the Union Labor party, "into which the Greenback party has practically merged, along with

some other labor organizations." While he had never joined the Democratic party, he had felt it to be his duty "to affiliate with that party in this House, in my State, and in my district, whenever it was practicable, through the action of separate conventions, because I believe the Democratic party is nearer to the people than the Republican party, and because I find more friends there for the principles which I represent than in any other party outside of my own.

"But while thus affiliating, it has been done in the frankest possible manner and with the distinct knowledge that I reserve my independence and the right to strike at wrong wherever found, and . . . . I have been fearless in the exercise of my independence. I have nothing to conceal here. Those old extracts have been read in all the campaigns in Iowa for the past decade, until they sound like extracts from ancient history. The Democrats there have said, 'Yes, he did hit us hard, but we hit him just as hard, and the account is square; and we prefer him to any monopoly Republican that can be put up in the State'."[235]

Developments in Iowa politics during these same years also throw light upon political conditions. Early in June, 1887, a State convention was held at Marshalltown under the name of Union Labor, although very few labor men were present. There was two factions, one led

by L. H. Weller and J. R. Sovereign, opposed
to fusion, and the other led by E. H. Gillette
and L. Q. Hoggatt, who were willing to unite
with the Democrats. The latter group, with
whom Weaver worked, far outnumbered the
Weller or anti-fusion forces, but Weller got a
resolution passed allowing those present from
any county to cast the full vote of the county,
and by this means the distant counties, though
slimly represented, had as much weight as the
sixth and seventh districts that had almost a
full representation. Thus the minority obtained at once a two-thirds vote, and Weller and
the anti-fusionists had control. The Weaver
men favored ex-Congressman B. T. Frederick,
a Democrat, for Governor; but Weller succeeded in nominating M. J. Caine.[236]

The defeated faction met at Des Moines late
in August and issued an address to farmers and
labor men, but made no nominations. In October a State committee, selected at Des Moines,
issued a short address regretting that the convention at Marshalltown had not been harmonious, but declaring that the platform was
satisfactory and advising members of the party
to support the ticket since it was too late to
name new candidates. The Greenback vote was
14,283, as compared with 23,013 for Weaver in
1883, the last year in which there had been a
straight Greenback ticket in the field.[237]

In 1888 there was in Iowa only one third party convention, which was held at Marshalltown in June and at which it was agreed to put a straight ticket in the field for the State election. The leaders were Weller, Gillette, and Sovereign, and there was considerable discussion over the endorsement of Weaver and Anderson for their action in Congress: Weller opposed the endorsement of the latter who had been elected as an Independent Republican. Several Iowa men were prominent in the National Union Labor convention held at Cincinnati in May. Among them were Gillette, Caine, Weller, and W. H. Robb. Apparently Weaver did not attend either the State or national convention. Probably he did not wish to be away from Congress during the debate upon the Mills Bill in which he took a great deal of interest. The vote at the State election showed a falling off of over 5000 from that of 1887.[238]

There was mention of General Weaver as a candidate for the United States Senate in 1888 to succeed James F. Wilson whose term expired in 1889. The Washington correspondent of *The Iowa State Register* was described by a contemporary as bringing out Weaver as a candidate, and it was added that "the big and the little organs of the republican party will engage in unceasing warfare upon Weaver, his senatorial ambitions and his proposed cam-

paign for election. Even the organs that have
so strongly urged the election of union generals
to the senate will oppose Weaver.'' The same
paper thought that *The Iowa State Register*
had an object in proposing Weaver, and that
object was to strengthen Hepburn who was being urged by that paper against Wilson.

Again, the same authority declared that if
Weaver should be endorsed by the Democratic
State convention as a senatorial candidate he
''and his friends will make a canvass of the
state that will surprise the opposition.'' Republicans feared trouble from him in the next
campaign and they had ''concluded that a democratic prejudice had better be worked up
against him before the canvass begins.''

The Washington representative of *The Iowa
State Register* was quoted as follows: ''Gen.
Weaver is mapping out a programme for the
democratic state convention this year, and,
judging the future by the past, it is safe to
assume that the convention will accept any plan
he may suggest, even though it may involve a
departure from the time-honored custom of the
party. In a recent conversation with a prominent democratic politician from Iowa, he said
that their convention this year would nominate
a candidate for United States senator and in
the election of members of the legislature, the
people would know who the successor of Sen-

ator Wilson would be in the event the democrats should secure a majority on joint ballot. He expressed great confidence in the result, and thought the democrats would have a safe working majority in the legislature, and the election of a democratic successor to Mr. Wilson would follow. It is believed here that Weaver expects to be named by the convention for the senatorial succession.''

In the same article in which this statement is quoted are to be found some suggestive comments. ''Iowa democrats will not be prejudiced against Weaver by such interviews. If the General made such predictions, they are certainly of such a nature as to encourage democrats. Being a member of congress, it is hardly possible that he would court a senatorial nomination — after the Nebraska plan — if he did not feel sanguine that he could and would make a successful race. It is possible that he does not wish the nomination, but if he does he will ask for it. If he receives it he will make the best effort he can make to win. His style of seeking office in the past has been commendable and by far too successful to please his republican opponents.''[239]

A Union Labor convention was held at Des Moines in September, 1889, in which a resolution was passed favoring the nomination of candidates for the United States Senate by the different political parties, and proposing the naming of General Weaver as the Union Labor candidate for Senator. There was a strong sentiment in the convention against fusion, as was shown in the vote upon the resolution introduced by Weller which was adopted by a vote of 150 to 30. The Union Labor candidates received votes varying from 5300 to 5800. The election of this year was notable because the Democrats elected their first Governor since the Civil War. Overshadowing the principles for which the Greenback and Union Labor parties contended, the prohibition issue was the chief feature of the campaign. Weaver's pronounced views upon prohibition made any fusion with the Democrats less probable than in the last few years.[240]

In August, 1890, there was held at Des Moines a nondescript convention composed of delegates from the Greenback and Union Labor parties, Knights of Labor, Farmers' Alliances, and Granges. The miscellaneous character of the gathering illustrated concretely the confused political conditions. There were still some who called themselves Greenbackers, the temporary Union Labor party had not entirely disappeared, and the elements which were the next year to be organized into the Populist party were actively at work. The name of Union Labor Industrial Party of Iowa was used to describe the convention of independents of this year. It added to its platform on motion of General Weaver a resolution for the election of United States Senators by direct vote of the people. ''And until we can properly amend the constitution in this behalf, we favor the nomination of United States senators in the State conventions, pledging in the same resolution all Representatives elected by our party to vote for the nominee at the meeting of the Legislature.''

General Weaver also addressed the convention, although a Republican newspaper claimed that he declined to serve on the platform committee because his close identification with such a convention would injure his standing with the Democrats in the seventh district. Such a statement hardly seems worthy of much consideration, for within two weeks of the meeting of the convention he declined a unanimous nomination for Congress by the Democrats of that district. He gave his reasons fully for refusing to accept in a letter written August 28, 1890.[241]

With characteristic frankness he wrote: ''Feeling at all times a warm sympathy for the great industrial movement now shaking the republic from center to circumference, I advised members of the alliance and other labor organizations to hold a conference in the district concerning congressional matters. Such a conference was held. . . . Friends attending the meeting were instructed not to allow my name to be considered. This conference designated Hon. Jas. H. Barnett as its candidate. You will readily see from this statement of facts that I cannot consent to stand as a candidate, and that if I should do so I would subject myself to the charge of bad faith, and I know that you would not knowingly place me in such a situation. These facts were unknown to the members of the convention when I was nominated, but I cannot ignore their force.

"I trust that the Seventh district and every other district in Iowa may be redeemed from republican misrepresentation at the coming election. There should be no division of sentiment in our state in view of the circumstances which confront the people. The republican leaders are determined at all hazards to perpetuate their power, and to do so they do not hesitate to trample under foot the plain letter of the constitution, the traditions of the fathers, and the liberties of the people. This is plainly shown by the passage of the Lodge bill through the house, the McKinley tariff bill, and the defeat of the bill for the unrestricted coinage of silver. The first of these measures takes the election of representatives out of the hands of the people where it has rested for more than a century and places it under the control of partisan officers appointed for life. The second, if it shall become a law, will increase the cost of nearly all the necessities of life without diminishing a single burden. The third demonetizes silver, reduces the country to a single gold standard and in conjunction with kindred legislation renders general business prosperity impossible. I trust the people of Iowa may break through all obstacles and elect a delegation to congress who will look after Iowa interests instead of the interests of money sharks, corporations and cutthroat combines.''[242]

Light is thrown upon the political situation by an editorial upon Weaver's declination of the Democratic nomination, in which after an expression of sincere regret, the statement is made that ''had Mr. Barnett been willing to withdraw his candidacy so that General Weaver might have had the united support of all the opponents of the republican ticket, he might have been prevailed upon to make the race. But Barnett would not do it. A nomination for congress, although coming from nowhere and representing no party nor no organization, being simply the act of sixteen independent men meeting in Des Moines, was a big thing for him, and he was as proud of it as a boy with a new toy.''

The result, declared the writer, ''will prove a grievous disappointment to the people of the district. They would have elected General

Weaver to congress. From every county in the district there came word of the enthusiasm among the people for him. He is the ablest and truest representative of all the people's interests that could be found in the state. He is known to be incorruptible and faithful. He would be a power in the canvass and a host in himself in congress."[243]

The results of the State and Congressional elections in 1890 showed that the estimates of those who predicted success for the opposition to the Republicans were not unwarranted if the various elements composing it could unite. As it was the Congressional delegation stood six Democrats and five Republicans, a loss of five for the Republicans, giving to the Democrats a majority for the only time since the Civil War. Furthermore, two of of the Republican districts were carried by very close votes. Had Weaver been a candidate for Congress, he would almost certainly have been elected, and had he been the Democratic and independent candidate for the Senate, he might have made a successful campaign which would have added to his already great prestige.

The election of 1890 was the first in which the new forces that were to form the Populist party attracted the attention of the country. The tidal wave of defeat that overwhelmed the Republicans was due to conditions in the West and South, particularly during the years just preceding. Farming was unprofitable, and with the best of management the average farmer in the West could not make both ends meet. The situation was somewhat different in the South, but widespread unrest there resulted in the formation of a political alliance between the two sections. Suddenly in 1890 a combination of circumstances produced the remarkable overturn of that year, and the country found itself face to face with a new popular movement, similar to the Granger and Greenback agitations, but much stronger and destined to have far-reaching effects upon the political situation.

In 1890 Iowa had only one Farmers' Alliance candidate for Congress — A. J. Westfall who received 4658 votes and nearly defeated the Republican candidate who won over his Democratic opponent by only 900 votes. There had been a Farmers' Alliance in Iowa since 1881, but it belonged to the so-called "Northern Alliance", the activities of which, like those of the Grange, were non-political in character. Early in 1891 steps were taken to establish the "Southern Farmers' Alliance" in Iowa. The chief differences between the two alliances were as to the participation of their members in politics and the use of some secret methods, such as grips and pass-words. Among the persons

21

active in the efforts to establish the Southern
Alliance in Iowa were General Weaver and
J. R. Sovereign. Evidently the organization
would receive the support of former Greenbackers and Union Labor party members.[244]

Early in May seventy-four "leaders of various labor and farmers' organizations" issued
a call for a "people's independent convention"
to meet at Des Moines on June 3rd. The convention was composed of 425 delegates from
sixty counties, the largest number coming from
the eighth, sixth, eleventh, and seventh Congressional districts in the order named. It adopted
the name of "People's Party of the State of
Iowa", and ratified and confirmed "the movement inaugurated at the Cincinnati conference,
May 19, 1891, and the wise and patriotic platform of principles there adopted." Weaver
and Sovereign were described as in control of
the convention, and the new party was declared
to be "composed of the same men who years
ago started out to reform the world under the
Greenback banner and later as the Union Labor
party."[245]

General Weaver attended the conference at
Cincinnati at which the "People's Party of the
United States of America" was formed on May
20, 1891. He was made a member of the national
committee which consisted of three men from
each State — the other members from Iowa

being M. L. Wheat and A. J. Westfall. He also presided at some of the sessions, relieving Senator William Peffer of Kansas who was permanent chairman. Senator Peffer, Congressman Jerry Simpson of Kansas, General Weaver, and Ignatius Donnelly of Minnesota were mentioned as prominent candidates of the new party for President at the next election.[246] It was assumed that the party would make an independent nomination in 1892, and its recent record indicated that it would prove a formidable competitor. Conceivably it might nominate a candidate who might be elected; actually it did help to defeat the Republican candidate and reëlect Cleveland.

There were a number of other preliminary meetings in the course of the formation of the new Populist party, and General Weaver seems to have attended all of them. He was at Indianapolis in November, 1891, where the Supreme Council of the Southern Alliance was in session, and was "called for and made a speech on the general situation, which was received with enthusiasm." Late in January, 1892, he was present at a Reform conference in Chicago, the purpose of which was, according to Miss Frances E. Willard, who presided, "to form a union of all the reform elements of the country." Weaver was described as speaking "at some length favoring the plan." He was also made a member of the committee which was appointed to present the recommendations of the conference to a larger gathering, called to meet at St. Louis on February 22, 1892. The recommendations favored greenbacks, denounced the saloon, urged government control of railroads, the limitation of land ownership, and municipal suffrage for women.[247]

The St. Louis conference was a very stormy affair. All sorts of "isms" struggled for recognition, among them prohibition and woman suffrage as well as the other economic and social reforms advocated by the successive third or independent parties. Approximately seven hundred and fifty delegates were seated, representing a great variety of organizations, while a considerable number of minor associations were excluded. Prohibition and woman suffrage were the topics of heated discussion, and a serious split was threatened over the question of independent political action, to which many Southern delegates were opposed. The concrete object of the controversy was the appointment of a committee to act with the committee of the People's party for the purpose of calling a national convention to nominate candidates for President and Vice President. The conference failed to act, but a mass-meeting of delegates held immediately after adjournment, with General Weaver in the chair, appointed this "much talked of committee". The delegates present at the mass-meeting acted without even leaving their seats after the adjournment of the conference. Weaver's selection as presiding officer and his willingness to act indicate his attitude in regard to the controversy. He favored independent action against the old parties whenever there was good ground for such action, but he was also ready to coöperate with the Democrats if they would accept his program. He understood that there were times when independent action was to be preferred, and other situations when fusion offered the only hope of success. A Republican paper in Iowa once declared that he never made a fusion in which he could not dictate the terms.[248]

Thus during the years from 1884 to 1892 General Weaver moved with the political development of the period from Greenbacker to Populist. In fact he was what one writer described as a "logical" Populist. He joined each of the succeeding minor parties because he hoped that each new one might prove to be the instrument by which his convictions and principles would be advanced. He was moving, largely unconsciously, toward a goal which he never reached, but which he made a little more feasible and hopeful for his successors.

XV

Second Campaign for the Presidency

1892

The formation of the Populist party in 1891 was followed by nominations for President and Vice President in 1892. At the time of its organization several leading men were mentioned as receptive or willing candidates, and among these was General Weaver. The others were either comparatively new men, like Peffer and Simpson, swept into public notice by the overturn of 1890, or like Donnelly with merely local or literary reputations. General Weaver was the only national figure who represented the new issues forcefully. His reputation as a public speaker and campaigner, together with his notable service in Congress, had given him a unique position. Likewise his candidacy in 1880 for the Presidency helped to make him seem to be the logical nominee of the new party.

Early in 1892 a ticket consisting of General Weaver and L. L. Polk of North Carolina was regarded by many of the well informed as altogether probable and suitable. Weaver would represent the West in the new alignment of forces, while Polk, who was the president of the Southern Farmers' Alliance, was identified with the South and its interests. Polk's death just before the Omaha convention removed his name from consideration and left open the nomination for Vice President. The only important opposition to Weaver came from those who hoped to induce some Republican leader, like Judge Gresham, to accept the nomination of the new party.

One of the earliest suggestions of Weaver as a candidate in 1892 came from a Kansas Congressman elected in 1890. During a visit to Washington in February, 1891, he was quoted as saying that he did not doubt but that the new party would have a national ticket in the field. "It may be too sanguine to expect to elect the president at this time, but we will try. Weaver of Iowa, for president and Polk, of North Carolina, for vice president are spoken of as the ticket. It is not unlikely that they will be nominated. No one can say what will be the result. It may throw the election into the house."[249]

It was in March that L. H. Weller in writing to a friend asked: "What will be the outcome at Omaha?" He indicated his opposition to the proposed ticket by adding: "but what can any man do when the tide sets strong in favor of any combination as it now appears for Weaver and Polk?" Weaver and Weller differed as to the advisability of fusion arrangements with the Democrats. Weller was much more of an extremist than Weaver and had less political insight. He was also jealous of Weaver's wider recognition and influence.[250]

In May, 1892, *The Review of Reviews* published pictures of Weaver and Polk, and in April of the same year the *Arena* gave prominence to the same men as leaders of the new party. General Weaver had an article in the March *Arena* on *The Threefold Contention of Industry*.[251]

These references show that well in advance of the meeting of the nominating convention at Omaha there had been developed a good deal of agreement that Weaver and Polk would make a strong ticket and ought to be named as the standard bearers of the new party. The only serious opposition came from those who tried to induce Judge Gresham to accept the Populist nomination.

Just before the Populist State Convention in Iowa in June, General Weaver returned from Oregon and Washington where he had taken part in the campaign preceding the election in those States. In an interview he described his meetings in Oregon as "wonderful", and said that the Republicans were on the run, and the Democrats greatly depressed by Governor Pennoyer's defection to the Populists, as he was very popular and was serving his second term. When asked about the Omaha and State conventions, he replied that "the backward spring will interfere with the attendance — you see the farmers cannot come, but we shall have a goodly gathering and will select fifty-two delegates to the Omaha convention." He refused to say whether he would be a delegate at large or a candidate for the Presidency.[252]

At the State convention General Weaver was recommended to the national convention as a candidate for President, and delegates were chosen who met after adjournment and selected M. L. Wheat to nominate General Weaver.[253]

A large element in the Omaha convention, led by Powderly and Hayes of the Knights of Labor, hoped to induce Judge Walter Q. Gresham to accept the nomination for President. They consequently tried to postpone nominations until definite word could be received from their candidate. Supporters of General Weaver were inclined to hasten the proceedings of the convention. As a result of these efforts, great confusion occurred and nominations were delayed until late in the evening.

General Weaver was nominated by M. L. Wheat, and his nomination was seconded by Mrs. Mary E. Lease. The balloting was a "struggle between the 'new blood', represented by Senator Kyle, of South Dakota, and the 'old

guard' of the Greenbackers represented by
Gen. Weaver" who won easily with nine hundred and ninety-five votes to two hundred and
sixty-five for Kyle.[254]

"From the very beginning of the roll-call
Weaver led all his competitors, and so overwhelming was the vote cast for him that his
nomination was practically assured before the
ballot was half completed. The Weaver infec-
tion seemed to spread as State after State cast
its vote unanimously for the Iowa man, the
Weaver people grew enthusiastic, and when the
result was announced the cheering was loud and
long continued."

The nomination was made unanimous in the
usual manner "with a hurrah and loud cheering, ending with calls for Weaver. The General
was not present, and a committee was appointed
to escort him to the hall." It was after one
o'clock in the morning when the nomination for
President was completed and the cheering
ceased. With little delay balloting for a Vice
Presidential candidate began: it resulted in the
selection of General James G. Field of Virginia.
General Weaver and General Field were
brought in and given a most enthusiastic reception. Each made an address, and at 3 A. M. the
convention adjourned.

In his address General Weaver declared this
to be "the grandest moment of our civilization.

JAMES BAIRD WEAVER

CANDIDATE FOR PRESIDENCY 1892

It is rallying the best hearts and heads of the Nation around the great contention of modern times — the great land problem, the great currency or financial problem, and the great and overshadowing problem of transportation. These are the centres around which this great movement is rallying. You are right, and you will be triumphant as certain as we are assembled in this hall. Your faith and your work will conquer.

"This is no longer a country governed by the people, and it is the great duty to-day devolving upon the party which you represent to rescue the Government from the grasp of Federal monopolies and restore it to the great common people to whom it belongs. I wish to thank you for the distinguished honor that you have conferred upon me, and to promise you that, in so far as it shall be within my power, your standard shall not be trailed in the dust or lowered during this campaign. And I wish to make you here and now a promise that if God spares me and gives me strength, I shall visit every State in the Union and carry the banner of the people into the enemy's camp."[255]

The Eastern press minimized or ridiculed the nomination of Weaver, as it did that of Bryan in 1896; but competent observers in the West recognized its importance and strength. The *Clinton Age* described his nomination as of greater significance than any third party nomination "since the birth of the republican party", and expressed the opinion that "the republican party would be injured far worse than the democratic party." The editor of this paper showed his political acumen by predicting the election of the Democratic candidates, although his political sympathies probably helped him to this decision since he was a Democrat.[256]

In another opinion relative to the nomination it was pointed out that General Weaver represented "the Western and Southern view of the political situation. His election would mean prosperity to these two sections without impairment to the East. Able, earnest and fearless . . . . He takes the field against the combined forces of the two old parties, at a time when their determination to strangle the last breath of liberal sentiment and the last throb of patriotism out of the minds of American citizenship, is demonstrated by their own declarations. Patriot, statesman and orator, he is the strongest man who could possibly have been nominated, and will go on to victory, and the Presidency because he is the standard-bearer of justice, honesty, principle and liberty, which have so long been pushed aside by dishonesty, corruption and oppression."[257]

A non-partisan reception was given to General Weaver in Des Moines about the middle of

July.   Judge C. C. Cole, a former prominent
Republican, presided, and "spoke for nearly an
hour upon political topics and the record and
character of General Weaver". He described
the meeting at Omaha as "a most remarkable
convention", and expressed appreciation of the
honor conferred upon Des Moines by the choice
of one of its citizens. After a number of other
speakers had addressed the gathering, General
Weaver was introduced: he thanked them for
the "demonstration" and for the "kind things"
that had been said of him, observing that "men
are secondary considerations. A score of years
hence your children will gather in meetings of
this kind, and perhaps under better auspices.
Men .will pass away, but principles are eternal . . . .

"The new movement proposes to take care of
the men and women of the country and not of
the corporations. This movement is a protest
against corporate aggression. It is a declaration of purpose to entirely obliterate sectional
prejudice. It is a declaration that we will not
tolerate any foreign interference with our financial system. Another principle is that workingmen have a right to organize to advance self-
interest. This is to be an exciting campaign.
Let us not be carried away by passion. Let us
approach the ballot box reverentially. In the
distribution of favors of the government we be-

lieve that those who stand nearest to the earth should be the first partakers. We make no war on property rights. We simply lay deep the principle that those who produce property should use it. The problem of the present is resolvable into three great questions — the land question, the money question and the labor question and they are now completely controlled by monopoly.

"The whole movement can be summed up in one sentence: 'Equal rights for all and special privileges to none.' It is simply a battle for liberty. Having secured the power we will work out the details.

"The great bulk of men of all parties are honest. That is as individuals. If you think your old party as a party is honestly trying in the right direction to remedy present evils cast your ballot for them. If you think our party is the one that is honestly striving in the right direction cast your vote with us. This is an educational campaign. We must resort to argument. The reason the principles, the same ones contained in the Omaha platform, have not made faster growth in Iowa is that our enemies have had control of the press."[258]

One of the first speeches of the campaign was made by General Weaver on July 20th at Vincennes, Indiana, where he spoke for two hours on finance, land, and transportation. He said that he was "standing with both feet upon the Omaha platform." He paid high tribute to and expressed great admiration for Judge Gresham. One of the subjects to which he gave considerable attention was the then recent industrial struggle at Homestead, where a battle between an armed Pinkerton force and striking workmen resulted in a considerable loss of life. At the close of the speech a collection was called for to meet the expenses of the national organization, and a "bushel basket was set out to receive the silver dollars that rained into it from all directions until it was half full."[259]

General Weaver's first long tour was through the West. He began at Denver on July 26th and remained in Colorado eight days, visiting nearly all the principal centers of population. From Colorado he went to Nevada, where he touched all the chief points in the State, holding a night meeting at Reno which was addressed by Senator Stewart and other State leaders in addition to the speeches made by Mrs. Lease and General Weaver. They were compelled to speak eight times in one day, so great was the interest in the campaign.

From Nevada they went to Los Angeles where the meeting numbered from 7000 to 9000 persons assembled from all parts of southern California. "At this meeting began to be manifest", according to General Weaver, "the pecu-

liar psychological phenomena which characterized the early Republican meetings throughout
the country in 1860." The people were deeply
in earnest, and their devotion to the cause was
of a religious nature. Their convictions of
right and justice had been awakened, and they
were ready to make any sacrifice necessary to
secure victory. From Los Angeles they went
to Fresno, where they met fully 6000 people in
the open-air.

On the following day they were at Oakland,
where they addressed an audience of 4000 to
5000 in the afternoon, and at night they spoke
in Mechanics' Pavilion at San Francisco. Here
the seating capacity of 12,000 was crowded to
its utmost limit. The next night they were at
Sacramento, where they had the largest audience that had assembled in that city for many
years.

General Weaver and his party, which consisted of Mrs. Weaver, Mrs. Lease, and three
others, next went to Portland, Oregon, where
two meetings were held, "one in the afternoon
composed of farmers about 3,000 strong, and
another at night, which could only be counted
by acres". From Portland they went to Ta-
coma where they expected simply to meet a few
friends, but instead were greeted by a crowd of
5000 people. At Seattle they were met by "an
innumerable crowd of enthusiastic people,

which filled the piazza and the streets leading
to it to an extent that made it almost dangerous
to alight from the cars. It was with great difficulty that we reached our carriages and were
finally driven to the place of speaking. Two
meetings were held at the same time, one addressed by Mrs. Lease and one by myself
[Weaver]. After each had spoken an hour, we
alternated so as to reach all the people. We
called it exchanging pulpits, and this had to be
done almost every day.''

From Seattle they proceeded to Spokane
where they had a very successful meeting.
From there they went to Helena and Butte.
They held three meetings in Butte, one in the
afternoon and two at night. ''The meeting in
the opera house was crowded to suffocation,
and the meeting out of doors covered about two
acres, solidly packed with people. We each
spoke an hour and exchanged audiences, and
spoke again for fully an hour. From Butte we
proceeded to Cheyenne, stopping for short
speeches at railroad stations through Idaho and
Wyoming. The Cheyenne meeting was the
largest ever held in Wyoming, and was characterized by the usual enthusiasm which had been
met with all along the line. Everywhere the
people gathered at the depot and cheered us on
our way. They covered us with floral tributes
and crowded our cars with refreshments, and

22

manifested their approval of our mission in every possible way. You may set down the whole group visited, consisting of eight states, as absolutely certain for the People's party national ticket.''

General Weaver expressed his approval of the work of Mrs. Lease in the highest terms. She spoke every day, and as often as he did himself. He described her as ''an orator of marvellous power and a phenomenal psychological force.'' Her hold upon the laboring people was something wonderful. They almost worshipped her from one end of the country to the other.

The general plan of campaign was for General Weaver to proceed next to Missouri, and then to Arkansas where he would remain until September. Mrs. Weaver and Mrs. Lease would join him, and they would travel through Texas, Mississippi, Alabama, Georgia, Tennessee, the Carolinas, Virginia, and West Virginia, reserving the last twenty-five days of the campaign for Iowa and the Northwest.[260]

The Southern tour was marked by some unpleasant experiences; indeed, a part of it had to be given up. General Weaver went from Missouri to Arkansas where he had an enthusiastic reception. Late in August he had a very successful meeting at Beebe in the northern part of the State. The audience which numbered over 5000 persons, consisted almost entirely of farmers, many of whom came from twenty to thirty miles to hear him: they came in wagons and on horseback, and occupied every available spot near the town with their camps. Weaver spoke for two hours, "arraigning the old parties for their sins of omission and commission, and predicted that the pending movement would never cease till plutocracy was overthrown and the shackles stricken from the limbs of the agricultural class and industries generally." He was followed by "Cyclone" Davis of Texas, who aroused the greatest enthusiasm by his burning words.[261]

From Pensacola, Florida, addresses were issued by Weaver and Field in which they formally accepted their nominations. They referred to the request made by the national committee "to visit the various states of the Union." Already one or both of them had visited fifteen States; and if health and strength were spared to them they intended to continue the work until the campaign ended. General Weaver had followed a similar plan of campaign in 1880; and it was as much because of his own inclination in the matter as because of the request of the committee that he made such a thorough canvass. The campaign of 1892 undoubtedly suggested the remarkable tour of Mr. Bryan in 1896, the first of the kind to impress itself upon the country and to set a new standard for presidential candidates. But such a method proves almost too strenuous for political leaders who are not such vigorous and effective speakers as Weaver and Bryan, and who have not been trained by years of experience upon the platform.[262]

About a week after the formal acceptance General Weaver addressed a letter to the chairman of the State committee of the People's party of Georgia in which he announced the abandonment of the campaign in that State. He described his experiences from the time of his entrance at the request of the committee. He found "the spirit of rowdyism, at some of the points within the State, so great as to render it inadvisable for me to attempt to fill the engagements at the points not already reached". He specified the treatment received at a number of places, culminating at Macon where rotten eggs were thrown, one of which struck Mrs. Weaver upon the head. "At Atlanta a similar crowd of rowdies gathered at the point of meeting, bent on tumult and disorder. Learning of this Mrs. Lease and myself refused to appear either in the forenoon or evening." Convinced that similar treatment awaited them at the points not yet visited, Weaver declined to continue the campaign.

The members of the Populist party, although

largely in the majority in the State, were unable to secure for them a peaceful and respectful hearing. Weaver called attention to the
fact that the disorder was almost exclusively
confined to the young roughs who infest the
towns and who were incited to violence by persons who kept in the background. The country
people were uniformly respectful and anxious
to hear. It was especially worthy of note that
the disorderly conduct did not proceed from
the ex-confederate soldiers, who were "manly,
almost without exception, in their conduct, and
generally in sympathy". The police force
seemed to make no effort to preserve order, and
in some instances gave open countenance to the
tumult. He added in conclusion that it was
"but fair to say that many good people who are
not in sympathy with the People's party openly
denounce these outrages, but they seem powerless to assert themselves."[263]

Undoubtedly the trouble was due to the political situation in the South, which was very
different from that in the West. The lines were
closely drawn between the Democrats in the
cities and the Populists in the rural regions.
The fight between the two groups was exceed-
ingly bitter, and back of the tense political situation was the race problem that has kept the
South from breaking up politically to the present day. Weaver had visited the South for

many years, and had never experienced any
difficulty before; but in 1892 he represented a
new movement which threatened to break up
the Solid South. Hence the bitterness which
led to rowdyism and disorder.[264]

Except for the unpleasant experiences in
Georgia, it seems that General Weaver and his
party had a satisfactory and successful Southern campaign. He travelled through the entire
section with the exception of West Virginia, and
found the people accepting Populist doctrines
"with avidity and turning from the old parties
almost in armies." His meetings in Mississippi were "everyone 5,000 strong", and in
Florida there was the greatest enthusiasm. In
North and South Carolina their meetings were
five times as large as those of General Stevenson, the Democratic candidate for Vice President: at Raleigh they had at least 10,000 audi-
tors and at one other place 12,000. The outlook
in the South he regarded as "magnificent".
The majority of the white people were with the
Populists, and with a fair count he was pretty
sure of success in every Southern State. He
added that he was determined to have a fair
count.[265]

The Southern tour closed at Pulaski, Tennessee, early in October. A determined effort
was made to induce Weaver to cancel his visit
there because of charges made against him as

military commander at that point during 1863 and 1864; but he refused to be deterred by the threats of trouble. He left Nashville in the morning accompanied by Mrs. Weaver, Mrs. Lease, and two others. When the train stopped at the station one hundred men on mules and horses formed an escort around his carriage. A band led the procession through the town, and out to the fair grounds a mile away where the speaking began at noon. The town was full of horsemen and men on mules, in cotton carts, and in road wagons. There were no weapons in sight. The Democratic leaders were working vigorously from sunrise to prevent trouble.

After discussing party issues General Weaver said: "I am not and never was afraid of anything on earth. They said I would not dare to come here. Some of the tenderest memories of my life are here, memories of the good people with whom I lived here. I was a subordinate officer, a military Mayor. I was the guest of the best families here and for the first time I am accused of tyranny while here. I did make a levy by orders and gave a receipt for every dollar. Men do not give receipts for property they steal.

"I am accused of extortion, of taking money to release men from prison, of selling passports, of putting women out of their homes, of abusing confederate soldiers. I do not care who said these things or who swore to them, they are absolute falsehoods. They are trying to beat me by fraud with the aid of a campaign liar, but they cannot do it. I have no apologies to make for doing my duty as a Union soldier, and want none from you who wore the gray."

This reply made the Populists cheer and the Democrats wince. Some one tried to make a disturbance, but he was suppressed. Mrs. Lease closed the meeting with a speech. Then the procession returned to town, and moved around the court house square where a Democratic meeting was in progress. The speaker denounced Weaver, and there were moments when a word or a gesture might have brought trouble and led to a general battle in the town. Before the meeting broke up resolutions were offered describing Weaver "as a military tyrant, a renegade legislator, and a scoundrel as a man."

When shown these resolutions Weaver said that "they were adopted by a small crowd of cowards and defamers, who refused to hear my answer to their charges. They were discomfited and whipped on their own ground. They slunk away conscious of their crimes." General Weaver and his party were then escorted to their train by four armed men mounted on mules. Mrs. Weaver declared that she had not passed "so anxious and awful a day since the war.'' This experience, like those in Georgia, resulted from a strained political situation to which recollections of Civil War controversies added local seriousness. General Weaver's fearlessness conquered the respect of the majority, leaving only a few who tried to stir up trouble.[266]

From Pulaski General Weaver went to St. Louis where the national headquarters of the Populist party were located. After a short rest he spent the day in consultation with chairman H. E. Taubeneck of the national committee upon the exigencies of the campaign. He filled a few appointments in Missouri, and then left to meet engagements in Illinois, Indiana, Iowa, Minnesota, South Dakota, Nebraska, and Kansas. He expected to conduct an energetic campaign up to the day of election. Of the West he believed the Populists were reasonably certain; and while he made no claims — not thinking it to be good politics — he asserted that the new party was quite strong in the East. The old parties represented the bitterness and cruelties of the past and must give way to the new order of things.[267]

Soon after the close of General Weaver's campaign in the South, Murat Halstead came out in an article in the *Cincinnati Inquirer,* commenting upon the treatment which he, as an old soldier, had received, saying that he could perform a great service by withdrawing his candidacy and denouncing the South. Such action would, of course, result in advantage to the Republican party.

About the same time General Weaver also received a long letter from Albion W. Tourgee, the novelist, containing a similar request. This letter suggested that if he remained in the field as a candidate "the election of Grover Cleveland, with the 'solid South', as his controlling force" was "possible, perhaps probable. Every vote for you increases this probability. That fact at this time, means the permanent establishment and entrenchment in the most impregnable legal forms, of that Southern spirit of intolerance and determination to rule or ruin, of which you and I have in our own persons had more than one exemplification." Mr. Tourgee then raised the question whether General Weaver could "not by withdrawing about Nov. 1st, assigning as a reason your deep conviction of the need of concentrating the active sentiment of the country on this subject, do a service to the country greater than you have ever done before or will ever have an opportunity to do again?" Furthermore, he asked if his "personal and political interests" would not be "enhanced thereby?" He pointed out that General Weaver had "always been credited by Republicans with a very strong sense of patriotism.

Even when farthest estranged, they have conceded that. Your honesty of motive and high impulse have been admitted under circumstances that are rather surprising.

"Should you take this course, the whole Republican party, nearly the whole of the Populist party at the North and a good many at the South, with a considerable portion of the Democrats, will admit the sincerity, propriety and patriotism of your action. You will compel attention to this subject that no other act of any other person could, and no one could charge that it was for any personal advantage. At the same time, it could not inure to your detriment."

At one of General Weaver's meetings in the South, at which Mrs. Weaver was present, two men appeared and sought to interest him financially in the withdrawal of his candidacy. Of course these men were dismissed very promptly. Nor is there any indication or reason to suppose that General Weaver gave serious consideration to Tourgee's proposal. All three incidents make it clear that his candidacy in 1892 was regarded as of serious importance, and that it was thought likely to have an important influence upon the results of the election.[268]

One of the methods used for raising funds to carry on the campaign was the sale of a book by General Weaver entitled *A Call to Action*. This

book was published in 1891 and embodied in
systematic form the principles and policies for
which he had been contending since 1877. It
was sold for $1.50 per copy. The preface states
that the author's object in publishing the book
was "to call attention to some of the more serious evils which now disturb the repose of American society and threaten the overthrow of free
institutions.

"We are nearing a serious crisis", reads the
preface. "If the present strained relations between wealth owners and wealth producers continue much longer they will ripen into frightful
disaster. This universal discontent must be
quickly interpreted and its causes removed. It
is the country's imperative Call to Action, and
can not be longer disregarded with impunity.

"The sovereign right to regulate commerce
among our magnificent union of States, and to
control the instruments of commerce, the right
to issue the currency and to determine the
money supply for sixty-three million people and
their posterity, have been leased to associated
speculators. The brightest lights of the legal
profession have been lured from their honorable relation to the people in the administration
of justice, and through evolution in crime the
corporation has taken the place of the pirate;
and finally a bold and aggressive plutocracy has
usurped the Government and is using it as a

policeman to enforce its insolent decrees . .
. . The public domain has been squandered,
our coal fields bartered away, our forests de-
nuded, our people impoverished, and we are
attempting to build a prosperous commonwealth among people who are being robbed of
their homes . . . . The corporation has
been placed above the individual and an armed
body of cruel mercenaries permitted, in times
of public peril, to discharge police duties which
clearly belong to the State. Wall Street has
become the Western extension of Threadneedle
and Lombard streets, and the wealthy classes
of England and America have been brought into
touch. . . .

"But the present stupendous uprising among
the industrial people of the new world con-
founds them. It is the second revolt of the
colonies. It required seven years for our
fathers to overthrow the outward manifesta-
tions of tyranny in colonial days. But our
weapons now are not carnal, but mighty to the
pulling down of strongholds. Their children
can vanquish the American and British plutocracy combined in a single day — at the ballot-
box. They have resolved to do it. . . .

"We have made no attack upon individuals,
but have confined our criticisms to evil systems
and baleful legislation. We have endeavored
to be accurate, but claim no literary merit for
our effort."[269]

This book was of course no patiently wrought out study of existing conditions: it comprised rather the substance of the matter which General Weaver had been presenting upon the platform and in Congress for many years. While many of his opinions about currency and finance which were impracticable and visionary have been wisely ignored, a careful and thoughtful examination of his book shows an astonishing amount of anticipation of real evils and abuses long before they became apparent to the country at large. To mention only a few instances the criticism of the Senate as influenced by corporations and made up of the very rich men, the autocratic power of the Speaker of the House of Representatives, the conservation movement, and the need of a more adequate and elastic currency and banking system provided for by the Federal Reserve Act of 1913 are all anticipated by this pioneer in social politics. The platform of 1880, the Weaver speeches in Congress, especially from 1885 to 1889, the platform of 1892, and *A Call to Action,* are the documents that paved the way for Bryan in 1896, for Roosevelt from 1901 to 1909, and which culminated in the Progressive platform of 1912: they are the real foundations for much of the accomplishment of the first administration of President Wilson and an important element in his reëlection in 1916. Demands of the progressives of both parties since 1900 have been based largely upon the demands of Weaver in his campaigns from 1880 to 1900. The election of 1916 resulted in the union of the West and South — the union that Weaver hoped for and worked for in 1892.[270]

At the general election in November, 1892, General Weaver received 1,027,329 votes out of a total of 12,000,000 — eight and five-tenths per cent compared with forty-six and two-tenths per cent for the Democratic candidates and forty-five and one-tenth per cent for the Republican. Of the four hundred and forty-four electoral votes he received twenty-two. For the first and only time since 1860 a third party candidate had won a place in the electoral college. The States that voted for him were Colorado four votes, Idaho three, Kansas ten, Nevada three, North Dakota one, and Oregon one. The Democrats nominated no electors in Colorado, Idaho, Kansas, North Dakota, and Wyoming, but voted for the Populist candidates. In Nevada they named a ticket, but voted generally for the Populist electors. In North Dakota and Minnesota there was partial fusion; and in Oregon the Democrats accepted one of the Populist electors. In Louisiana the Republicans and Populists fused. Negotiations for fusion between Democrats and Populists in Iowa failed, because the Populists insisted that the

Democrats must indorse their electoral ticket
in full. The vote for Weaver in his home State
was 20,595 out of a total of 443,159, or about
four and one-half per cent.[271]

The only section of the country that came up
to Weaver's hopes and anticipations was the
Far West, especially the mining States of Colorado, Idaho, and Nevada, where the production
of silver was the chief industry. His enthusiastic campaign produced concrete results in the
electoral votes cast for him by the States of
that section — ten out of the twenty-two.

Kansas was, of course, the banner State of
Populism and gave him the largest support of
any single State. The economic conditions of
the farmers in Kansas in the early nineties
explain the strength of Populism there.

Weaver's expectation of a large Populist
vote in the South proved altogether too optimistic, although Texas, Alabama, North Carolina, and Georgia contributed over 270,000 to
the popular vote. The situation in the South
was described in a letter written to Weaver by
A. M. West from Holly Springs, Mississippi, in
September, 1892. He said that "we [the Popu-
lists] have the country vote. The democrats
have the town vote *and the Count* and, I am persuaded, will use the same regardless of right or
justice to perpetuate democratic rule in this
state. The cunningly devised provisions of our

state constitution and statutory laws establishes an absolute Party despotism, in this state, as intolerant and tyrannical as human ingenuity can make it, under the supremacy of the constitution of the United States. It is truly fearful to contemplate the decay of patriotism and political honesty and the all pervading corruption of party leaders. They do not hesitate to adopt and execute any methods to accomplish their unholy purposes. They are oblivious to the sublime teachings and examples of the founders of the republic. They are unscrupulous in their defamation of human character. In their mad pursuit of power they ignore social and religious ties and make the supreme rule of their party the God of their worship. For these reasons we work, in this state, with no expectation that the vote, however cast, will be counted otherwise than for the democratic party. I admire and honor you for your heroic struggle in the great work of reformation and trust that your efforts will ultimately be crowned with a glorious success."[272]

The States that gave the largest popular votes for General Weaver were the following:

KANSAS	163,111 VOTES	WEST
TEXAS	99,418 VOTES	SOUTH
ALABAMA	85,181 VOTES	SOUTH
NEBRASKA	83,134 VOTES	WEST
COLORADO	53,584 VOTES	FAR WEST

23

NORTH CAROLINA	44,732 VOTES	SOUTH
GEORGIA	42,937 VOTES	SOUTH
MISSOURI	41,213 VOTES	SOUTH
MINNESOTA	29,313 VOTES	WEST
OREGON	26,965 VOTES	FAR WEST
SOUTH DAKOTA	26,544 VOTES	WEST
CALIFORNIA	25,311 VOTES	FAR WEST

Of these States five were Southern, four Western, and three Far Western, indicating that the Populist strength was widely distributed through the West and South. Evidently there were latent possibilities for the formation of a strong sectional party. Weaver's vision foresaw the development of such a party, as he had seen the Republican party emerge in 1854 and 1856. What actually happened has been the permeation, first of the Democratic and then of the Republican party until American politics have become social. Weaver's intuition was sound in essentials, although we still await the establishment of a social democratic party. The campaign of 1892 was merely the prologue to that of 1896 and 1912.

General Weaver published an address to the people which was dated at Des Moines, November 16, 1892. He pointed out to "the friends of reform throughout the Union" that the new party "unaided by money" had achieved "surprising success at the polls. We are but little behind the Republican party in the number of

States carried. As a result of the late election we will doubtless hold the balance of power, in the Senate of the United States. We have doubled the number of our adherents in the House of Representatives, secured control of a number of State governments, hold the balance of power in a majority of the States of the Union, and have succeeded in arousing a spirit of political independence among the people of the Northwest which cannot be disregarded in the future. . . .

"The accession of the other party [Democratic] to power is the result of violent reaction and not, I am sure, of the deliberate judgment of the American people. The battle leaders of the triumphant party are without any well-defined policy, except that of contemptuous disregard for every element of reform within the ranks of their own party, and among the people at large. The new administration will ignore the great contentions of modern times relating to land, money and transportation, and will not attempt to solve either. In fact, the whole force of the new regime will be exercised to prevent reform in these important matters. The urgent demand of the people for the free coinage of silver is to be disdainfully ignored, and new obstacles will, doubtless, be interposed to further restrict the use of the white metal. . . .

"The issues pressing for solution are simply

tremendous, and the situation portentious. Our party has not made its advent too soon. Its mission is to restore to our government its original and only legitimate function, which has been well nigh lost by non-use, that of assuring to all its citizens — the weak as well as the mighty — the unmolested enjoyment of their inalienable rights." Referring to the relations between labor and capital as "now upon a war footing", he declared that the repressive policy "will not work well in the nineteenth century . . . . It denies to labor the right to organize, relies upon the military arm to sustain corporate pretentions, and when labor organizations defend themselves against armed mercenaries, it adjudges the members to be guilty of treason. . . .

"The violent political storm of 1888 and 1892, which first swept the Democratic candidate, then the Republican party from power in spite of the weight of patronage which they carried, signify a turbulent condition of the political atmosphere which plainly foreshadows an approaching crisis. It were better that it be not hastened by the enactment of measures which savor of usurpation and the extension of class privileges.

"I sincerely trust that the work of organization and education may now be pushed with energy throughout all the States. The field is ours and we must occupy it without delay.''[273]

At another time he described the Populist party as ''the coming factor in national politics, and its advent to national supremacy before the dawn of the twentieth century is assured. It holds the key to the political situation in America, and will battle again next year with the strength of a young giant in every state in the union for the free coinage of silver and the whole range of economic reforms now crying for solution. The future of free coinage of silver is assured and free coinage will follow. This is the first reform to be accomplished, and we [will] make short work of it.''[274]

Again he spoke of the situation in the United States as ''parallel to the conditions that led to the French Revolution. We have our noblesse the same as France, and, as in the days of Louis, the United States has its third estate.'' In answer to the question whether he thought the third party was increasing in strength, he replied that he certainly did. ''There is every evidence of prodigious growth. There will undoubtedly be a rapid consolidation of all industrial forces with the great body of business men throughout the Union. The trades unions are already on the move for political action, and the Knights of Labor and the various farmer organizations are already so. The tendency is unmistakable everywhere. I consider a great political revolution inevitable. It promises to be both peaceful and conservative."[275]

Later, while in New England upon a lecture tour, General Weaver was interviewed in Boston. He looked "the picture of health", and appeared "not the least affected with the largeness of his vote in the late election". In reply to questions upon the political situation, he answered that in his opinion the Republican party was "permanently disabled in the West as was the Whig party in 1852". It had "fallen to pieces in the presence of the overshadowing issues that have been evolved in the last quarter of a century's growth". The return of the Democratic party to power was "a mere accident", and "not the result of the deliberate purpose of a majority of the people of the United States. . . .

"The Republican party will rapidly disintegrate everywhere — in fact it is doing so now — and the anti-monopoly elements in both of the old parties will affiliate with the Populists, just as the Free Soil elements affiliated with the Republicans between 1856 and 1860. . . .

"The old parties represent the past. They are like two hostile armies inspired with bitterness and stained with blood. The Populists have a different mission, thank fortune.

"Their face is turned toward the glorious future, and they are trying to introduce the golden rule into politics and to lift the people to the plane of the sermon on the mount."[276]

General Weaver contributed to a symposium devoted to a consideration of the election results in *The Iowa State Register* early in December, 1892; Hon. W. W. Witmer represented the Democrats; and Hon. W. M. McFarland spoke for the Republicans. The discussion presented excellently the point of view of the three parties. General Weaver's contribution was given first place and was first in importance. It was the only one that undertook a real analysis of the situation and tried to get at fundamentals; the others played upon the surface of things or repeated political platitudes. Mr. Witmer did not mention the new political party represented by General Weaver, and Mr. McFarland devoted two lines to it.[277]

XVI

From Populist to Democrat

1893-1896

The results of the election of 1892 made General Weaver a political factor of considerable importance, since the rallying of over one million voters to the standard of the new party in its first national campaign aroused a good deal of apprehension among the leaders of the old parties which had been quite evenly balanced in the recent presidential elections. For the time being it seemed possible that the Populist party was at the stage of development of the Republican party in 1856, and that it might be about to replace one of the older parties as that party had replaced the Whig party.

Under the disturbed political conditions the new party was likely to be earnestly courted by its older competitors. To gain its support both Democrats and Republicans would be ready to make proposals and concessions. Political accident happened to give the Democrats the first opportunity, and they absorbed most of the Populist vote in 1896. Weaver's place in the alliance of Populists and Democrats could not but be an important one after he had turned over the million votes of 1892 together with the additions made since that year.

Soon after the election the *Clinton Age* referred to a prediction by a Des Moines paper that General Weaver would be the next United States Senator from Iowa. The opinion was based upon the supposition that he would work up fusions in counties where the Populists held the balance of power, and that these representatives would be the deciding factor in the next General Assembly. If the Democrats continued to vote for Populist candidates, his election would be very likely to result.[278] The union of Democrats and Populists, by the former supporting the candidates of the latter, was suggested in this statement instead of what did actually happen — the absorption of the Populists by the Democrats. Weaver was always ready to coöperate with other parties provided they were willing to support the principles in which he believed. Immediately after the success of 1892 it was easy to anticipate the growth of the Populists by accessions from the Democratic party. Actual developments from 1892 to 1896 turned the movement in the opposite direction — in any event the more probable course in view of party history in this country.

Weaver's attitude towards fusion at this time is shown by his opinion of the election of

a free-silver Democrat as Senator from Kansas
by a combination of Democrats and Populists.
He thought "that the very best possible result
was accomplished . . . . Judge Martin is
a man of splendid character and first-class ability. He has for years been openly in accord
with the doctrines of the People's party and
hence incurred the bitter opposition of the
machine Democrats in his own state . . . .
The judge is a free silver man, opposed to the
National banks and in favor of an increase of
the circulating medium until the volume is sufficient to place the business of the country on a
cash basis. I trust, however, he is the last so-
called Democrat to be elected by Populists'
votes."[279] His judgment in a concrete case,
when he was in a most optimistic frame of mind
as to the future of the new party, makes it plain
that he had not changed his settled conviction
as to the value of fusion between parties working for the same purposes. Throughout his
career as an independent he was ready to co-
operate if thereby the principles in which he
believed would be advanced.

During 1893 he continued the campaign of
education in which he had been engaged for
many years, and which had simply been en-
larged and accentuated in 1892. Late in January and early in February he made a tour of
Arizona, speaking at a number of points and

receiving the most courteous and hospitable treatment. He found the people unanimous for free silver and coming into the Populist party in large numbers. ''Since the November election the Republican party is a thing of the past, while anti-monopoly free silver Democrats have more sense than to look to a Wall street administration for their cherished reforms.''[280]

A letter written just after his return from Arizona described his position and plans at that time. He was going East for a series of meetings, which were to begin at Cooper Union in New York City and from there extend through Connecticut, Massachusetts, New Hampshire, Maine, and New Jersey. It was his ''purpose to represent the silver interests in all these meetings and start the current of public opinion in the right direction in those localities. The Silver Club is the proper form of organization as it is comparatively easy to secure pledges from the voters as . . . . in Colorado, not to vote for any candidate for an important office who is not in favor of the free coinage of silver. This is the line upon which the battle should be fought. It is the line of the least resistance and we should hurl our forces against it at every point. I shall reach home about the first of March and shall then take up the work of club organizations which will mean time be in progress of formation throughout the State.'' He referred to the work in behalf of free silver throughout the country and expressed his willingness to coöperate with it at all times.[281]

During July free silver meetings were held in Des Moines, and among the speakers were General Weaver and Congressman William J. Bryan of Nebraska. These meetings were a part of the silver propaganda which had its chief source in the silver-mining States of the Far West. There was a national organization known as the American Bi-metallic League which was closely associated with the Populist party. During 1893 meetings were held at Washington in February, at Chicago in August, and at St. Louis in October. The session at Chicago reported forty-two States and Territories represented and eight hundred and ten delegates in attendance. Bryan was associated with this agitation, and in connection with it he gained the experience that enabled him in 1896 to carry the Democratic convention by storm with his "Cross of Gold" speech. There was widespread dissatisfaction among the people of the West and South, due to the economic conditions of the period, and the free silver orators were eagerly listened to when they presented their panacea.[282]

While in Detroit in August it appears that General Weaver was interviewed by a representative of the *Detroit Free Press* in the course of which he indicated his position in regard to the political situation as it had developed since the election. Incidentally he also gave an account of his recent activities. He described himself as "engaged in visiting various states, talking to the people. I have put in thirty days in Kansas, Missouri, North Carolina, and New York. The meetings have been large, something like 2,500 to 10,000 every day. A great political revolution is pending among the people — the greatest I have ever seen. The financial situation has increased the public interest in political matters. I find that the Republican party has been largely destroyed as a factor in national politics and the Democratic party is badly crippled . . . . At present the free silver and anti-monopolist elements and all who believe that America should have an independent system of finance are coming together without regard to party. There is no necessity for the two gold parties in this country . . . . The Republicans and Democrats will join hands during the present session to repeal the Sherman act, to destroy silver and to establish the single gold basis. The financial situation is deplorable. The country is losing twice as much money per day by the enforced idleness of our people as it was at any time during the late war. Autumn is almost here and winter is approaching and millions of our industrious people are without food or employment.

"The administration and its advisers are as oblivious to the situation as was Louis XVI. at the beginning of the French Revolution. The most fearful consideration of the whole affair is that even with best intentions it would be difficult to provide relief before winter sets in. But no relief will be provided by the present administration. The most that is looked for is the repeal of the Sherman act and a few more privileges granted to the national banks. In order to secure the repeal of the Sherman law the bank interests may conclude to let the south have a few state banks of issue and may permit the repeal of the ten per cent. tax on issue of state banks. Rely upon it, everything will be done to enable the banks to control the volume of money of the country."

When General Weaver was asked about the future of the Populist party in the same interview he replied: "It is the only party that polled votes in every state. It is growing prodigiously, and is the only party fighting for an American system of finance and the increase of our volume of money. It is the only party making an honest effort to shake the trusts, corporations, syndicates and combines from the throats of the people. It is impossible that an industrial nation should disregard such an organization. They must give it their support."

He described the old parties in Iowa as "disorganized — the Democratic party on the silver question and the Republican party also on that question, with the additional affliction of disagreement on the prohibition matter."[283]

The Populist State Convention met in Des Moines in September. It was a noisy and irregular acting body, according to *The Iowa State Register,* which also declared that General Weaver controlled it, drew up the platform and presented it.[284] Undoubtedly the platform represented his views put in concrete form for campaign purposes in 1893. It was devoted to the money question very largely as "the one overshadowing, all-absorbing issue". The only party that voted "as a unit against the tricks of the millionaires is the People's party. There are only two parties to-day — the People's party and the gold party."

Other resolutions favored the election of President, Vice President, and United States Senators by direct vote of the people; demanded the abolition of all trusts and unlawful combinations in trade; denounced the attacks made upon pensions "as a part and parcel of the monied conspiracy which demands that no money shall pass from the government to the people without first passing through the toll gates of the banks''; and referred to ''the utter demoralization of the Democratic and Republican parties . . . . in their attitude toward the liquor question. They are engaged in an attempt to outbid one another for the support of the saloon element in the state, and are seeking to drown by their cry for the saloon every other important consideration relating to the public welfare. We demand that the present law shall remain until such time as it can be replaced by what is known as State and National control with all profits eliminated — which we believe to be the true method of dealing with the question.'' A final resolution urged ''equal political rights for all adult citizens without regard to sex.''[285]

This platform includes the chief items in which Weaver was interested in those years, and it roughly indicates the order of their importance in his opinion. The crisis of 1893 and the struggle then going on over the repeal of the silver purchase clause of the Sherman Act concentrated popular attention upon the money question and drew the lines more and more closely between the advocates of free coinage of silver and those who saw safety only in the single gold standard.

The year 1894 was one of industrial and social unrest in the United States, due largely to the prevailing business depression that followed the crisis of the preceding year. Bodies of men known as "Coxey" or "industrial" armies crossed the country from the Pacific Coast to Washington during the months from March to June. They were described by one writer as "but the byplay of the social movement." Much more serious were the labor controversies of the year, reaching a climax in the great railroad strike of July. Some slight disturbances occurred in Iowa as a result, but the State was not seriously involved. One of the industrial armies, the so-called "Kelly's Army", passed through during April and May; it was in Des Moines from Sunday, April 29th, to Wednesday, May 9th.

General Weaver devoted almost his entire time to the army while it was in Des Moines and vicinity. He drove out to the temporary camp near the city on Sunday morning and spoke to the men, who gave him a cordial greeting. He told them that as long as they did not violate any law their "marching petition" was invincible. He was in full sympathy with the objects of the movement and so were the great majority of the people in his opinion. He advised them to "keep on and get work. When you get work that is all you want."

Monday night General Weaver addressed a meeting in the interests of the army at the Trades Assembly Hall at which "General"

24

Kelly, its leader, also spoke. The hall was so crowded that the meeting was forced to adjourn to the court house square. Among other things Weaver urged appropriations to open the arid lands of the West so that homeless people could make homes for themselves. The next afternoon a meeting at the Opera House was addressed by Weaver, Kelly, and Sovereign. On Thursday morning about three hundred laboring men marched to the Capitol to ask the Governor for transportation from the State. General Weaver was described by the *Clinton Age* as "master of ceremonies". Governor Jackson read letters from the railroads refusing to carry the men for less than regular fare, but he promised to lay the matter before the Executive Council, and he thought that funds might be obtained to take the army by boats to the Mississippi River. This plan was finally adopted and the army started down the Des Moines River. The citizens of Des Moines paid the cost of the boats and furnished one day's provisions.[286]

The Midland Monthly for June, 1894, contained a short article by General Weaver under the title of *The Commonweal Crusade,* in which he gave his opinion of the significance of the invasion of Iowa. While General Weaver presented a sympathetic view of the "crusade", another article in the same number of the maga-

zine disclosed a radically different attitude.
General Weaver regarded the industrial armies
as representative of millions of hungry, pov-
erty-stricken people working at starvation
wages without hope of any improvement in
their condition. They were "a forecast of the
great conflicts and reforms" which were to
make "the closing years of the nineteenth and
the early years of the twentieth centuries the
most important epoch which has ever dawned
upon Christian civilization."

The lasting achievements of the American
and French revolutions were the declarations
of human rights but these rights had been made
merchandise of in the United States, wrote General Weaver. This was "the prime cause and
origin of the whole difficulty in a nutshell." The
appeal of these armies was not selfish. They
protested against wrongs which had become
universal and intolerable, and the safety of
society at large depended upon speedy and
proper adjustment. The armies declared for
the commonweal: they represented the vast
excluded multitude. "They can not till the
earth in their own right, for they have been
fenced out by land monopoly. They can not
pass rapidly to and from the seat of government to present their grievances, for they are
excluded from the great highways by their poverty . . . . They are denied the right to labor.

Employment cannot be found . . . . Their
written petitions are spurned with derision,
and when they attempt to march in person to
present their grievances they are pursued by
the wolf of hunger and beset with armed militia
and the policeman's club. . . .

"Every student of our times knows what they
want. They want labor, independence, homes,
and the ready money which these indispensable
factors will bring. Society, through state and
national government, is abundantly able to
quickly solve the whole vexed problem. If we
hesitate, we will pay the penalty at a very early
day".[287]

In 1894, as in the preceding year, General
Weaver took an active part in the proceedings
of the Populist State convention — which met
at Des Moines early in September. After the
organization of the convention and the appointment of committees, General Weaver was called
for and made a speech in which he expressed
his satisfaction at the presence of so many persons devoted to the interests of "our glorious
young party." He criticised the Republican
party and pointed out that more persons were
killed and wounded each year upon the railroads under the interstate commerce law passed
by that party than in the battle of Shiloh. He
said that was the way the Republicans protected the workingmen. He urged breadth and

liberality "to build up a great party. You can't have all honest men in any party — it would live forever, and no party ought to live more than three terms of power. 'I am a middle-of-the-road man, but I don't propose to lie down across it so no one can get over me. Nothing grows in the middle of the road'."[288] He concluded by declaring that it was possible for the Populists to elect seven members to Congress with the aid of the Democrats.

A resolution was proposed for "the adoption of a comprehensive amendment to the federal constitution, which shall reënact all valuable portions of the constitution of 1789 as subsequently amended and incorporate therein those necessary reforms which are now constitutionally impracticable, including elective United States senators, a single term of the presidency, determined by popular vote, an elective supreme court holding office for a definite term, with similar subordinate courts, direct legislation by the people through the initiative and referendum, and such broad extensions of popular rights as shall set the people absolutely free to govern themselves in their own way and to conduct in their national or local capacity such industries as may be withdrawn by monopoly from individual competition, and such other enterprises as may meet the public approval as properly subject to popular conduct." The resolution closed with a call for "a mass convention of the American people to assemble in . . . . Des Moines on the first Monday in December, 1894, to consider the necessary amendment of the fundamental law of the land."

The reasons for the proposed amendment are given in the preamble in these words: "We share the admiration which moved a great modern statesman to declare our present federal constitution the most perfect work ever thrown off by the human mind at one time; but we hold that it is now essentially a product of a by-gone age, too inflexible for the varied conditions of modern life, warped, blurred and burdened by judicial construction, and practically not open to amendment except as the result of war or supreme, universal and protracted effort."

When this "sweeping constitution-repealing resolution" was brought up General Weaver characterized it as "conservative", and he favored its adoption. One of the delegates described it "as a very singular thing", and moved to lay it on the table. "The viva voce was close, and a standing vote was called for which laid the resolution on the table by a large majority."[289]

The opinion entertained by General Weaver that the Populists might elect seven members of Congress in 1894 is emphasized by the fact that

he had already been nominated for Congress in
the ninth district, although he had been a resident of Des Moines since 1890. The selection
of a non-resident is noteworthy, since it exposed
him to criticism during the campaign and may
have weakened him as a candidate. If elected
he planned to remove from Des Moines and take
up his permanent residence in Council Bluffs
but his defeat put an end to such a change.[290]

His nomination for Congress was probably
the result of the growth of sentiment for the
free coinage of silver in the West. The national administration by its course was arousing the antagonism of many western Democrats.
The friends of the administration, aided by
Federal office-holders, maintained control of the
State conventions until 1896; but in many Congressional districts the majority pronounced in
favor of free coinage, nominating free silver
Democrats, or fused with the Populists and
endorsed their candidates. There was no
serious effort to bring about fusion upon the
State ticket, but fusion candidates were agreed
upon in five districts — the third, seventh,
eighth, ninth, and tenth. The movement that
was to lead to national fusion in 1896 thus
began in Iowa two years earlier.[291]

The Congressional convention met at Council
Bluffs on August 8th and endorsed Weaver's
candidacy by a vote of seventy to twenty. He

was described as the choice of none of the Democrats individually, but of three-fourths of them collectively. The majority of the committee on resolutions reported in favor of the free coinage of silver, while a minority report was made by the anti-silver men who withdrew immediately thereafter, claiming that the majority report was a packed affair and demanding another deal. There were many threats of the nomination of an anti-silver candidate, but nothing of the kind materialized. Weaver undoubtedly represented the majority in the district. The chief strength of the anti-silver forces was probably among the Democratic office-holders.[292]

General Weaver had a tremendous fight on his hands. The Republicans put forth especial efforts to save their candidate and to defeat Weaver, and in addition he could not count upon the support of the anti-silver Democrats. Senator Allison and Congressman Dolliver were sent into the district; and leading Republicans, like McKinley of Ohio and Reed of Maine, were regarded as necessary to save the day for the Republicans. Charges were also made that considerable money was used to secure Weaver's defeat. He devoted much of his campaign to a discussion of the free coinage of silver, which he maintained would remedy the need for more money, and would not pro-

duce the evils that its opponents prophesied.
He also urged the reduction of the tariff, government control of railroads, an income tax,
and the election of United States Senators by
the direct vote of the people.[293]

The election resulted in Weaver's defeat by a
vote of 18,817 to 21,874; but he received a larger
vote than any of the other fusion candidates for
Congress. In every county but one in the district he polled more votes than were cast for
both the Democratic and Populist party tickets,
using for comparative purposes the number of
votes received by the candidates of those
parties for Secretary of State. Weaver's hope
for seven fusion Congressmen proved wide of
the mark as the Republicans returned a solid
delegation of eleven. The contest attracted
national attention. *The Review of Reviews*
referred to his defeat as a "notable incident".
Mr. Samuel Gompers wrote, expressing gratification at his nomination because of his "sturdiness in advocating reforms in the interest of
labor and the masses generally". Eugene V.
Debs regretted his inability to help him in his
campaign, and declared himself "in hearty
accord with the People's Party and wish it and
you, as the veteran champion of *all* labor's
hosts, the greatest measure of success."[294]

After the election General Weaver was interviewed and expressed himself freely concerning

the political situation and the results of the
contest. He remarked that he felt no regrets
about his own defeat, as his vote was greater
than the combined vote of the two organizations
which supported him. Many Republicans also
voted for him as was shown by the official count.
He lost the election by only about two thousand
votes; whereas if the landslide had struck his
district as hard as it did other parts of the
State, he would have been defeated by ten thousand votes. "He was simply caught under the
outer rim of a tremendous landslide which was
general throughout the country, but which was
much heavier in other parts of the republic than
it was in the Ninth district. It was not a personal defeat and hence was easy to be borne."

He described the general defeat of the Democrats as "simply a tremendous cyclone of discontent"— the result of "idle labor, low prices,
a tight money market and corporate arro-
gance." The Republicans had "not triumphed
because of any affirmative policy which they expected to inaugurate, but because of a universal
discontent for which they have not even a pretended remedy . . . . This party in its
leadership and machinery, in every state in the
nation, is a unit against every reform now
pressing for solution. It is emphatically the
party of the corporations and the gold power.
Its only purpose is to hold its position and in

the late election it drew to its support the single gold standard advocates from all quarters and they will remain with it permanently. This is a wonderful fact of the widest possible significance when we come to forecast the future.

"Everybody can see now that the failure of the democratic party is due to the fact that it is hopelessly divided upon all the great questions of the day, while its enemy is a unit . . . . and all can now see clearly that there is neither call nor room for two corporation and gold standard parties in this country . . . . The advent of the corporate power and that of the money kings took place under republican rule and all their vast growth is due to republican legislation, and the two can never be separated . . . . Under great leadership the democratic party should have comprehended these things and taken the field as the champion of the plain people."

With his usual optimism General Weaver regarded the future of the Populist party as "hopeful and full of promise. We have emerged from the storm with our vote largely increased in every state . . . . It is now clear that the populist party has come to stay and henceforth must be reckoned as a formidable factor in American politics. It is not to be judged by the ill-considered utterances of some of its over-zealous, radical and unbalanced men.

The republican party, in its early days, flourished in spite of the extreme utterances of the ultra men of that time, and it still retains a measure of power in spite of a host of concededly bad men who occupy very high position in its councils. All reform movements attract to their ranks men of radical and extreme views.

"The new party will be judged by what it promises to do. The measures which it advocates are all eminently rational and conservative. Its cardinal doctrines are: Free bimetalism at the ratio of 16 to 1; the overthrow of trusts, monopolies and excessive taxation; the issuance of all money by the government instead of through banking corporations; the election of senators by the people; the control of transportation facilities by whatever lawful means shall prove necessary to that end; and a graduated income tax. The American people are in favor of all these reforms and will so express themselves when given a fair opportunity to do so . . . . Before another congress is chosen, the people who favor the above reforms will unite, and they will choose a congress which represents their wishes and then, and not until then, will we get relief.

"The great duty of the hour is a close union of all classes of men who substantially believe alike, and we can now all see clearly the necessity for such a union of forces. The times call aloud for it and now let all good men and women work for it with zeal."[295]

The elections of 1894 represent the high-water mark in the electoral strength of the Populists. Compared with the results in 1892 there was a gain of forty-two per cent — from 1,027,329 to 1,471,590 votes. So great a success made more inevitable its absorption by one of the older parties — the usual result in the United States.[296]

The year 1895 was occupied with preparation for the presidential contest of 1896. Free coinage of silver was the one great issue. The control of the Democratic party machinery in Iowa by the Federal administration through Federal office-holders led the free silver Democrats to attempt by a preconvention union of forces to assert themselves more effectively than in the preceding year. Accordingly, in June silver conferences were held at Des Moines in which General Weaver took an active part. These conferences were intended to bring together all the advocates of the free coinage of silver regardless of their party affiliations. By such accessions of strength the free silver Democrats hoped to gain control of the State convention. The silver conferences were also a part of the national propaganda of the silver forces which had as its object the fusion of all the supporters of free coinage into a compact party. General Weaver was understood to be one of the leaders in the effort to secure such a union, and to have the coöperation of such men as General A. J. Warner of Ohio and Congressman Bland of Missouri. The plan would bring together the Populist party, the free silver Democrats, and the silver organizations of the country — a result accomplished in 1896.[297]

Apparently General Weaver was inclining more and more to emphasize the single issue of free coinage of silver, and to undertake to unite those favoring such a policy regardless of their party relations. It was fusion in a different form, and it aroused the opposition of the more extreme Populists who wished to build up a separate party organization.

Rumors were also current of a secret plan of the Populist leaders to fuse with the Democrats to control the next General Assembly in the interest of General Weaver as a candidate for the United States Senate to succeed Senator Allison, whose term would expire in 1897. Senator Gear had also been seriously ill, and there was a possibility of the election of two Senators in the near future. Such an opportunity would give an excellent chance for a well arranged fusion. In August the plan was said to have been under consideration for four months and had been carried into the silver conferences and into the Populist State Convention. The middle-of-the-road Populists opposed it, as they did the proposal to make silver the only issue and mainly for the same reasons — because it would endanger the continued existence of their party. General Weaver was at the State convention and assisted in straightening out the party finances.

Soon after he wrote the candidate for Governor assuring him of his support and stating that reports printed in Chicago papers to the contrary were "absolutely false. There is but one difference of opinion within our party in this state or elsewhere . . . . and that relates to the method of securing a union of the reform elements for 1896, and there is ample time in which to review our present attitude and for calm reflection between now and the convention of next year".[298]

Early in August the Democratic State Convention met at Marshalltown, the State committee and the temporary organization being in control of the gold men. The first test of strength of the two factions came over the election of the permanent chairman, and the nominee of the State committee was chosen by a vote of six hundred and sixty to four hundred and seventeen. A free coinage amendment to platform was voted down by practically the same vote. The gold Democrats proceeded to complete the business of the convention by the nomination of a gold man for Governor and a silver man for Lieutenant Governor. There was much dissatisfaction with the conduct of the convention because of the presence and prominence of Federal office-holders. This dissatisfaction added to the growing strength of the silver faction in the State: it helped to give the control of the convention of 1896 to the free silver Democrats. The union of the silver forces behind Bryan in 1896 was brought one step nearer.[299]

As the campaign of 1896 approached Weaver became more and more earnest in his advocacy of a union of reform forces. He felt sure that neither the Republican nor the Democratic party could hope to poll a united vote for their tickets in 1896. Millions of free silver Republicans would bolt a gold standard ticket, while about one-half of the Democrats favored free silver at sixteen to one, the abolition of national banks, and the issue of legal tender paper currency by the government. The other half were devoted to "the gold standard and the British system of finance". These parties were hopelessly divided and would eventually disappear, making possible the formation of new parties. "Just how the union of the reform element is to be effected is a little difficult to forecast. I think, however, that the ticket will be the point of union. The populists will of course hold their national convention and the country may fairly hope for broad and liberal action on their part. . . . This will lead them to nominate men like Mr. Sibley of Pennsylvania and Judge Caldwell of the United States circuit court. The first is of democratic antecedents; the latter a republican. These men are of the Lincoln and Jackson type. . . . Such a ticket would likely unite all reform elements. The great question of the hour is how to get together. We are past the platform period and are confronted with great tactical questions which always precede great conflicts like that which awaits us in 1896."[300]

Again, at another time Weaver elaborated his reasons for urging a union of reform forces. In a private letter to a friend he declared that they must secure at least 5,500,000 votes in addition to the Populist vote of 1892 "in order to stand any reasonable show of success." Such a result could only be accomplished by a policy of "mutual concessions". He thought that "the money plank in all its fullness, and Sibley at the head of the ticket, afford a reasonable basis of union." He took a cheerful view of the political situation and was confident that "good sense and patriotism" would "finally triumph in all the reform parties and elements that sin-

25

cerely long for the speedy overthrow of the British Gold Power."[301]

The union of reform forces in 1896 was regarded by General Weaver as "an alliance, not fusion . . . . made up of Populists, Democrats and Republicans. It will first agree upon a platform, then declare its union perpetual until the objects in view are secured. If this is done, they will, of course, agree upon a ticket . . . . The formation of this alliance is not likely to be contingent upon the action of the Republican and Democratic parties . . . . the Republican slogan for 1896 is quite certain to be gold and national bank paper, sugar-coated with the hope and promise of possible international bimetallism. Most of the western and middle States Democratic leaders will endeavor to commit the remnant of their party to the same policy. Failing, they will flock with meagre following to the Republicans. They nearly all carry cards of admission now . . . . The American bimetallic movement, recently inaugurated at Washington . . . . suggests the four-pronged money question as a basis for union, unrestricted gold and silver coinage at the present ratio, without waiting for the action of any other nation; legal-tender Government paper, no banks of issue and no bonds. This furnishes a platform wide enough for the greatest civic struggle we have ever known.

"If the kindred but now divided factions shall have the good judgment to accept and act upon the timely suggestion — stripping themselves for the time being of everything else, no matter how important — they will close the century with the grandest battle ever fought and crown it with the greatest victory ever won for commercial supremacy and industrial freedom. If they do not unite, the gold power will march its forces over the field and settle the whole question in its own way without firing a gun . . . . A Democratic or Republican uniform no longer has any meaning. There may be a silver man or a gold man, a bank man or an anti-bank man, or a bond man underneath it . . . . This is very confusing, and a change is necessary. At present the reform line is good enough for scouting purposes, but too lengthy for battle . . . . We must now huddle and fight and see to it that the other fellows do the running."[302]

A letter published in the *Farmers' Tribune*, Weaver's own paper and the State organ of the Populist party, was evidently a reply to Populist criticism of his insistence upon a union of reform forces in 1896. He began by the statement that he would not "quarrel with any person within the party, use hard names or hurl epithets at others who may differ with me. Nor shall I reply to those who may assail me with such weapons. If we cannot treat each other with respect we certainly may not hope to draw to us those who are not within our ranks. We are not making platforms now, but there will have to be some expression of opinion if we are to have a consensus of judgment when we meet in convention. This requires time. By all sensible men expressions of opinion are given in the nature of advice and are intended simply to be persuasive instead of authoritative. What are all the letters you are publishing, and the thousands of editorials of the Reform Press, but expressions of opinion intended to act persuasively upon the minds of those who read them? Has any member of the party lost his right to express an opinion? In my judgment the great work of our next national convention will be tactical, and relate to marshalling our forces rather than to the formulation of doctrinal matters. We know now what we want. The question will be how best can it be secured? I have nothing to conceal in this matter. Viewing the public situation as it exists to-day, unless some material changes shall occur, while considering fully and unreservedly the great importance of our other planks, I shall favor going before the people in 1896 with the money question alone, unincumbered with any other contentions whatsoever. Not on the silver issue alone, but distinctly favoring unrestricted coin-

age at the ratio of 16 to 1, and legal tender
government paper, with neither bonds nor banks
of issue . . . . Meantime let us keep our
guns trained upon the common enemy and let
each other alone. Concerning our proper attitude toward other forces that may be forming
to grapple with the money power, I commend
the reading of Luke 9: 49, 50.''[303]

The great event of 1896 politically was the
adoption of free coinage of silver as an issue by
the Democrats and their nomination of Bryan
as a candidate. To the country at large these
events came as surprises; but as a matter of
fact they had been in preparation for several
years. The large vote of the Populists in 1892
gave them encouragement, while it alarmed
the older parties; but the more experienced
leaders like Weaver realized that to add by
gradual growth enough votes to obtain a majority was a difficult task.

Furthermore, the committal of the Democratic party in 1893 to the fight against silver
left the free silver Democrats of the West and
South in an awkward position, for there was no
place for two gold parties, and the most of their
constituents were hostile to such a course. The
Democrats by adopting free coinage, and nominating a candidate favorable to it, might hope
to concentrate all the elements opposed to gold.
The wide-spread demand for silver in the West

and South made such a course seem really likely to result successfully. The large vote for Bryan proved that the judgment of those who urged it was by no means entirely unwarranted and mistaken.

General Weaver's part in this development was important. As the standard bearer in 1892 he was the recognized leader of his party and exercised a large influence. He had for some time been urging a union of the reform forces. The endorsement of the Democratic nominees would accomplish his purpose. To such a conclusion, therefore, he gave his support in the months preceding the conventions. Bryan's nomination was by no means entirely spontaneous and due to his dramatic speech: it had been worked for and anticipated by some of the members of both conventions. Among these workers General Weaver occupied an influential position.

The Populist State Convention met in Des Moines in April to nominate delegates to the national convention to be held in St. Louis. General Weaver was temporary chairman and made one of the principal addresses. He declared that he had come two thousand miles from Oregon, where he had been campaigning, to attend the State convention and to get it to unite with all the silver parties. They must get four and a half million votes by November to

win, and if they did not win this year, the party
would fail. Evidently there was considerable
opposition, for when L. H. Weller moved to
make the temporary organization permanent,
some one objected, although General Weaver
had just stated that he would not accept the
chairmanship unless the action was unanimous.
He was also a member of the committee on resolutions which by a vote of seven to three recommended that the delegates to the national
convention ''do all in their power to secure a
union of all reform forces on a common ticket
or a platform embodying the fundamental principles of the Omaha platform and in addition
recommend the adoption of the initiative and
referendum.'' The minority report omitted all
reference to the union of reform forces. A
motion was made and carried by acclamation
that General Weaver should be one of the delegates at large to the national convention.[304]

In the national convention Senator William
V. Allen of Nebraska and General Weaver were
the ''foremost advocates'' of the nomination of
Bryan by the Populists. Their opponents were
largely Southern delegates who were hostile to
the Democracy as the dominant party in their
section. There were also some northern Populists who feared that the endorsement of Bryan
would mean the disappearance of their party
as a distinct organization: the Iowa delegation

was divided upon this point. General Weaver
was chosen chairman of the delegates favoring
Bryan, and of the "steering committee" to
canvass delegates upon their arrival and to do
missionary work among them. The results of
these efforts were shown in the election of Allen
as permanent chairman by a vote of 758 to 564,
and the appointment of Weaver as chairman of
the committee on resolutions.

The next conflict between the two groups
came over the nomination of a candidate for the
Vice Presidency. Arthur Sewall of Maine,
Bryan's running mate upon the national ticket,
was an eastern bank president, and had been
known as a free silver man only about a year.
He was a man of wealth and a director in railroad and other corporations. His selection was
a matter of political expediency, and was not
favorably regarded by the rank and file of the
Democrats. The Populists rejected him altogether, and nominated in his place Thomas E.
Watson of Georgia. After this action Bryan's
candidacy was endorsed by a vote of 1042 out
of about 1300 delegates.[305] The nomination of
a separate candidate for the Vice Presidency
showed the existence of a strong minority in
the party opposed to Weaver's policy of alliance with the Democrats, and it was this
minority that constituted the Populist party
after 1896. The majority were absorbed into

the Democratic party, Allen and Weaver acting
with the Democrats after the campaign of that
year.

General Weaver made the chief nominating
speech for Bryan, and in it he gave his reasons
for such action and explained its relation to the
movements in which he had been a leader for so
many years. He described the year 1896 as
"the most critical period" in the history of the
Populist party. He had only "two aspirations
in connection with that party. The first is incorporated with my life work. It is to preserve
untarnished and unsullied to the American
people the great principles that we have contended for for the last twenty years. My second
purpose is to preserve the organization for
present and future usefulness in every part of
this Union. . . .

"For twenty years we have been pleading
with the people to espouse the sacred cause
which is at stake in this campaign. We have
constantly urged through good and evil report
that our principles were more important than
party associations, were above all considerations of private fortune or the petty and fever-
ish ambitions of men. We have thus far suited
our action to our words. Through five presidential campaigns, stretching from 1876 to
1892, you correctly estimated the purposes of
old party managers, and events have sustained

every specification in your indictment against them . . . . To your devoted efforts is largely due the revival of economic learning in this country, which has enabled the Democratic party to assume its present admirable attitude. Your work now promises much to mankind, and is about to break forth in complete victory for the industrial masses. Though oft repulsed by the multitude, whom we would have liberated, though crucified in return for our kindness, yet through it all we have steadily confided in the righteousness of our cause and the final good sense of the people. We still believe that this nation has a mission to perform which bad men will not be permitted to destroy, and recent events indicate that the nineteenth century is not, after all, to close with the friends of freedom despondent in the western hemisphere.

"This country has recently witnessed a new Pentecost, and received another baptism of fire. The recent convention at Chicago sounded a bugle call for union which can neither be misunderstood nor go unheeded. In its patriotic utterances and action it swept away all middle ground, and opened the road to a formidable organic alliance. They not only made union possible — thank heaven, they have rendered it inevitable.

"From the very beginning our organization has made party fealty subordinate to principle.

We will not here reverse ourselves and refuse to accept victory now so easily within our reach. We will not refuse the proffered assistance of at least 3,000,000 free silver Democrats, and not less than 1,000,000 free silver Republicans, simply because they have shown the good sense to come with an organized army fully equipped and manned for battle. Let them have their own divisions and army corps. The field of glory is open to all competitors who are fighting for the same principles. . . .

"If we would be victorious we must make common cause with the heroic men who dominated the Chicago convention. No other course is either prudent or desirable. We are not asked to abandon our party, nor would it be wise to do so. If it is to be preserved we will, in my judgment, be compelled to take the course which I am about to indicate. The silver Democrats have lined up as an organization. Now let the Populists, free silver Republicans, and the American silver party do likewise. . . .

"After due consideration, in which I have fully canvassed every possible phase of the subject, I have failed to find a single good reason to justify us in placing a third ticket in the field. The exigencies of the hour imperatively demand that there shall be but one. I would not endorse the distinguished gentleman named at Chicago. I would nominate him outright, and make him our own, and then share justly and rightfully in his election . . . . Take this course, and all opposition will practically disappear in the Southern and Western states, and we can then turn our attention to other parts of the field. Take any other, and you endanger the entire situation and strengthen the arm of our common adversary.

"If you allow the present happy juncture to pass, all the heroic work of twenty years will be thrown to the winds. Our guiding hand will disappear in the momentous conflict just when it should be stretched forth to steady the ark of our covenant. We would prove to the world that we are devoid of capacity to grasp great opportunities, and lacking in strength to grapple with prodigious emergencies. The people have a gallant champion in the field, who is leading a revolt against the plutocracy of Christendom. Every oppressor, every plutocrat, in two hemispheres has turned his guns upon him. The subsidized organs have openly proclaimed that he must be crushed by any means and at whatever cost. The confederated monopolies have laid aside their parties and their politics and are marching in hot haste against him. Let us signal to him to hold the fort — that we are coming — and then hasten to his relief."[306]

The active part taken by General Weaver in

the nomination of Bryan by the Populists made him the recipient of many attentions by the Democrats. At the State convention of that party held at Ottumwa in August, he was named as elector-at-large with ex-Governor Boies upon the fusion ticket of Democrats and Populists. After the completion of the nominations he was called for and made a speech. He said that "there was a political miracle being performed . . . . The Chicago convention was a political miracle and it still continued." He rubbed it into the Democrats just a little. He told them that the Populists had been "fighting for years for the principles you incorporate in your Chicago platform, but there is no jealousy; God bless you, we welcome you. Take the lead, and if you can plant the flag one foot nearer the citadel of plutocracy than we did, do it, and we will help you." He said there was no distinction or difference between Democrats, Populists, and free-silver Republicans, and the convention cheered him. He prophesied the greatest victory since the foundation of the country, which would be a victory of the people, guided by a divine hand". Then he called for three cheers and after they were given the convention adjourned. He was described as the hero and dictator of the convention, and as dividing the honors with ex-Governor Boies.

Mr. Bryan stopped over in Des Moines on his

way to New York to open the campaign. Here
he referred to General Weaver in most eulogistic terms, describing him in connection with
Boies as "that other gallant man, who for
twenty years has fought and, whether we have
agreed with him or not on all the things, there
is not an honest man here but must concede
that where Weaver fought he fought with the
strength of a giant."[307]

During the same month of August in which
he was honored by the State convention and the
national standard bearer of the Democratic
party, he was also tendered a place upon the
national Democratic campaign committee. He
also accompanied Mr. Bryan upon parts of his
spectacular campaign of the country, which was
really only an extension of his own campaigns
of 1880 and 1892, made possible by better facilities for travel and more ample finances.[308]

XVII

The Later Years

1896–1912

THE result of the election of 1896, though disappointing to General Weaver and those who worked with him, was still near enough to victory to give encouragement for another campaign along the same lines. A contest lost by only about half a million votes out of a total of over thirteen million was a very close approach to success when all the circumstances are taken into consideration. It is not surprising, therefore, that a man of Weaver's optimistic temperament should anticipate a victory in 1900. Repeatedly between 1896 and 1900, he indulged in such prophecies and he worked continually for such an outcome during the intervening years.

His description of the political situation preceding the Congressional campaign of 1898 explained his position and gave reasons for it. He believed that the people were misled in 1896 by the promises of the Republicans, and that they had begun to understand the real state of affairs "before the smoke of battle had fairly

cleared away." In his opinion the victory was
won by "lavish promises, reinforced at the critical juncture by the corrupt use of money,
fraud, and intimidation." He declared that
"the overwhelming popular revolt" against
Cleveland "was not against the person, but the
policy of the administration. It was his gold
bonds and bank schemes, his attempt to retire
the greenbacks, the revenue deficits under the
Wilson tariff law, and his pro-Spanish-Cuban
policy." In all essential respects, McKinley's
administration was "an exact duplicate of
Cleveland's minus the latter's backbone." He
pointed out that the "same evil counsellors"
were "all powerful", and if there was any difference between the administrations, "the trust
magnates" were "more potential" than they
had been under Cleveland.

Weaver was confident that "the triple alliance between the Bryan Democrats, Populists,
and Silver Republicans" would soon result in
"complete triumph", and he urged the strength-
ening of this alliance in every part of the
country with the object of gaining control of
the House of Representatives in 1898. The
contest in 1898 would mean "the initial mobili-
zation" for 1900. He hoped every member of
the alliance would support "our great leader,
Bryan . . . . He is at war with the classes
and the common people love him. His heart is

as true as that of Old Hickory, and his head as
clear as that of the immortal Jefferson."[309]

In 1898 General Weaver was again a candidate for Congress from the sixth district
against Lacey who had defeated him in 1888.
He was nominated on the first ballot by a vote
of fifty to forty-seven in a convention made up
of Democrats, Populists, and free silver Republicans. The Populists were satisfied with the
nomination, but at least half the Democrats
were said to be "sore". The Populists believed
that he could defeat Lacey, but the Democrats
were less sanguine. It was generally conceded
that he would make the strongest possible campaign against the Republican candidate. The
contest ended with Weaver's defeat by a vote of
18,267 to 19,738, a plurality of 1,471 for
Lacey.[310]

The references made by General Weaver to
the "pro-Spanish-Cuban policy" of Cleveland,
as one of the causes of the popular revolt
against his administration, indicated his attitude upon the War with Spain in 1898. He was
among the first to offer his services to the government; and there is a letter in his correspondence from Governor L. M. Shaw, acknowledging
the tender of his services to the State and
nation in the event of a war with Spain.
Weaver's letter was written on March 17th.
There is also a letter from the War Department

26

acknowledging a similar tender made in a letter dated March 25th.[311] These letters are noteworthy because of his later position upon imperialism. The freeing of the Cubans from Spanish rule appealed to his democracy, while the later extension of American government over the Philippines was contrary to his ideals.

While the insurrection under Aguinaldo was in progress General Weaver discussed "Imperialism" before a Des Moines audience. He undertook to maintain two propositions: (1) that the position of the national administration in regard to the Philippine Islands was contrary to the law of nations; and (2) that its position was also contrary to the spirit and the letter of the Declaration of Independence. He closed his address by stating what he regarded as the duty of the United States towards the Filipinos. He would "invite Aguinaldo to meet under a palm tree somewhere" to talk things over, and he would then "tell him to go back and organize his congress and take charge of the administration of the affairs of his country." Incidentally in the course of his remarks, he referred to President McKinley as "worse than a Spaniard".[312]

In December, 1899, he wrote to *The Des Moines Leader* in regard to an article which had appeared in that paper under the title of *Militant Clergymen*. He declared that it recalled to his mind the conversation between Christ and Pilate just before the crucifixion. "It was an apostacized church and a prostituted imperial government that united to blot out the hope of mankind at the crucifixion. And it is the Caesars and Pilates of to-day, backed by a widely subservient pulpit, who are crucifying the devoted Boers in the Transvaal and the bleeding Christian Filipinos in the Orient. And for what reason? Simply because they dared to exercise, in their own country, the love of liberty and self-government which our common Father has implanted in the breast of every human being . . . . If there is a man in this world who deserves the scorn of mankind it is the so-called minister of the gospel or the so-called Christian who is in sympathy with the bloody and merciless slaughter now raging in the Philippines and the horrible English butchery now being committed in the Transvaal . . . . Our bishops and ministers who support the wars of conquest now flagrant in Africa and the Philippines have reached a point where the divine methods of conquering the world by justice and love are too slow for them. Such methods keep out of view commercial advantages. For the present these gentlemen seem to prefer the policies of Caesar and Pilate. They could have given the Galilean valuable pointers if they had been present at his trial."[313]

Again in May, 1902, he protested against
some resolutions adopted at the G. A. R. encampment "endorsing the policy of the administration in the Philippines and covertly com-
mitting us to an indorsement of the atrocities
which have been perpetrated upon the Filipino
people. It is an attempt to commit the old
soldiers of Iowa to an endorsement of these
atrocities and the introduction of politics into
the encampment which is wholly unjustifiable.
There are thousands of democrats belonging to
the Grand Army of the Republic in Iowa who
do not endorse the policy of the administration
in the Philippines and thousands of Republican
veterans who feel the same way. The resolution was passed without discussion. I was not
present or they would undoubtedly have heard
from me."[314]

After 1896 Weaver described the relation of
the Populists to the Bryan Democrats and free
silver Republicans as a continuance of "the
triple alliance" of that year. In reality it meant
practically the absorption by the Bryan Democracy of the other elements. The Populists, who
opposed the nomination of Bryan and insisted
upon the naming of Watson instead of Sewall
in 1896, came to be known as Middle-of-the-
Road Populists, and they were naturally opposed to the continuance of the alliance. By
1900 the two wings or factions had been devel-

oped and organized as fusionists and anti-
fusionists — the latter having its chief strength
in the South. Weaver acted with the regular
or fusionist faction in 1900.

Associated with him in this wing of the party
were Senator Allen of Nebraska, Senator
Marion Butler of North Carolina, "Cyclone"
Davis of Texas, and Thomas M. Patterson of
Colorado. His intimate connection with party
management is shown in his correspondence
during 1900. A letter from J. H. Edmisten,
chairman of the State committee of the People's
Independent party of Nebraska, urged a meeting of the national committee at Lincoln in
February, and asked Weaver's support for it
as the best place "to secure a large attendance,
and also have the moral support of those supporting the union of forces at the point where
a meeting could be held. In the event of the
meeting being located at Lincoln, I shall call
our state executive committee together and will
send out invitations to 200 or 300 of our leading
men to be present on that occasion, which I am
sure they will do. This will give us a strong
influence at the time of the meeting. Of course
should the meeting be located at some other
point, we would be unable to tell what influences
we could surround it with. I think it would be
well for you to write Mr. Butler urging him to
lend such influence as he can for Lincoln as the

place to hold the meeting, if you have not already written him." The Lincoln meeting was held on February 19th and resulted in the complete separation of the factions. In spite of the predictions of the Nebraska chairman, the fusionists were in a minority at Lincoln — the fusionists had forty-two, while the anti-fusionists had fifty-seven delegates.[315]

S. B. Crane, chairman of the State committee of the People's party of Iowa, wrote Weaver in March in regard to "a speaker of national reputation for an evening meeting after the convention", and suggested Allen, Weaver "or some one that could create some inthusiasm . . . . I would like to go to Sioux Falls with a strong delegation of inthusiastic men." In April Senator Butler wrote that the Associated Press had asked him to furnish them an outline of the remarks that he would make in calling the convention to order, and also to have the temporary and permanent chairmen do the same as soon as possible, as telegraphic communication with Sioux Falls was limited to two wires, and they could give more space if they could have the matter in hand in advance than if they were forced to get the speeches from the convention.

"Of course I cannot control who will be permanent Chairman of the Convention," wrote Butler, "but permit me to say that there is a

general consensus of opinion among those of
us who are here that you [Weaver] ought to be
permanent Chairman, therefore permit me to
suggest that you at once prepare a synopsis of
the speech that you will make as permanent
Chairman, if you are elected. Or at least prepare what you are willing for them to publish as
a report of your speech.''

A letter from George H. Shibley, dated May
2nd, reminded Weaver that he was a member of
a committee of five on platform appointed at
Lincoln in February, presumably to prepare a
preliminary draft for the Sioux Falls convention.[316] In connection with this appointment, it
is interesting to note that the Sioux Falls platform contained four planks vigorously condemning the new imperialistic tendencies of the
United States, and expressing sympathy for the
Boers, while no references to these matters
appeared in the platform of the other faction.
We may safely infer that Weaver had a hand in
the drafting of these resolutions.

The two wings of the Populist party held
national conventions at the same time in May
— the regulars at Sioux Falls, South Dakota,
and the Middle-of-the-Roaders at Cincinnati,
Ohio. Weaver, of course, went to Sioux Falls
where the nomination of Bryan was a foregone
conclusion; but the question of naming a candidate for Vice President gave rise to a serious

contest, the friends of Bryan opposing such a nomination in advance of the meeting of the Democratic national convention. After a warm struggle Charles A. Towne of Minnesota was nominated; but later in August he withdrew, and the national committee substituted the nominee of the Democrats, Adlai E. Stevenson. It hardly needs to be added that General Weaver was opposed to the nomination of any candidate for Vice President, since a complete alliance could not be brought about without the acceptance of the same candidates by the allies. There was not the same reason as existed in 1896 for such action, for the other wing of the party nominated a separate ticket made up of Wharton Barker of Pennsylvania and Ignatius Donnelly of Minnesota.[317]

The Weaver correspondence after the convention at Sioux Falls again reflected his position and relation to party affairs. On May 16, 1900, George S. Canfield of St. Paul wrote him that he was "very sorry that matters went against your judgment at Sioux Falls, and feel certain that you appreciated our position as to Minnesota. It was apparent from the start that some nomination must be made. Knowing that you reflected the sentiments of our leaders, we appreciated your position, and the fact that your great personal strength with all members of your party was unable to stem the tide, is all the more proof that nothing could have brought about any different action.

"Myself and others outside of the delegation bore from Mr. Towne his most urgent advice that a conference was a better plan. When a nomination was unavoidable, of course, the nomination of an outside man was the best possible thing to do. You will be glad to be reassured, as we are, from Mr. Towne since the convention, of the receptive attitude which he maintains and his lofty purpose to take such final action as may be deemed best in the final consideration."[318]

A few days later a letter to Weaver from T. M. Patterson of Colorado, permanent chairman of the Sioux Falls convention, declared that their views as to the nomination of Towne were the same, and yet he would like very much "to see them proved wrong. Towne would make a strong second to Mr. Bryan in all of the middle, mountain and far western states, and I think, from what Mr. Bryan said, whom I saw on my way back from Sioux Falls, he would be more than pleased to have Mr. Towne on the ticket with him. I have no means of judging what the democratic sentiment generally will be about Towne, except as it is developed here in Denver. Most of the Democrats are Mr. Towne's warm admirers, but they almost uniformly say that they believe it will be unwise to

nominate him at Kansas City under the circumstances. They do not believe that a great party
should be in the position before the entire people of the country — of accepting their full
presidential ticket ready made at the hands of
another political organization. And then you
know Populism is very unpopular in the South
and the East. The single fact that he comes to
delegates from those sections of the country as
a Populist nominee I fear is enough to destroy
his chances. Towne's nomination was the outcome, in my opinion, of a combination between
Mr. Bryan's friends and enemies; a large number of those who supported him are sincerely
Mr. Bryan's friends, but I think there were
some marplots there with their pockets full of
proxies — who would really rejoice to see Mr.
McKinley re-elected."[319]

E. H. Gillette, who had been elected to Congress with Weaver in 1878, representing the
Des Moines district, and who had been associated with him politically ever since, asked his
advice in June in regard to the need for his
attendance at Kansas City to urge the nomination of Mr. Towne by the Democrats. Gillette
wrote that he had not intended to go and had
"felt highly elated for two months to think"
that he would not have to test his "physical
endurance" and "hold on life by thrusting"
himself "into that seething July cauldron.

That is a place where you'd grow young, but
where I'd grow old. However if it should happen that there was any Dem. there whom I
could persuade to do the right thing, which I
very much doubt, I might be tempted as a matter of duty . . . . to make a sardine of
myself for a week."[320]

The Kansas City convention nominated
Bryan unanimously upon the first ballot, and
completed the ticket with only a slight contest
by the selection of Adlai E. Stevenson of Illinois as its candidate for Vice President. Towne
received only eighty-nine and one-half votes
compared with five hundred and fifty-nine and
one-half for Stevenson and two hundred for
David B. Hill of New York.[321]

The friction between Democrats and Populists and between the two Populist factions
made the alliance less complete in 1900 than it
had been four years earlier. The entrance of
the issues arising from the Spanish War confused the situation, while the return of business
prosperity reduced the urgency of the monetary
questions. The result was an increased vote
for the Republicans and a falling off of the
Democratic vote. The hopes for the success
of "the triple alliance" in a second campaign
were doomed to disappointment. Changed conditions were chiefly responsible for the failure,
and a new program was necessary.

General Weaver's position after the election of 1900 was stated in a letter to the *Omaha World-Herald,* answering an address recently issued regarding the future of the Democratic party. He believed that "under the leadership of Mr. Bryan and in the hands of its absolutely loyal committee, the democratic party is a reform party — a new and mighty reform force — and its leadership cannot revert to objectionable hands unless the 7,000,000 reform voters commit the stupendous blunder of disbanding in face of the enemy for the vain purpose of attempting a re-organization.

"The way to insure a complete union of the reform forces is for the elements which rallied to the support of Mr. Bryan to stay together. The work of the unification is already accomplished, and our leader is the best known and best beloved man on earth to-day. A new organization could not muster one-half of the mighty host who gave us their support in 1900, and plutocracy would hail the advent of a new party with peans of joy. It would insure their supremacy for a quarter of a century. If the various reform elements that supported our leader in the memorable conflict of the present year desire to exert salutary influence in political circles in the future let them resolutely stand by their guns and await events."[322]

Evidently General Weaver was satisfied to

remain a member of this "union of reform forces", as he regarded it, and apparently he continued to act with the Democrats during the rest of his life. Probably the close friendship with Mr. Bryan had a great deal to do with his permanent association with the Democratic party. During all these years Bryan was the unquestioned leader of the Democracy, and Weaver's opinions and sympathies coincided with his own. He recognized, too, the pioneer services of Weaver in preparing the way for his own leadership from 1896 to 1912. Bryan and La Follette and Roosevelt were all long preceded by Weaver. Bryan fully and freely acknowledged his indebtedness to the "Grand Old Commoner of Iowa".[323]

In July, 1904, General Weaver was one of the delegates at large from Iowa to the Democratic national convention at St. Louis. The delegation were instructed by the convention to vote for William R. Hearst of New York and were bound by the unit rule to support him. The State convention also voted down the reaffirmation of the Kansas City platform of 1900. The domination of the Hearst supporters was very distasteful to the older leaders who opposed the instruction of the delegates. General Weaver advocated the instructions; and one of the district delegates, W. W. Baldwin of Burlington, a sound money Democrat, wrote him immediately afterwards, expressing his "unqualified admiration" of his ability as a political debater. "I thought that your speech for instructions at Des Moines was a model of adroit and skillful appeal." In the convention the votes for the four delegates-at-large who were elected were as follows: J. M. Parsons 611; E. M. Carr 596; S. B. Wadsworth 562; and Weaver 521.[324]

Although Hearst failed to receive the Democratic nomination at St. Louis — his chances of success were never good — General Weaver seems to have turned to the support of Parker with remarkable willingness. Probably with Bryan he was ready to give the conservative Democrats a chance to show their weakness with the hope that in 1908 the party would turn again to progressive leadership. At any rate he took an active part in the campaign.

His opinion of the situation was given in an interview one week after the St. Louis convention. He described the Chicago convention of 1896 as "the vernal equinox", and that of 1904 as "the autumnal of the great struggle for democratic reform"; but he believed that "balmy spring" would come again. "Bryan, the loftiest democratic leader that ever lived, still survives, towering like the Alps, and is to-day the greatest positive individual force of the New Century.

"Everybody was accorded a fair hearing at St. Louis. Not only the opportunity to be heard was granted, but each side was actually and completely heard and hence there is not left the shadow of an excuse to bolt. We did not get all we wanted either as to candidate or platform . . . . But we secured much that is good, and our platform of promises, when compared with the republican platform of silence on the one hand and vicious performance on the other, amounting together to a denial of hope, is sufficient to give us a united democracy in every state of the Union.

"The platform is anti-imperial, anti-trust, is opposed to militarism, calls for tariff reform, election of United States Senators by the people, strikes at military despotism in Colorado, calls for trial by jury and a return to the safeguards of the constitution. Judge Parker's plutocratic entourage is not pleasing to me. But it is, to say the least, equally as good as the surroundings of President Roosevelt. We can accomplish nothing by flying apart into fragments at this juncture of affairs; neither can we best serve our country and age by fleeing to the camp and standard of the adversary. Good judgment and patriotism alike call for the united support of Parker and Davis. The promise of reform and the great body of reformers who are tactful in their methods will be found under this banner in spite of the plutocratic influences which forced the nomination."[325]

General Weaver also seriously considered running for Congress from the sixth district again in 1904. His correspondence contains a number of letters, either urging him to be a candidate, or expressing pleasure at the prospect and promising support if he were nominated. Nothing came of this proposal and he occupied himself with the campaign for Parker. Late in the campaign he gave as a reason for his failure to run the short time allowed for the contest. He liked to open a campaign January 1st and keep it up to December 31st. Some of his friends believed that many Republicans would vote for him as they had done in the past, others advised him to "have nothing to do with the deal at all" because many Democrats were "very sore", and some made "no bones of saying right out that they will vote for Roosevelt straight so that the vote will be over-whelming for him as against the re-organizers and the Wall-street gang."[326]

When the Democrats nominated Bryan for a third time in 1908 there could be no question as to Weaver's position. His friendship for Bryan and his belief in the coming success of the reform forces made him optimistic again. As in 1896 and 1900 he looked forward to the

long-deferred victory for which he had been
laboring in season and out since 1877. There
seemed to be good grounds for such hopes, for
the Democratic party was more completely
united behind Mr. Bryan than it had been in the
two previous campaigns when he was the standard bearer. Weaver was active in the campaign, being especially associated with John W.
Kern, the candidate for Vice President. Afterwards Kern wrote to him expressing his appreciation of his "splendid efforts during the
campaign. I look back upon that part of it, in
which I traveled and communed with you, as by
far the most pleasant of it all. I don't want to
be a flatterer, but I feel that I would like you
to know that I admire you immensely and want
you to register me on the list of your best
friends. If I gave you my reasons for liking
you so well, you would blush."[327]

General Weaver was also talked of as a candidate at the primaries for the Democratic
nomination for Governor. Apparently the
perennial talk about his nomination for Congress occurred, since his old colleague, E. H.
Gillette, wrote him in June and asked him, if
he did not know that "the man who silenced
the Speaker (Sam Randall) and sent him to the
cloak room for a drink; the man who opened
Oklahoma; the man who exposed the National
Bankers to the contempt of mankind, and made

27

the fakirs and Trusts tremble is a marked man,
and when he shows his head it gets hit? Did
you imagine they'd ever let you into a legislative assembly again? Did you imagine they had
forgotten? *Not much!* Don't be a target for
'em but hit 'em again."[328] General Weaver's
age made it rather unlikely that he would ever
be a candidate again.

But his interest in politics remained keen to
the very end. In the summer of 1911, while on
a visit to one of his daughters in Seattle,
Washington, he expressed the opinion that the
progressive movement was becoming "formidable". He pointed out that the progressives
had cut loose from corporate and trust control.
They were making war upon the "interests",
and in effect were "forming a new party by
trying to transform the old one, [and] they will
succeed. The old regime had better stand from
under." Referring to the popular election of
Senators, which he had urged during his three
terms in Congress, he said the progressives
were doing "the next best thing" by nominating them in the primaries.[329] Evidently he
saw that they were doing for the Republicans
what Bryan had done for the Democrats. He
recognized that both movements were working
along the same lines along which he had campaigned for so many years.

On his way home a month later he discussed

the political situation in an interview at Salt
Lake. He believed that if La Follette was nominated for President he would sweep the country, and that if President Taft should be
renominated he would certainly be defeated.
He described "the Democratic presidential outlook" as "somewhat chaotic. The Harmon
people are keeping their forces well in hand.
Woodrow Wilson has ingratiated himself with
the Democrats of the country. Champ Clark,
however, would seem to be the popular choice."
He planned to take the stump for the Democratic presidential nominee in 1912.[330]

During the last months of his life he was
much interested in the campaign of the candidates for the Democratic nomination for President in 1912. Early in November, 1911, Judge
A. Van Wagenen of Sioux City wrote him that,
after diligent study for four or five months, he
had reached the conclusion that Woodrow
Wilson was "the most fundamentally rooted of
any progressive in the country." He expressed
a desire to know how Weaver's thoughts were
running "on the important question of who
will make the right kind as well as the strongest
leader." A few days later Judge Van Wagenen
replied to a letter from Weaver, which he had
"read and studied carefully. I like Champ
Clark splendidly but I am just like you I am
afraid of his poise. They tell me in this respect

he has been better for some time but poise is a thing that comes with a life long habit . . . . Still we must give Clark credit for having done a wonderful lot of good. I haven't said to any one or to myself just what I am going to do, but I am like you the more I think the more strongly I am about settling upon Wilson."[331]

Late in December, 1911, and in January, 1912, letters to Weaver indicate a leaning towards Champ Clark. W. D. Jamieson, a former Democratic congressman from Iowa, wrote him that "it did my heart good to find that you are so emphatically with us in the effort to get an Iowa delegation for Mr. Clark, and with the kind of a fighting spirit that you have for the things that you believe to be right, I am sure you will be glad to write a few letters." He mentioned a number of persons to whom he would like to have Weaver write. About three weeks later he wrote again and urged him to make a statement of his views for publication. "As the man who had more than a million votes as a presidential candidate, and one of those to whom Wilson undoubtedly referred as the 'alien' element which was to be eliminated from the democratic party, I think it would be well for you to try the case out very exhaustively, setting forth clearly and at length your reasons and arguments for your present position. You are recognized everywhere as being one of the very earnest and substantial leaders of the radical fight of the country, and as being one of the very earnest and honest and reliable democrats.''[332]

His last expression of opinion upon public affairs was an endorsement of Champ Clark as a candidate for the Democratic nomination for President, written upon a scrap of heavy manilla wrapping paper. The letter was written to W. D. Jamieson on January 26th. He had taken time to think over the political situation in Iowa and had reached the conclusion that the State ought to support Champ Clark. ''This is emphatically Clark territory. His versatility and wide experience as a legislator, his long acquaintance with the public men of the country and his thorough understanding of the motives of those who represent the almost omnipotent 'interests'— motives which are never willingly disclosed or admitted — preeminently qualify him for the high position. Mr. Clark should have every vote of our delegation without division. I say that not with any resentment toward other candidates. They are all eminent men and small things should not be introduced and considered. The path of duty is plain. Let us follow it. With charity for all I am resolutely and unalterably for Mr. Clark, and trust sincerely that Iowa will so align herself at Baltimore.''[333]

General Weaver's death occurred in February, 1912, before the contest between Wilson and Clark had assumed definite form. Without doubt he would have followed Bryan in his support of Wilson when events developed as they did in the Baltimore convention. One can not but regret that he could not have lived another year to witness the election and inauguration of a Democratic President, who would have seemed to him to represent the triumph of that union of reform forces for which he had toiled and waited for more than thirty years.

IN March, 1901, General Weaver was elected mayor of Colfax, the town in which his later years were spent. Under the circumstances his choice for the position was an indication of the regard in which he was held by his friends and neighbors. Political lines were not drawn to any great extent, and he received the support largely of those desiring a cleaner administration of local affairs. This election as mayor was the first of a series of events during the last years of his life which showed very plainly that he had won the recognition and esteem of the people of the State. There was nothing partisan in this tardy appreciation of his services. A letter from his son-in-law, H. C. Evans, in February, 1903, informed him that he would be renominated for mayor, unless he "immediately" wrote "some one at home" to stop it. General Weaver was still actively interested in State politics, and the same letter refers to his "boom for governor" as "big".[334]

The golden wedding anniversary of General and Mrs. Weaver was celebrated in July, 1908.

No formal invitations were issued and only a
simple notice inserted in the press a few days
before the event. The guests were received
upon the lawn of the unpretentious home at
Colfax, and the afternoon and evening witnessed a continuous procession of persons who
called to pay their respects. General and Mrs.
Weaver were assisted by all of their children,
except Mrs. Laura Ketchum of Seattle, Washington, who found it impossible to be present.
The six children present were Mrs. Maude Rob-
inson of Colfax, Mrs. Susan Evans, Mrs. Ruth
Denny, and Mr. James B. Weaver, Jr., of Des
Moines, Mrs. Esther Cohrt of Traer, and Mr.
Abram C. Weaver of Aberdeen, South Dakota.
A delegation from Des Moines, where General
Weaver had lived from 1890 to the time of his
removal to Colfax, presented a beautiful library
chair as a gift from the Polk County Democracy.

During the evening the people of Colfax
turned out in large numbers. An informal program also was given during the course of the
evening. A present of $50 in gold — one gold
dollar for each year of wedded life — came
from the citizens of Colfax. General Weaver
responded "in a speech replete with humor,
pathos and the expression of the thanks of himself and wife for the many kind words and
deeds of the day.

In the course of his remarks he paid a fine tribute to Mrs. Weaver, who throughout their married life had been in perfect sympathy with his understanding of the issues involved in his public career. She had been a leader in the temperance and suffrage movements in the State, and an active associate and helper in all of his reform work. General Weaver related the story of how when he asked Mrs. Weaver if she had heard the news of Lincoln's call for troops in 1861, she answered, "Yes, James, and I want you to go". They were financially very poor at that time. Their first child had been born in 1859, and another was expected in August, 1861.

Mr. W. S. Moore of General Weaver's old regiment, the Second Iowa Volunteer Infantry, was called out and responded in a witty and effective speech. There were many presents from friends and relatives. .' . . Singing closed the evening that will be a delightful recollection to all concerned."[335]

The custom of hanging the portraits of the famous men of the past upon the walls of public buildings is an old and widely accepted one. When the Iowa Capitol was completed in 1882 Charles Aldrich began to urge the collection of the portraits of noted Iowa men to be hung upon the walls of the offices and corridors. The portraits of a score of governors, judges, and other officials had been hung on the walls in the Capitol before the gallery of the Memorial Historical and Art Building was opened. The popularity and value of the plan, originated by Mr. Aldrich for the Capitol, led him to emphasize this feature after the erection of the Memorial Historical and Art Building. He felt very strongly that oil paintings of the prominent men of Iowa ought to be preserved, and he made the securing of such portraits one of the chief objects of the Historical Department of which he was Curator. Without funds for this specific purpose, the only method of acquisition was by gift. Many of the pioneers and distinguished men to whom Mr. Aldrich issued his invitations could not afford or were too modest to present their portraits. Among those who received such an invitation from Mr. Aldrich was General James B. Weaver; but neither response nor refusal came while Mr. Aldrich lived.

Soon after Mr. Aldrich's death in March, 1908, Mrs. Charles Dupree Smith noticed the absence of a portrait of General Weaver in the gallery of the Historical Memorial and Art Building. She at once conceived a plan for providing and presenting such a portrait, and immediately communicated her ideas to General G. M. Dodge, Hon. Fred E. White, General James S. Clarkson and a number of other eminent men, all of whom cordially approved the

MR. AND MRS. JAMES BAIRD WEAVER

FROM A KODAK FILM 1911

plan. Thereupon Mrs. Smith began a campaign to collect the necessary funds. The friends and admirers of General Weaver, in and out of Iowa, responded readily and generously. Mr. Charles A. Cumming of Des Moines was commissioned to paint the portrait, which was ready for presentation in February, 1909.

A committee of subscribers was appointed, consisting of Hon. Jerry Sullivan, Hon. Carroll Wright, Hon. H. W. Byers, Rev. J. F. Nugent, Mrs. Charles Dupree Smith, with Mr. Edgar R. Harlan as chairman, to arrange a program befitting the occasion. The board of trustees of the Historical Department asked that the exercises be given under their auspices, and the House of Representatives by resolution offered the use of their hall for the purpose. The Speaker of the House appointed a committee of three to act with the general committee. The afternoon of February 15, 1909, was selected as the time for the public unveiling and presentation. On the evening of the same day a memorial banquet in honor of General Weaver was given at the Savery House, Des Moines, under the auspices of the Democratic members of the legislature. Both occasions were intended to be of a non-partisan character, and were participated in by men of all parties. Together they constituted a unique testimonial to the career and a sincere recognition of the worth of a man who had only occasionally held office and whose public activity had usually been with the minority.

The afternoon program, over which Governor B. F. Carroll presided as chairman of the board of trustees of the Historical Department, consisted of an address by Rev. J. F. Nugent presenting the portrait on behalf of the friends of General Weaver. Immediately following came the unveiling of the picture by two of his granddaughters. After this ceremony Major John F. Lacey, a long time friend and political opponent in the sixth district, paid special tribute to the military record and character of his former antagonist. Mr. William Jennings Bryan was then introduced, and his address was ''a sermon on goodness and nobility of character, and an application of these traits to the life of the speaker's friend.'' In a few well chosen remarks Judge H. E. Deemer accepted the portrait on behalf of the trustees of the Historical Department. An audience of twelve hundred persons was present at these impressive exercises.

Just before the close of the proceedings, Mrs. Smith presented to General Weaver a ''beautiful, hand-tooled, Morocco bound volume'' containing the many letters which had been received in the course of the preparation of the portrait. General Weaver rose and with deep emotion received the book with a few words of thanks. He declared that the one feature that he appreciated more highly than anything else was the fact that it was "strictly non-partisan" and came from "loving friends of all political faiths". After the conclusion of the exercises in the hall of the House of Representatives General Weaver held a reception in the rooms of the Speaker.[336]

The memorial banquet in the evening was attended by about four hundred persons. State Senator and Congressman-elect W. D. Jamieson was the toastmaster, and Hon. Jerry Sullivan, Governor B. F. Carroll, Ex-Governor Warren Garst, Colonel Lafayette Young, Attorney General H. W. Byers, Senator J. A. De Armand, Representative W. L. Harding, Judge M. J. Wade, and Hon. G. F. Rinehart responded to toasts. Following this list of speakers, General Weaver and Mr. Bryan closed the program with addresses upon *Brotherhood* and *Retrospect and Prospect, America* being sung between the two speeches. The banquet was a fitting climax to a really wonderful occasion which will go down in Iowa history as "Weaver Day".

"General Weaver's speech was full of the feeling of gratitude that had been evident throughout the day. As he expressed his thanks to his friends for the tributes of the day, his voice trembled with the emotion he could not conceal, and as he pledged his life long gratitude and that of his children, the heart of every hearer was touched by his earnestness and the realization of what this homage means to him after a life long struggle in which, as he said, he was not merely usually in the minority but in the 'minor minority'."

The honors of the day were shared with Mr. Bryan. "When he was introduced . . . . at the banquet the applause was as long as that which had greeted General Weaver. Mr. Bryan first gave his attention to Col. Lafe Young, who had preceded him on the programme and had turned some pointed stories his way. He referred to Mr. Young's declaration that he had been a greenbacker at twelve years of age, but had changed soon afterward to a republican. 'We are told in the Bible', said Mr. Bryan, 'that truth is revealed to babes.' Shouts of laughter greeted the sally, and Mr. Young joined in the storm of applause." Though it was after midnight when Mr. Bryan concluded his address very few had left the hall at that time, the interest having been remarkably well sustained throughout the long evening.[337]

At the reunion of the Pioneer Lawmakers' Association held in Des Moines a few weeks after the unveiling of General Weaver's portrait, Mr. Isaac Brandt, the Secretary of the Association, declared that he had attended "all

the presentations of these notable pictures . .
. . and I want to say that I believe there
never was such a day in the State of Iowa as
was the day that Gen. Weaver's picture . . . .
was presented to the State of Iowa . . . .
Those grand tributes that were paid to him by
Father Nugent — it was magnificent. His manuscript was grand, but when he laid down his
manuscript and spoke from his heart . . . .
the audience arose almost en masse and cheered
it. And then, the tribute that Mr. Bryan paid
to him was grand, and I must say that of all the
functions I ever attended there was none that
pleased me so fully and completely as the tribute that was given to Gen. J. B. Weaver.''[338]

The bound volume of correspondence presented to General Weaver by Mrs. Smith contains a wealth of eulogy and praise of his
character and career. One of the most suggestive contributions was an original poem with
the title of *The Skirmisher,* sent by the author,
Herbert Quick, then of Sioux City. It was dedicated to General Weaver and aptly described
his rôle in politics.

The battle thunders all along the line;
The mustered myriads drink its draught like wine!
We charge in lusty squadrons unafraid
Cheered by the bellow of our cannonade
Still stands th' embattled host of Vested Wrong,
Unshaken, unabashed, unconquered, strong;

But Right has now her fields of clustered spears,
And shakes the air with trampling and with cheers!
The fight seems dubious; yet one thing we know:
The fight shall not be lost without a blow!
The soldier dies; but as his senses swim
He sees the line sweep on, with eyes grown dim.
The wounded lie and bleed — their faces shine
As billowing cheers come swelling down the line!
All now is glory, conquest, conflict, thrill;
The great war dims the sky and shakes the hill;
The very mass of battle bears us high
In generous resolve to do or die —
And we forget in the tense urge to win
The skirmishers that drove their pickets in!
They fought in the gray dawn, cold and alone,
A hardy few, darting from tree to stone.
No fife and drum, no touch of elbow cheered —
They saw no following host with flags upreared;
And that which wrung their valiant spirits most
Was the dread doubt, "There is no following host!"
Yet through the fearsome jungle forth they went,
Felt for the foe, and drove him to his tent;
And in the splendid faith that one good blow
Is each man's legal debt to every foe,
They struck. The sparse fire crackled through the
    dawn,
Grew, greatened, roared — and the great war was
    on!
So let us honor, 'mid the battle's din
The skirmishers that drove their pickets in!

Harvey Ingham, editor of *The Register and*

Leader, wrote that Mr. Quick "fitly designates the General 'The Skirmisher'. It is a happy suggestion. He has been on the skirmish line of every reform for a lifetime, and he has driven in many of the pickets of entrenched wrong."

Another very noteworthy expression of regard and esteem came from General James S. Clarkson, Weaver's old journalistic opponent of the days of his prime when battles royal were waged by the two men — one the champion of the party in power, the other the apparent leader of a forlorn hope. Clarkson was in complete sympathy with the plan "to pay fitting honor to one of the worthiest and most distinguished of Iowa men. There is very much in the brilliant career of General Weaver to stir the pride of every Iowa citizen, as well as to win popular admiration and affection. After the differences of the time shall have passed away and a full perspective of his life and work shall have been gained, he will be ranked and go into history among the dozen stronger Iowa men in several fields: in that of the law, his own profession; in the lists of oratory, where he has been among the foremost in public life in times of peace, where he has always made a superior record; most of all, in the war to preserve the Union, where his great record is a peculiar source of Iowa pride; and in later years in the

28

highest fields in politics, where he has borne a very prominent national part, as well as a leading part in local, or Iowa, affairs. General Weaver had by nature many of the elements of actual greatness, and these natural qualities he improved by application and experience. It may be said that he achieved eminence in all the larger fields except that of commercial success and money-making. His failure in that is to be credited to his generous nature and his lifelong desire to help others rather than himself. Indeed, the finest thing to me in his whole career of many achievements is that he has always been the willing and valorous and effectual friend of the weak, the oppressed and the needy. Great as he could have been by applying himself as a lawyer, he could have achieved great fortune and made money in many other ways. It is to his credit that he preferred to be useful to his fellow men rather than to achieve money and fortune for himself.''

An interesting combination of circumstances made it possible for three Republican Governors of the State to write letters of approval of the plan for the presentation of General Weaver's portrait, each writing while actually in office, and all within about three months of each other: Governor A. B. Cummins wrote October 3, 1908; Governor Warren Garst wrote December 9, 1908; and Governor B. F. Carroll

wrote January 25, 1909. The non-partisan
character of these testimonials is emphasized
when we remember that General Weaver was at
the time a Democrat, and had left the Republican party thirty years before.

Another confirmation of the absence of anything of a political character from this correspondence is to be found in a letter from
W. W. Baldwin of Burlington. He regarded
the placing of General Weaver's portrait in the
gallery of the Historical Department as "certainly appropriate", because he represented
"the patriotic sentiment of the state, for he was
a splendid soldier in the War for the Union; he
stands for ability in public debate of a high
order, and he has upheld his political convictions with courage and fidelity in the face of
many defeats, and much disappointment and
personal loss to himself.

"I have not always agreed with his views and
theories of government and politics, but I have
never failed to admire the charm and vigor with
which he defended them, and have always been
glad to call him my personal friend.

"Some of the earliest recollections of my boyhood are connected with General Weaver . .
. . I shall never forget the lofty sentiment
with which he inspired me as a youth when, in
an important law-suit, he denounced a notorious
social miscreant in words that fairly flamed

with eloquent indignation and won a substantial verdict. Forty years later, I could not conceal my admiration for the masterly skill with which he argued through a State convention a proposition to which I could not agree at all. The same old fire of speech was there, delivered in the same old captivating way.''

W. D. Jamieson, Congressman-elect from the eighth district and a political friend and associate, wrote that he admired General Weaver ''for the temptations he has withstood. At one time he was taken up into the high mountain and offered a seat in the United States Senate from Iowa if he would — not swerve actually — but by his silence *appear* to swerve from the course ahead of him that his conscience had mapped out . . . . On every occasion his character has stood out clear and true — four square to every wind that blew. I first saw General Weaver when I was a little fellow ten years old. My impression of him then was that he was a mighty smart man, and I thought he was *honest*. An added acquaintance of a quarter of a century, more or less intimate, has deepened my child's estimate in both regards.

''His preacher told me one time that he went to prayer meetings on Thursday evenings, and that he worked at his Christianity. I believe this is true, for I have never yet seen a single act of his that I thought was otherwise than in

conformity with his conception of the right. I
was called upon, not long ago, to introduce him
at a political meeting, and almost without thinking of what I was saying I told the audience
that he was the one man who was a factor in
our political life, whom I had introduced up to
that time, of whom I could say that he believed
in the sermon on the mount, and that he took
that sermon into his every day political life".

Mr. N. E. Kendall, Republican Congressman-
elect from Weaver's old district, the sixth, described him as "one of the most remarkable
men Iowa has ever produced. His career has
been unquiet, because his nature has been uncompromising. He is not inclined to perceive
an abuse without attacking it with all his vigor,
and he is not disposed to observe a reform without espousing it with all his ability . . . .
Upon all problems public or private, upon all
issues social or religious, upon all questions
moral or political, his yea is yea, and his nay is
nay. Throughout all the decades which have
intervened since that memorable day nearly
half a century ago when he enlisted as a soldier
for the Union in the Second Iowa Infantry, he
has been constantly engaged in battle with some
system, or some principle, or some opinion.
He has not always triumphed, and yet he has
been victorious, for this is true: that never
once in all his long and laborious life has his

sterling integrity been assailed, his stalwart
rectitude questioned, his steadfast fidelity im-
peached. In the bitterness of repeated political
campaigns men have challenged the correctness
of his conclusions, but they have never impugned the sincerity of his convictions. When
the impartial history of his generation is compiled he will be awarded adequate credit as a
powerful, aggressive and incorruptible influence for patriotism, for temperance, for religion. He has been

Patient of toil, serene amid alarms,
Inflexible in faith, indomitable in arms.
And he comes to twilight and evening star with
honor, love, obedience, troops of friends, to
accompany his old age.''

Brief quotations from other letters in the
same collection simply add emphasis to the
testimony already presented. Henry Wallace
of *Wallace's Farmer* wrote that he knew ''of
no man in the state more deserving of a place
in the hall of fame of the State of Iowa. However honest men may have differed from him in
their conviction or their views of public policy,
all will concede to him honesty of conviction,
sincerity of purpose and a supreme desire to
benefit his fellow men''.

Lafayette Young of *The Des Moines Capital*
expressed his pleasure that General Weaver
was to be given ''proper recognition in Iowa's

Hall of Fame", and referred to him as "the old
hero. . . . We all love him because he is a
patriot and because he is a fine specimen of
western citizenship, virile and active."

State Librarian, Johnson Brigham, declared
that he had never heard General Weaver's
"patriotism and courage questioned, and his
honor impugned. I have read with keen appreciation the story of his bravery in battle and
his endurance in camp and on the march, and
have listened to his oratory with admiration,
even when his eloquence was directed against
my party. There is nothing more helpful to
the party in power than the honest criticism of
its opponents."[339]

XIX

Final Tributes

General Weaver died at the home of his daughter, Mrs. H. C. Evans, in Des Moines, on Tuesday, February 6, 1912, at 1:15 in the afternoon. His death came unexpectedly after an illness of only a couple days. He had suffered an attack of indigestion on the Sunday morning preceding, which affected the heart acutely. He seemed to be recovering, when he experienced a fainting spell about noon on Tuesday from which he never rallied. From that time his life ebbed away calmly and peacefully. He retained consciousness to the last. His wife and all his children, except one daughter, were with him when he passed away.[340]

The funeral was held on Thursday, February 8th at 2:30 P. M. at the First Methodist Church in Des Moines. From noon until the time fixed for the services the body lay in state. Behind the family reservation the pews were filled by more than one hundred and fifty citizens of Colfax. At the right members of the Woman's Christian Temperance Union were seated and behind them the Yeomen. The nave of the church was occupied by the friends and ad-

mirers of the dead statesman. On the left sat a
hundred veterans of the Civil War, including
survivors of General Weaver's own regiment.
The pallbearers were: J. B. Weaver, Jr. and
A. C. Weaver, the two sons; H. C. Evans,
Edward Cohrt, and Charles Sullenberger, the
three sons-in-law; and D. H. Payne, a nephew.
Two songs were sung during the services —
Lead, Kindly Light by a quartette before the
prayer at the beginning, and *Does Jesus Care*
by Mr. F. V. Evans before the benediction.

Rev. Edward Pruitt of Colfax, pastor of
General Weaver's home church, spoke of the
life of the deceased and of his influence in the
town where he had lived for nearly sixteen
years. He had often thought "how desirable it
would be to be wholly at peace with God", and
had "wondered if it could be true in any life".
The example of "this godly man" had convinced him that his "religion was a part of his
life", and that he regarded religion as "a necessity and not a convenience." He discovered
that he had "a pronounced sense of the needs
of the common people from the religious side",
and constantly "was reading before them the
word of God. No matter what kind of a meeting he was in, he found place and time to say a
word for his Master . . . . and often when
he was speaking to the old soldiers he would
open the book and preach to them . . . . He

never asked would the task be difficult? Is it
possible for us to succeed? But he always
asked, is it right? and the price was not too big
to pay if it was right."

The next speaker was the Rev. Orien W.
Fifer of the Grace Methodist Church, Des
Moines. He described General Weaver as
"essentially democratic, at home with the common people, reading their minds and feeling
their heart beats as if gifted with superhuman
skill, and above all one with them in aspiration,
purpose and affection. He was the great commoner, like product with Abraham Lincoln of
these western prairies . . . . Illinois gave
Lincoln, the man of incomparable compassion.
Nebraska has given Bryan, the man of un-
swerving honesty and consistency. Iowa is no
less proud of Weaver, the dauntless crusader of
unflinching courage . . . .

"He was the tribune of the people. For them
he was voice and heart. From some lofty
height of vision or inspiration he came down to
plead for the men who toiled, the true home-
makers of America. The causes he advocated
were in the interest of that class which has no
great lobbyists, no strong organizations, no
skillful friends at court. If any of the causes
he advocated were not perfect in plan there can
be no doubt that the purpose of every cause was
the uplift of the man who had no influential

friends. Reared on soil of Iowa, widened by the greatness of the times in which he lived, perfected in compassion by the scenes of the Civil War, he was drawn near to the heart of humanity. The greatest tribute one can bring is this — that out of all his public career, he made no fortune, gained no store of riches, but multiplied his friends by the thousands and died beloved by friend and respected by foe.

.   .   .   .

"But it was as a Christian man that his quality appeared in highest worth. Generous to a fault, faithful to a degree involving risk of health in attendance upon the church he loved, fervent in the devotional habits of a Christian, stalwart and unfailing in aiding every good work, naming and honoring his Lord in private and in public without ostentation or intrusion, making himself a winner of souls, a teacher for years of the things of Christ, the fairest flower of his character was the red rose of spiritual devotion. For nearly sixty years he was a member of the church."

Father James Nugent, pastor of the Church of the Visitation of Des Moines, made the final address. Speaking extemporaneously as a close friend of General Weaver for more than thirty years, he devoted himself to an eulogy of the man. He had learned to look upon him "as a man of sterling character", and in "following

his life work on the platform and the hustings'',
he had come ''to recognize in him the ring of
the true man. He was an orator of unusual ex-
cellence, and one of the best proofs of an orator
is that he says what he means and he means
what is right . . . .   There is, I think, no
man in the country who has ever heard General
Weaver's speeches, could say when he finished,
'I wonder if the General believes that'. We all
knew that he did. . . .

"If any man ever thought that God and one
made a majority, he was that man, and he
fought with that idea in his head. His life is
now a part of his country's records, but it is
useless to dwell here on this solemn occasion
upon his history. He wrote it large himself in
the annals of his country. He was honorable in
the highest degree. He lived a clean life as a
citizen. An intelligent man, always religious
— intensely religious. . . .

"We have learned to respect the man on account of his integrity; and if I were going to
say one thing in special honor and praise of
James B. Weaver, I would say that he was a
conscientious man . . . .   Had it not been
so, he might have been a rich man. He had the
talent and he had the ability, and he had the
world opening before him. Avenues of wealth,
honor and fame spread out around him, but,
like the high priest of the temple, he clung to

his ideals and offered a sacrifice no less than the sacrifice of a noble life. To-day his country reveres his name, and the highest gift that is left to his family is the clean; unspotted reputation of a noble soldier and a noble citizen."[341]

Many telegrams of sympathy were received by the family from men prominent in public life who knew General Weaver and were shocked to hear of his death. Among those who sent messages were Speaker Champ Clark and Charles W. Bryan, brother of William J. Bryan, who was in Texas en route to Arizona, and who could not be reached in time for him to attend the funeral. Many marks of respect were shown to General Weaver in Colfax and Des Moines at the time of the funeral.[342]

Under the caption *A Giant Fallen*, Bryan's *Commoner* declared that the death of General Weaver removed "one of the giants of the political forest. He represented all that is highest in citizenship and noblest in manhood. For three score years almost he was a warrior, fighting the battles of the common people. His strong body, his active mind and his great heart — all were at the service of his fellows. He was a pioneer in the reforms which are now marching on to victory and his last days were gladdened by the consciousness that he had not labored in vain. Happy man to have lived to see the harvest ripening in the field in which he toiled so faithfully. He was more than an exemplary citizen; he was a man of the purest and most exalted type. In every relation of life he played his part with fidelity. He did not amass wealth, but he left his family what money cannot buy — a spotless name and a secure place in the hearts of his countrymen."[343]

In an editorial upon the death of General Weaver, *The Register and Leader* referred to the Civil War as "the determining factor in his life. On the battlefield his nature was set. He became a fighter for the right, and a fighter for the right he was to his last breath, perhaps not always seeing the right with unerring vision, but pursuing it with unabating zeal and sacrifice.

"Coming from the war with military honors fairly won, the slave freed, he stepped into civil life at a time when faith in humanity was strong, and human rights were uppermost. The first hint that the money the boys at the front had taken at a discount was not good enough for the bondholders stirred him to the core. His whole subsequent political career was marked out as he took leadership in the greenback movement. He saw the logic of the situation, and he never wavered. In fifty years he was never at outs with himself.

"It is probably true that Iowa has produced no man who was his equal in debate; certainly in his prime there was not in the United States his superior. No man ever crossed swords with him on the stump or in congress and got away to boast of the encounter. On the contrary, he often won a signal victory when public sentiment was plainly against the cause he advocated. He owed more than one election to his powers of presentation and persuasion. He was witty, bold, and eloquent, always on his feet. He lost no battles through lack of generalship. . . .

"He lost a republican nomination for governor because of his too early alignment against the saloon. The convention was for him, and his nomination was conceded. But the political managers, exerting the power of the old days, decided that it would be unwise to commit the party to so advanced a position. Had he been named and elected, Iowa might have been leading an insurgent movement twenty years earlier. That is one of the 'ifs of history' of engaging interest.

"Take him all in all, as pioneer, as soldier, as fighter for the right, as worker in the church, as enemy of the saloon, as father and friend of his family, as orator, as leader of movements, dying without an unclean dollar sticking to his palm, without an unclean record to suppress, how shall we estimate his seventy years in Iowa? His failure to be with the majority, to win the honors of place and power, may be the measure of his failure to properly judge the needs of his time. And, again, it may mean merely that he was somewhat ahead of his time, a skirmisher 'who drove the pickets in'."[344]

Major John F. Lacey, Weaver's political opponent in the sixth district in 1888 and 1898, emphasized the fact that he was criticized "for his radicalism but lived to see the wildest of his political principles competed for by opposing political parties each claiming to have 'seen it first'. Gen. Weaver had a fine sense of humor and in the last few years greatly enjoyed the spectacle of his old political opponents masquerading in his old clothes . . . . He had seen many victories and many defeats, but I think the victory of his life was when his two little granddaughters pulled the cords that exposed his portrait to the view of the assembled multitude."[345]

The *Sioux City Tribune* described General Weaver as a man of "prophetic vision. Social, political and industrial evils which he pointed out years ago are today acknowledged to exist by every person familiar with current national affairs, and to their extermination is being devoted the best thought and the highest statesmanship of the United States.

"When General Weaver began his crusade

as 'the first insurgent', he met the usual scorn
and contumely heaped upon men who are in
advance of their time. Interests which his agitation threatened, combined with a public as
yet unawakened to the evils which Weaver so
clearly perceived, joined in making him the
most unpopular man in Iowa, and for years he
was the target for ridicule, abuse, contempt and
hatred.

"Times have changed and so has the public
attitude toward General Weaver. Men have
come almost universally to recognize that the
evils and dangers which he emphasized and
condemned were and are real. It is unnecessary to agree with all his political views to concede that in him were elements of a high order
of greatness, nor need it be admitted that the
remedies he suggested were infallibly wise and
practical. But the fact remains that he fought
his fight according to the best light given him;
that he kept the faith, and lived to see most of
the ideas which were once ridiculed as the
dreams of a crank become the accepted political
doctrines of the people of Iowa and of the country at large . . . . In his closing years
there must have been consolation for him in the
fact that the old bitterness with which he was
once regarded had passed away, and that he
had come to enjoy the esteem, confidence and
admiration of his fellow citizens of the Hawk-
eye state."[346]

Congressman N. E. Kendall, who represented
the sixth district from 1909 to 1913, announced
General Weaver's death to the House of Representatives on February 8th in the customary
way. He spoke of his career as "in many
notable respects . . . . without parallel in
the political history of the American Republic.
From the day of his youth, when he volunteered
as a private soldier in the Second Iowa Infantry, to the day of his death at three score and
nine years, he was constantly on the firing line,
advancing some policy which he enthusiastically favored or combating some principle which
he earnestly condemned. He was a natural
polemic, whether in official position or in honorable retirement, always amply armed for any
controversy, and challenging conflict with any
adversary he might encounter. He never hesi-
tated to espouse a cause unfamiliar or unpopular, and he would struggle to the uttermost to
vindicate the beliefs he entertained. While he
did not always achieve victory, he never con-
fessed defeat . . . . many men differed
from the opinions he defended, but all men recognized his sincerity of conviction and his
integrity of purpose. His life is an inspiring
illustration of extraordinary ability, of unex-
ampled energy, of unblemished character — all
devoted with unfaltering fidelity to the welfare
of his fellow men."[347]

Another recognition of Weaver's life and work came three years after his death when his old home in Bloomfield was dedicated for public use by the Davis County Chautauqua Association as Weaver Park. The purchase of the old homestead was the completion of a plan conceived four or five years earlier to provide suitable grounds for the association which had been established in 1905 and had had remarkable success under rather adverse financial conditions. The old Weaver homestead had from the start been looked upon with a great deal of favor as a site for the purpose, and a year before a few enterprising men of the county had started a subscription list to raise funds. The ground was purchased for $4500, and an option was held by the association upon some adjoining land which would cost about $1400. It was estimated that to improve the grounds, beautify them, and build a coliseum, would cost nearly $9000.

The plan was to preserve the house built by General Weaver, and occupied by him for a number of years as his home. Part of it would probably be used by the caretaker, and the rest would form a kind of community home. The plan was not confined to the Chautauqua alone, although it had taken the initiative, but it was "a movement on behalf of the people of the county to buy and convert into a park the home of its most distinguished citizen as a perpetual memorial to that great statesman, brave soldier and true reformer, a man whose relation to his wife, to his family and neighbors was pure and in every way ideal''. The people of the county were asked to help in two ways — by patronizing the Chautauqua liberally, and by subscribing for the stock of the association which was sold at $10 a share. About one hundred and fifty residents of the county had already subscribed for from one to twenty-five shares.

The dedication of the Weaver Park occurred on August 18, 1915, and the program consisted of introductory and explanatory remarks by Congressman-elect C. W. Ramseyer, a statement concerning the history of the grounds by James B. Weaver, Jr., and the dedicatory address by William J. Bryan. Governors Carroll and Clarke were prevented from coming by previous engagements. Of the Congressmen living in the district, all of whom had been invited, ex-Congressman F. E. White and N. E. Kendall sent their regrets, while ex-Congressman D. W. Hamilton and Congressman Sant Kirkpatrick were present. The members of the Weaver family who attended, in addition to J. B. Weaver, Jr., were Mrs. Susan Evans, Mr. Evans, and two daughters, Mrs. Ruth Denny and daughter, Mrs. Esther Cohrt and Mr. Cohrt.

Mr. Bryan began his address by commenting upon the undertaking embodied in Weaver Park "as a splendid thought and a credit to the one into whose mind it first came". He felt sure that, if General Weaver could speak from the grave, he would be especially gratified with the plan "to make of his home a civic center". He then referred to the pleasure with which he had participated in the presentation of General Weaver's portrait a few years ago. He also volunteered to help in the financing of the enterprise and subscribed for five shares.

"You who loved General Weaver while he was among you as a citizen may have had more intimate acquaintance with him, so far as it pertains to the details of his life, and you have had more opportunity than I have had to talk with him and to profit by his conversation, but none of you were ever nearer to him than I felt that I was, and I feel sure that none of you ever felt more benefit from what he said and did than I did, and it is a pleasure to me to associate myself and my family with this movement that is to commemorate his name and perpetuate his memory. His son, who has the distinction to bear his full name has told you some of the secrets. I will let you into one.

"If I had been elected in 1896 he would have had a new honor added to those already upon him. I had not much time to think or plan, but

I had time enough to decide that, if I became President, General Weaver would be a member of my cabinet. In that campaign none was more devoted to my interests politically than he, and since then none has been more loyal in his personal relationship or more congenial in his companionship than he was, up to the day of his death. I had the honor as well as the pleasure of meeting him on many occasions both in public and private; at banquets and at his home table, and the memory — the sweet memory of that man whose life was large enough to embrace all the interests of humanity — that sweet memory will always remain with me. . . .

"I am glad that I am able to be here and to participate with you to-day in doing honor to the memory of a really great man, a man who had a conviction — a man who was in advance of most of the people of his time in regard to the things that stood in the way of the people's good, the things that must be removed before the people might walk forward as rapidly as they ought. I have long regarded General Weaver as one of the great pioneers of the later days. I have been given a great deal more credit than I deserve for work that I have done. Some of the things that I have been pioneering, and most of the things that I have been following, have been things that others have suggested before I did."

Mr. Bryan then gave "a list of some of the
things that were advocated by General Weaver
when he ran for President in 1880", and remarked that he himself was only twenty years
old at the time, and took "a very minor part"
in the campaign. The list of measures included a graduated income tax, postal savings
banks, the initiative and referendum, the popular election of United States Senators, an
eight hour labor law, sanitary conditions in
industrial establishments, the prohibition of
child labor, the establishment of departments of
Agriculture and Labor, the reduction of the
powers of the Speaker and more democratic
rules for the House of Representatives, prohibition of speculation in government lands, a
sufficient volume of currency, and the expansion of the powers of government. He believed
in making "the government an instrument for
the accomplishment of the peoples' will and the
peoples' good. . . .

"Now those are some of the things he advocated thirty-five years ago, and then as he went
along he kept advocating other things as he
came in view of them. Among the things that
he advocated in that time were woman suffrage
and the submission to a vote of the people of
the questions of the manufacture and sale of
liquor. You will find he had confidence in the
people; that he trusted them; that he was will-

ing to let them decide the questions affecting them, and, my friends, that is the test of democracy . . . . The real test of a democrat is his willingness to trust the people. The more democratic a man is the more completely does he trust the people, and General Weaver, no matter by what party name he called himself . . . . trusted the people. He believed, as every true democrat must believe, that the people have the right to have what they want in government, that the people have the right to make their own mistakes, for unless you concede to them the right to make their own mistakes, the more apt they are to make mistakes. . . . . General Weaver understood this and therefore he appealed to the people as the source of power and wanted them to decide the questions, knowing that when the people decide the questions they will be determined largely upon the principles of morality. When a question is settled on the basis of moral character, it is settled for good, but not until then."[348]

The presentation of the portrait in 1909 and the dedication of Weaver Park in 1915 constitute a very remarkable recognition of the life and work of a man who, as he expressed it, was usually in the "minor minority". He was fortunate in that he lived to see the two great parties adopt a large number of his own measures and enact them into law. He was fortunate, too, in the time of his death which happened to occur when the so-called "progressive movement" seemed to be reaching a climax, and when a majority of the people of the country seemed to have arrived at the position towards which he had been working for thirty years. The campaign of 1912, on the eve of which he died, was the logical result of his own campaigns of 1880 and 1892, and also of that of 1896, in which he really shared with Bryan the honors of leadership through his contribution of his support of 1892 and his part in the nomination of Bryan by the Populists. The near approach to success of the "alliance" of 1896 undoubtedly stimulated the progressive movement in the Republican party, led by La Follette and later in the national sphere by Roosevelt. The pioneer of 1880 lived to see the 300,000 voters of that year conceded to have been the skirmish line in an advance which had developed into the great army of progressive voters of 1912. He himself had driven in many of the pickets of conservatism, and many more had been driven in by the fresh forces which he had rallied and stimulated in his campaigns of education, waged throughout the country almost continuously from 1880 down to his death in 1912.

His last important public address at a memorial service in honor of the late Carroll

Wright, shortly after his death in October,
1911, brings out very clearly his fundamental
beliefs and the principles which controlled his
personal and public life. In this address
General Weaver declared that "the most wonderful and fascinating phenomenon in the
whole sphere of human association is personality. The thing we cherish most in history is
not so much the record of events as the revelation of men and women.

"A country is great, not through its magnificent scenery, delightful climate and varied
resources, but because of the men and women
who give it its national character. More than
our traditions, memories, poetry, literature and
art are our personal heroes. In our own private life, what we value most is not our homes,
lands, commerce, wealth, culture and progress,
but our friends — our loved ones.

"It is the crowning charm of revelation that
God has revealed himself to man in the personality of Jesus — a being of real flesh and blood,
a hero of heroes, who could be seen and who
walked, talked, worked, ate, slept and wept. It
is a constant source of thankfulness that he is
not mere cold abstraction or principle, but a
real person whom we can touch with our consciousness and embrace with our arms of faith
and love.

"Association reveals personality and acquaints us with character, discloses the ideals which guide our lives and which intensify and in fact transfigure us and those with whom we associate."[349]

General Weaver requested of his children that if an epitaph should ever be used in his memory it should consist simply of the words "He was a friend of the poor". The night before he died, as his son sat at his bedside reading to him extracts from famous writers, he asked that one passage in particular be read over three times. The passage was as follows: "I am the man who prays for whoso fares lonely in the world, the folk that go lost for a friend's hand or a woman's breast on aching journeys, and for all who know no lights at evening, put I up my prayers." Indeed "this sentiment was really an expression of the dominating passion" of his life—"that he might be of service to the bereft of the world."[350]

NOTES AND REFERENCES

NOTES AND REFERENCES

CHAPTER I

[1] *The New York World*, July 10, 1892, in the *Weaver Scrap Book*, p. 21.

[2] This account of James Baird Weaver's early life is taken largely from an unpublished manuscript entitled *Memoranda with Respect to the Life of James Baird Weaver* which was prepared by Mr. Weaver himself. It covers the period from 1833 to 1859.

[3] *The New York World*, July 10, 1892, in the *Weaver Scrap Book*, p. 21.

[4] *Memoranda with Respect to the Life of James Baird Weaver.*

[5] The Mexican· War closed with the conclusion of peace in February, 1848. Mexico City was occupied in September, 1847. It is probable that Mr. Weaver refers to the practical end rather than to the time when peace was actually concluded. Otherwise his dates are incorrect.

[6] The account of the California journey is taken from three articles by General Weaver, published in *The World Review*, January 18th and 25th and February 1, 1902.

[7] *The New York World*, July 10, 1892, in the *Weaver Scrap Book*, p. 21.

[8] *Memorandum in regard to the Graduation of General Weaver at Cincinnati College; The New York World*, July 10, 1892, in the *Weaver Scrap Book*, p. 21.

CHAPTER II

[9] *Memorandum in regard to the Graduation of General Weaver at Cincinnati College.*

[10] Rhodes's *History of the United States,* Vol. II, p. 58. See *In Memoriam,* published by the Loyal Legion of the United States, 1912, p. 3.

[11] Rhodes's *History of the United States,* Vol. II, p. 59; Salter's *The Life of James W. Grimes,* pp. 33, 54.

[12] *Memoranda with Respect to the Life of James Baird Weaver.*

[13] Comment by J. B. Weaver, Jr., upon *Memoranda with Respect to the Life of James Baird Weaver;* the *Weaver Scrap Book,* p. 153.

[14] *Memoranda with Respect to the Life of James Baird Weaver.*

[15] Herriott's *The Republican State Convention* in the *Annals of Iowa* (Third Series), Vol. IX, pp. 409, 410, 411.

[16] Herriott's *Iowa and The First Nomination of Abraham Lincoln* in the *Annals of Iowa* (Third Series), Vol. VIII, p. 93.

[17] Herriott's *Iowa and The First Nomination of Abraham Lincoln* in the *Annals of Iowa* (Third Series), Vol. VIII, p. 217.

[18] *The New York World,* July 10, 1892, in the *Weaver Scrap Book,* p. 21.

[19] Clipping from a Des Moines paper dated July 13, 1908, in the *Weaver Scrap Book,* pp. 152, 153.

In *The Cyclopedia of American Government,* Vol. I, p. 136, it is stated that the expression was "used first by Oliver P. Morton indicating the calling up of the issue of the Civil War for partisan purposes."

[20] The *Weaver Scrap Book,* p. 152.

CHAPTER III

[21] *Memorandum of James B. Weaver, Jr.;* the *Weaver Scrap Book,* p. 31; *Kirkwood Military Letter Book,* No. 1, p. 8.

[22] The *Weaver Scrap Book,* p. 31.

[23] *Roster and Record of Iowa Soldiers in the War of the Rebellion,* Vol. I, p. 91; Ingersoll's *Iowa and the Rebellion,* p. 33; Byers's *Iowa in War Times,* p. 60.

24 *Roster and Record of Iowa Soldiers in the War of the Rebellion*, Vol. I, p. 92; Byers's *Iowa in War Times*, p. 109.

25 Ingersoll's *Iowa and the Rebellion*, p. 35; Byers's *Iowa in War Times*, p. 482.

26 Ingersoll's *Iowa and the Rebellion*, p. 36; Byers's *Iowa in War Times*, pp. 95, 96.

27 Hosmer's *The Appeal to Arms*, pp. 88–92; Rhodes's *History of the United States*, Vol. III, pp. 581–593.

28 *Roster and Record of Iowa Soldiers in the War of the Rebellion*, Vol. I, pp. 92–94; Ingersoll's *Iowa and the Rebellion*, pp. 38–45; Twombly's *The Second Iowa Infantry at Fort Donelson* (pamphlet); statement of James B. Weaver, Jr.; Byers's *Iowa in War Times*, pp. 96–104; *Kirkwood Military Letter Book*, No. 4, pp. 105, 106; Clark's *Samuel Jordan Kirkwood*, pp. 227–229.

29 *In Memoriam*, published by the Loyal Legion of the United States, 1912, p. 2.

30 Letter of James B. Weaver to his wife addressed from Fort Donelson, February 19, 1862.

31 Twombly's *The Second Iowa Infantry at Fort Donelson*, pp. 16, 17.

32 Twombly's *The Second Iowa Infantry at Fort Donelson*, p. 10.

33 Ingersoll's *Iowa and the Rebellion*, pp. 45, 46; *The War of the Rebellion: a Compilation of the Official Records of the Union and Confederate Armies*, Series I, Vol. VII, p. 168.

34 Hosmer's *The Appeal to Arms*, pp. 96–98; Rhodes's *History of the United States*, Vol. III, pp. 617–620.

35 Ingersoll's *Iowa and the Rebellion*, p. 46.

36 Rhodes's *History of the United States*, Vol. III, pp. 620–625; Hosmer's *The Appeal to Arms*, pp. 99–107.

37 *Roster and Record of Iowa Soldiers in the War of the Rebellion*, Vol. I, pp. 94, 95; Ingersoll's *Iowa and the Rebel-*

lion, p. 46; Byers's *Iowa in War Times*, pp. 122–145; Rich's *The Battle of Shiloh.*

38 Letter of James B. Weaver to his wife addressed from Pittsburg, Tennessee, April 9, 1862. The account in this letter does not agree with statements made by Rhodes and Hosmer. The size of Confederate forces estimated is double the actual numbers. The report of the victory at Corinth was also unfounded. The city was not occupied by Union troops until late in May.

39 Hosmer's *The Appeal to Arms*, pp. 109, 218–229; Rhodes's *History of the United States*, Vol. IV, pp. 97, 173–180; Byers's *Iowa in War Times*, p. 149.

40 *Roster and Record of Iowa Soldiers in the War of the Rebellion*, Vol. I, p. 95; Ingersoll's *Iowa and the Rebellion*, p. 47; Twombly's *The Second Iowa Infantry at Fort Donelson*, p. 19.

41 Statement of James B. Weaver, Jr.; *Roster and Record of Iowa Soldiers in the War of the Rebellion*, Vol. I, p. 222.

42 Statement of Captain John M. Duffield in the *Weaver Papers; Kirkwood Military Letter Book*, No. 4, pp. 130, 245.

43 *Roster and Record of Iowa Soldiers in the War of the Rebellion*, Vol. I, pp. 95, 96.

44 Letters of James B. Weaver to his wife from Corinth, October 6, 1862, and from Rienzi, Mississippi, October 12, 1862.

45 *Roster and Record of Iowa Soldiers in the War of the Rebellion*, Vol. I, p. 96; Ingersoll's *Iowa and the Rebellion*, pp. 48, 49.

46 Ingersoll's *Iowa and the Rebellion*, p. 49; Twombly's *The Second Iowa Infantry at Fort Donelson*, p. 19; Byers's *Iowa in War Times*, pp. 482, 483.

47 Ingersoll's *Iowa and the Rebellion*, pp. 50, 51; *Roster and Record of Iowa Soldiers in the War of the Rebellion*, Vol. I, p. 96; Twombly's *The Second Iowa Infantry*, p. 20; Byers's *Iowa in War Times*, p. 483.

CHAPTER IV

[48] *In Memoriam*, published by the Loyal Legion of the United States, 1912, pp. 2, 3; the *Weaver Scrap Book*, p. 27; Byers's *Iowa in War Times*, p. 483.

[49] Stuart's *Iowa Colonels and Regiments*, p. 76. Praise of Weaver's bravery by this author is the more noteworthy because he also refers to his "vanity" and "affectation in delivery".

[50] The *Weaver Scrap Book*, pp. 44, 113.

[51] The *Weaver Scrap Book*, pp. 36 (cartoon entitled candidate Weaver's war record), 43, 76, 99, 113.

[52] Letter of General G. M. Dodge to Weaver, dated New York City, October 14, 1892, in the *Weaver Papers;* the *Weaver Scrap Book*, p. 85.

[53] Letter from Theo. Harris, Sr., dated "near Fayetteville, Tennessee", July 20, 1892, in the *Weaver Scrap Book*, p. 50.

[54] The *Weaver Scrap Book*, p. 113.

CHAPTER V

[55] Moore's *Davis County Disturbances* in *Report of the Adjutant General of the State of Iowa*, 1864–1865, pp. 1419–1428; Byers's *Iowa in War Times*, pp. 474, 475; Gue's *History of Iowa*, Vol. II, pp. 58, 82–94, 112–114.

CHAPTER VI

[56] *Burlington Weekly Hawk-Eye*, September 2, 1865, January 20, 1866.

[57] *Charles City Intelligencer*, June 22, 1865; *The Keosauqua Weekly Republican*, June 22, 1865.

[58] *Burlington Weekly Hawk-Eye*, October 14, 1865.

[59] *Burlington Weekly Hawk-Eye*, June 30, 1866; *The Fairfield Ledger*, July 12, 1866; *The Keosauqua Weekly Republican*, July 5, 1866.

[60] *Iowa Official Register*, 1915–1916, p. 845; *Weekly Gate*

City (Keokuk), October 24, 1866; *Bloomfield Democrat*, March 12, 1874.

61 *Burlington Weekly Hawk-Eye*, October 13, 1866; *Weekly Gate City* (Keokuk), October 17, 1866.

62 Gue's *History of Iowa*, Vol. IV, p. 280; *Report of the Commissioner of Internal Revenue*, 1867, p. xiii; *Annual Report on the State of the Finances*, 1873, pp. 62–64.

63 *Burlington Weekly Hawk-Eye*, September 28, 1871.

64 *Bloomfield Democrat*, November 25, 1875; *Burlington Weekly Hawk-Eye*, August 29, 1872.

65 *The Weekly Iowa State Register* (Des Moines), July 24, 1874.

66 *The Weekly Iowa State Register* (Des Moines), July 24, 1874.

67 *Bloomfield Democrat*, July 23, August 6 and 13, 1874.

68 Clarkson's *The Stampede from General Weaver in the Republican Convention of 1875* in the *Annals of Iowa* (Third Series), Vol. X, No. 8, pp. 564, 565; Letter of John Mahin to Weaver, October 31, 1911, in the *Weaver Papers*, refers to boasts made by his opponents that they had ''defeated that d——d Methodist''.

69 *The Weekly Iowa State Register* (Des Moines), July 2, 1875; Gue's *History of Iowa*, Vol. III, pp. 72, 73; Clark's *The History of Liquor Legislation in Iowa* in *The Iowa Journal of History and Politics*, Vol. VI, p. 361.

70 Clarkson's *The Stampede from General Weaver in the Republican Convention of 1875* in the *Annals of Iowa* (Third Series), Vol. X, No. 8, pp. 564–568. See Weaver's letter in *The Register and Leader* (Des Moines), October 30, 1911.

71 *The Weekly Iowa State Register* (Des Moines), July 2, 1875.

72 *Bloomfield Democrat*, July 15, 1875.

73 *Bloomfield Democrat*, September 2, 1875.

74 *Bloomfield Democrat*, September 23, 1875.

[75] *Bloomfield Democrat,* October 7, 1875.

[76] *Bloomfield Democrat,* October 14, 1875.

[77] *Bloomfield Democrat,* October 21, 1875. Weaver received 1459 votes to 1596 for Wonn. His vote in his own township compared with that for Kirkwood was as follows: Kirkwood 364, Weaver 353. His vote in the county compared with Kirkwood's was as follows: Kirkwood 1485, Weaver 1459.

[78] *Bloomfield Democrat,* November 4, 1875.

[79] *Bloomfield Democrat,* October 28, 1875.

[80] Quoted in the *Bloomfield Democrat,* November 25, 1875.

[81] *Bloomfield Democrat,* January 13, 1876.

[82] *The Weekly Iowa State Register* (Des Moines), July 21, 1876.

[83] The *Weaver Scrap Book,* p. 112. A reprint in 1898 of a correspondence originally printed in the *Bloomfield Republican* in 1876.

[84] *The Weekly Iowa State Register* (Des Moines), September 8, 1876.

[85] The *Weaver Scrap Book,* p. 112.

[86] *The Weekly Iowa State Register,* February 23 and June 29, 1877.

[87] *The Weekly Iowa State Register* (Des Moines), July 20, 1877.

[88] A copy of General Weaver's letter and the reply of Mr. Gear are preserved among the Weaver papers. A printed copy of General Weaver's letter is to be found in the *Weaver Scrap Book,* p. 135; *Congressional Record,* 1st Session, 50th Congress, p. 6147; *The Register and Leader* (Des Moines), October 30, 1911.

[89] *The Weekly Iowa State Register* (Des Moines), September 28, October 5, 12, 19, 1877; Stiles's *Recollections and Sketches of Notable Lawyers and Public Men of Early Iowa,* pp. 148, 149. According to *The Register,* Weaver ''was to have been Senator

if the Greenbackers had carried the Legislature. The political trouble with the General now is that he has always been one of the Was to Have Beens.''

90 Statement of James B. Weaver, Jr.; Stiles's *Recollections and Sketches of Notable Lawyers and Public Men of Early Iowa*, p. 148.

91 The quotations are from a letter from Judge Robert Sloan, dated at Keosauqua, June 19, 1918, and addressed to Benj. F. Shambaugh. Judge Sloan first knew Weaver in 1855 and, in referring to their relations, he describes them as ''personal friends for many years, although differing politically in later years of his life. I valued his friendship very highly. He had many excellent and lovable qualities.''

CHAPTER VII

92 *Daily Press* (Iowa City), March 1 and July 2, 1878.

93 *The Weekly Iowa State Register* (Des Moines), October 4, 1878.

94 *Daily Press* (Iowa City), November 12, 1878; *The Weekly Iowa State Register* (Des Moines), October 4 and November 15, 1878.

95 *The Weekly Iowa State Register* (Des Moines), August 23 and 30, 1878.

96 *The Weekly Iowa State Register* (Des Moines), August 23, 1878, contains Trimble's letter reprinted from the *Ottumwa Democrat*. It is dated at Bloomfield, July 15, 1878.

97 *The Weekly Iowa State Register* (Des Moines), October 11 and 18, 1878. See the writer's *Third Party Movements Since the Civil War*, pp. 165, 166.

98 *The Weekly Iowa State Register* (Des Moines), December 20, 1878, January 10 and 17, 1879.

99 *Appleton's Annual Cyclopaedia*, 1879, pp. 838, 839. A letter signed by Weaver for the executive committee of the national Greenback Labor party was sent to Democratic and Republican members of the House, giving the names of mem-

bers for whom the independent members of the House of Representatives were willing to vote for Speaker just before the opening of the session.

100 *Congressional Record*, 1st Session, 46th Congress, pp. 3, 5, 397; McLaughlin and Hart's *Cyclopedia of American Government*, Vol. I, p. 391.

101 *Congressional Record*, 1st Session, 46th Congress, pp. 225–227.

Incidentally Weaver referred favorably to a constitutional amendment giving the President power ''to approve a part of a bill and veto the rest of it. It is a very nice constitutional question, however, whether he has not that power already.'' He also opposed ''the concentration of so much power in the hands of the Committee on Appropriations'', and favored its distribution to various committees.

102 The *Weaver Scrap Book*, p. 25.

103 *Congressional Record*, 1st Session, 46th Congress, pp. 363, 364.

104 *Congressional Record*, 1st Session, 46th Congress, p. 1164.

105 *Congressional Record*, 1st Session, 46th Congress, pp. 1197–1202.

106 The *Weaver Scrap Book*, p. 26. This account probably appeared in the *Chicago Sentinel* as ''special correspondence'' from Washington, dated May 11, 1879. This speech was reprinted during the 1894 campaign of General Weaver for Congress in the ninth district.— See the *Weaver Scrap Book*, p. 93. *Congressional Record*, 2nd Session, 46th Congress, Index to Vol. IX, pp. 6, 8.

107 *Congressional Record*, 1st Session, 46th Congress, p. 1370.

108 *Congressional Record*, 1st Session, 46th Congress, p. 1500.

109 *Congressional Record*, 1st Session, 46th Congress, p. 1530.

110 *Congressional Record*, 1st Session, 46th Congress, p. 2169.

111 *Congressional Record*, 1st Session, 46th Congress, pp. 638, 1088, 2047.

CHAPTER VIII

[112] *Congressional Record*, 2nd Session, 46th Congress, pp. 22, 59, 170, 171, 473, Appendix, pp. 279–283, Index, p. 945.

[113] Weaver's *A Call to Action*, pp. 57–59; the *Weaver Scrap Book*, p. 29.

[114] *Congressional Record*, 2nd Session, 46th Congress, p. 1198.

[115] *Congressional Record*, 2nd Session, 46th Congress, pp. 1234–1236; the *Weaver Scrap Book*, p. 29.

[116] Weaver's *A Call to Action*, pp. 60, 61.

[117] *Congressional Record*, 2nd Session, 46th Congress, pp. 2139–2142. For another reference to these resolutions see the *Congressional Record*, 2nd Session, 46th Congress, p. 1432, and for speeches on the same resolutions see Appendix, pp. 109–114 and pp. 117–121 — speeches by E. H. Gillette of Iowa and Gilbert De La Matyr of Indiana.

[118] *Congressional Record*, 2nd Session, 46th Congress, pp. 22, 112, 186, 285, 924, 1392, 1563, 1570, 1673, 2526, Index, p. 818.

[119] *Congressional Record*, 2nd Session, 46th Congress, pp. 475, 476.
Weaver was given ten minutes by Buckner of Missouri who was in charge of the bill for the committee on banking and currency, and at the expiration of that period four minutes were added by another member after a motion to give fifteen minutes had been refused by Buckner who wanted to dispose of the bill that day.

[120] *Congressional Record*, 2nd Session, 46th Congress, Appendix, pp. 185–189.

[121] *Congressional Record*, 2nd Session, 46th Congress, pp. 724, 725. Weaver favored increasing the limit from $500 to $2000 for allowing transfers from State to Federal courts.— See pp. 846 and 847 of the *Congressional Record*, 2nd Session, 46th Congress.

[122] *Congressional Record*, 2nd Session, 46th Congress, pp. 767, 768, 925, 1641, 1686, 2326, 3248, Index, pp. 6–9.

[123] *Congressional Record,* 2nd Session, 46th Congress, pp. 3405, 3406.

CHAPTER IX

[124] *Congressional Record,* 2nd Session, 46th Congress, p. 4227.

[125] *The Weekly Iowa State Register* (Des Moines), March 21, 1879.

[126] *The Weekly Iowa State Register* (Des Moines), August 1, September 19, October 10, 1879. See the writer's *Third Party Movements Since the Civil War,* pp. 171–174.

[127] *The Weekly Iowa State Register* (Des Moines), January 16, 1880.

[128] *The Weekly Iowa State Register* (Des Moines), May 21, 1880.

[129] Weaver's *A Call to Action,* pp. 83–85.

[130] *The Weekly Iowa State Register* (Des Moines), May 28, 1880.

[131] *The Weekly Iowa State Register* (Des Moines), June 18, 1880; *The Daily Inter Ocean* (Chicago), June 9–11, 1880; the *Weaver Scrap Book,* pp. 1–3, 128.

[132] *The Weekly Iowa State Register* (Des Moines), August 6, 1880.

[133] The *Weaver Scrap Book,* p. 116; McPherson's *A Hand-Book of Politics for 1880,* pp. 196–198; *The Weekly Iowa State Register* (Des Moines), July 9, 1880.

[134] The *Weaver Scrap Book,* pp. 6–8; *The Weekly Iowa State Register* (Des Moines), September 3 and 24 and October 22, 1880.

[135] The *Weaver Scrap Book,* pp. 4, 5; *The Weekly Iowa State Register* (Des Moines), October 29, 1880.

[136] The *Weaver Scrap Book,* p. 5; *The Weekly Iowa State Register* (Des Moines), October 15, 1880; *Iowa State Press* (Iowa City), October 13, 1880.

[137] McPherson's *A Hand-Book of Politics for 1882,* p. 186.

[138] *Congressional Record,* 3rd Session, 46th Congress, pp. 308, 309.

[139] *The Weekly Iowa State Register* (Des Moines), November 19, 1880.

[140] *The Weekly Iowa State Register* (Des Moines), November 26, 1880.

CHAPTER X

[141] *Congressional Record,* 3rd Session, 46th Congress, p. 2433.

[142] *Congressional Record,* 3rd Session, 46th Congress, pp. 297–311.

[143] *Congressional Record,* 3rd Session, 46th Congress, pp. 328–335.

[144] *The Weekly Iowa State Register* (Des Moines), December 31, 1880.

[145] *Congressional Record,* 3rd Session, 46th Congress, pp. 386–388, 564, 565, 615, 616, 618, 661, 733, 742, 766, 773, 2308, 2324, 2325. Weaver took part in the debate on January 6, 12, 13, 15, 18, 19, and March 1, 1881.

[146] *Congressional Record,* 3rd Session, 46th Congress, Index, p. 456. See Bryce's *American Commonwealth,* Vol. I, p. 97.

[147] *Congressional Record,* 3rd Session, 46th Congress, Index, pp. 456, 457.

[148] *Congressional Record,* 3rd Session, 46th Congress, p. 280.

[149] *Congressional Record,* 3rd Session, 46th Congress, p. 2181.

[150] *Congressional Record,* 3rd Session, 46th Congress, p. 2090.

[151] *Congressional Record,* 3rd Session, 46th Congress, p. 2035.

[152] The influence of third parties in an election is always difficult to estimate. General Hancock always believed that General Weaver's participation in the election cost him the presidency in 1880. A few years later General Hancock meeting him said: ''But for you I should just about this time be vacating the White House''.— The *Weaver Scrap Book,* p. 118.

186 *Congressional Record*, 1st Session, 49th Congress, p. 5378.

187 *Congressional Record*, 1st Session, 49th Congress, pp. 6250, 6251, 6290, 6291. General Weaver and B. W. Perkins of Kansas each accused the other of being the paid attorney of the interests they defended. Perkins declared in reply to the charge of Weaver that he had never ''taxed'' the poor settlers while ''loafing about the Departments at Washington''. Weaver retorted: ''I will tell the gentleman what he is: His voice is the voice of Jacob, but his hand is the hand of Esau.'' For another reference to the ''Oklahoma boomers'' see *Congressional Record*, 1st Session, 49th Congress, p. 2308.

188 *Congressional Record*, 1st Session, 49th Congress, p. 7172.

189 *Congressional Record*, 1st Session, 49th Congress, p. 384; Commons and Andrews's *Principles of Labor Legislation*, p. 137.

190 *Congressional Record*, 1st Session, 49th Congress, pp. 2959, 3761; Dewey's *National Problems, 1885–1897*, pp. 42–44.

191 *Congressional Record*, 1st Session, 49th Congress, pp. 2965, 2966.

192 *Congressional Record*, 1st Session, 49th Congress, p. 384.

193 *Congressional Record*, 1st Session, 49th Congress, Index, pp. 629, 630. See Weaver's remarks in the debate over relief for Francis W. Haldeman, pp. 4261, 4262.

194 *Congressional Record*, 1st Session, 49th Congress, pp. 384, 4490–4492, 4973, 5321–5325.

195 *Congressional Record*, 1st Session, 49th Congress, Index, pp. 629, 630.

196 *Congressional Record*, 2nd Session, 49th Congress, pp. 818–822.

197 *Congressional Record*, 2nd Session, 49th Congress, p. 116.

198 *Congressional Record*, 2nd Session, 49th Congress, pp. 192, 225.

199 *Congressional Record*, 2nd Session, 49th Congress, pp. 672, 673.

200 *Congressional Record*, 2nd Session, 49th Congress, p. 1737.

201 *Congressional Record*, 2nd Session, 49th Congress, pp. 2700, 2701.

CHAPTER XIII

202 *Iowa Official Register*, 1888, pp. 72–74.

203 *Congressional Record*, 1st Session, 50th Congress, pp. 6, 280; McLaughlin and Hart's *Cyclopedia of American Government*, Vol. I, p. 392.

204 Dewey's *National Problems, 1885–1897*, pp. 64–73.

205 *Congressional Record*, 1st Session, 50th Congress, pp. 4258–4261. His list of "trusts" was taken from "standard authorities". He referred "to an article by Henry D. Lloyd in the North American Review for June, 1884, and to a recent work on 'Trusts' by William W. Cook, of the New York bar." See also *Congressional Record*, 1st Session, 50th Congress, pp. 7358, 7359.

206 *Congressional Record*, 1st Session, 50th Congress, pp. 4773, 4774, 4783, 5005, 5006.

207 *Congressional Record*, 1st Session, 50th Congress, pp. 4823, 4824.

208 *Congressional Record*, 1st Session, 50th Congress, pp. 4972, 4973. Weaver also took part in the debate upon the Mills Bill, July 11th and 19th.— See *Congressional Record*, 1st Session, 50th Congress, pp. 6144–6147, 6536.

209 *Congressional Record*, 1st Session, 50th Congress, pp. 5429, 5440, 5932.

210 *Congressional Record*, 1st Session, 50th Congress, p. 5555. In March it appears that Weaver interested himself especially in the great coal fields of Pennsylvania, declaring that the "large cities, and in fact the whole country, is at the mercy of a few coal barons". The words seem almost prophetic in the year 1917.— See *Congressional Record*, 1st Session, 50th Congress, pp. 2457, 2458.

[211] *Congressional Record*, 1st Session, 50th Congress, pp. 5591–5594.

[212] *Congressional Record*, 1st Session, 50th Congress, pp. 8508, 8509.

[213] *Congressional Record*, 1st Session, 50th Congress, pp. 8116, 8117, Index, House Bills, p. 442.

[214] *Congressional Record*, 1st Session, 50th Congress, pp. 6740, 8906.

[215] *Congressional Record*, 1st Session, 50th Congress, Index, House Bills, p. 384.

[216] *Congressional Record*, 1st Session, 50th Congress, pp. 2323–2325. In May, 1888, Weaver made an illuminating remark in regard to political contributions by Federal officeholders.— See *Congressional Record*, 1st Session, 50th Congress, p. 4678.

[217] *Congressional Record*, 1st Session, 50th Congress, Index, p. 782.

[218] *Congressional Record*, 1st Session, 50th Congress, pp. 1597–1600. September 17, 1888, he introduced a bill "to prohibit the deposit of public moneys in national banks or other banks except in certain cases".— See *Congressional Record*, 1st Session, 50th Congress, p. 8657.

[219] *Congressional Record*, 2nd Session, 50th Congress, pp. 606, 629–632, 650, 651, 676–686, 708, 744–751. A concise account of the filibuster is given upon pp. 747, 748. There are several articles about the filibuster in the *Weaver Scrap Book*, pp. 22, 25, 140.

[220] *Congressional Record*, 2nd Session, 50th Congress, pp. 1338–1358, 1363, 1378–1388, 1400–1402, 1501, 2010, 2287; McLaughlin and Hart's *Cyclopedia of American Government*, Vol. II, p. 577.

[221] *Appleton's Annual Cyclopaedia*, 1889, pp. 675, 676; *Congressional Record*, 2nd Session, 50th Congress, Vol. XX, pp. 2367–2369, 2399, 2400, 2414, 2724; *United States Statutes at Large*, Vol. XXV, p. 1005; *The Register and Leader* (Des Moines), October 30, 1911.

Congressman Weaver described the action taken in a ''dispatch'' from Washington, dated March 4, 1889, as follows: ''The Creek and Seminole cessions are ratified and authority given to open them to settlement by proclamation of the President. We accomplished this on an Indian appropriation bill. It was a flank movement on our part and proved successful in spite of the cattle men who have control of the Senate''.— See *Iowa Tribune* (Des Moines), March 6, 1889.

222 H. C. Evans in *The Yeoman Shield* in the *Weaver Papers;* McLaughlin and Hart's *Cyclopedia of American Government*, Vol. II, p. 577.

223 *Congressional Record*, 2nd Session, 50th Congress, p. 85.

224 *Congressional Record*, 2nd Session, 50th Congress, Appendix, p. 40.

225 *Congressional Record*, 2nd Session, 50th Congress, p. 2084.

226 Dewey's *National Problems, 1885–1897*, pp. 81, 82.

227 *Congressional Record*, 2nd Session, 50th Congress, pp. 194, 195; Dewey's *National Problems, 1885–1897*, p. 82.

228 *Congressional Record*, 2nd Session, 50th Congress, p. 2218.

229 The *Weaver Scrap Book*, p. 22.

230 The *Weaver Scrap Book*, pp. 115, 140.

CHAPTER XIV

231 The *Weaver Scrap Book*, p. 25; Pammel's *Major John F. Lacey*, p. 5.

232 Pammel's *Major John F. Lacey*, pp. 6, 25, 48, 49.

233 *Iowa Official Register*, 1889, p. 195.

234 *Congressional Record*, 1st Session, 49th Congress, p. 2966.

235 *Congressional Record*, 1st Session, 50th Congress, p. 6147.

236 *Iowa State Press* (Iowa City), June 8 and 15, 1887.

237 See the writer's *Third Party Movements Since the Civil War*, pp. 195, 196.

238 Ruggles's *The Greenback Movement in Iowa;* see the writer's *Third Party Movements Since the Civil War,* pp. 196, 197.

239 The *Weaver Scrap Book,* p. 26; Clark's *History of Senatorial Elections in Iowa,* p. 212.

240 Ruggles's *The Greenback Movement in Iowa; Appleton's Annual Cyclopaedia,* 1889, p. 450.

241 Ruggles's *The Greenback Movement in Iowa; Iowa Official Register,* 1891, pp. 84–87.

242 The *Weaver Scrap Book,* p. 23.

243 The *Weaver Scrap Book,* p. 22.

244 *The Weekly Iowa State Register* (Des Moines), March 27, May 1, 1891.

245 *Clinton Weekly Age,* May 12, 1891; *The Weekly Iowa State Register* (Des Moines), June 5, 1891; *Iowa Official Register,* 1892, p. 171.

246 *Clinton Weekly Age,* May 22, 1891; *The Weekly Iowa State Register* (Des Moines), May 29, 1891; letter from L. L. Polk, May 2, 1891, in the *Weaver Papers.*

247 *The Weekly Iowa State Register* (Des Moines), November 20, 1891; *Clinton Weekly Age,* January 29, 1892; the *Weaver Scrap Book,* p. 39.

248 *Clinton Weekly Age,* February 26, 1892; *The Weekly Iowa State Register* (Des Moines), October 15, 1880, March 4, 1892; the *Weaver Scrap Book,* pp. 32, 38, 100, 101; letter from L. L. Polk, May 2, 1891, in the *Weaver Papers.*

CHAPTER XV

249 The *Weaver Scrap Book,* p. 39.

250 *The Weller Papers* in the library of the State Historical Society of Wisconsin.

251 *The Review of Reviews,* Vol. V, pp. 391, 392; *The Arena,* Vol. V, pp. 427–435.

31

252 *The Weekly Iowa State Register* (Des Moines), June 10, 1892.

253 *The Weekly Iowa State Register* (Des Moines), June 17, 1892.

254 *The Weekly Iowa State Register* (Des Moines), July 8, 1892; the *St. Paul Globe*, July 2 and 5, 1892, in *Personal Scrap Book* in the *Donnelly Collection* in the library of the Minnesota Historical Society, Vol. XIII.

255 *The New York Times*, July 6, 1892, in the *Weaver Scrap Book*, p. 89.

256 *Clinton Weekly Age*, July 8, 1892; *Brooklyn Eagle*, July 5, 1892, in the *Weaver Scrap Book*, p. 111.

257 The *Weaver Scrap Book*, p. 49.

258 The *Weaver Scrap Book*, p. 88; *Clinton Weekly Age*, July 12, 1892; *The Weekly Iowa State Register* (Des Moines), July 29, 1892.

259 The *Weaver Scrap Book*, p. 50.

260 The *Weaver Scrap Book*, pp. 41, 44, 52, 53, 58–70, 84, 87. There is a statement about Mrs. Lease in Weaver's own handwriting in the *Weaver Papers*.

261 The *Weaver Scrap Book*, pp. 44, 80. James Harvey Davis was member-at-large from Texas in the Sixty-fourth Congress, and was defeated for renomination in July, 1916, because the name ''Cyclone'' was not allowed on the ballot.— See *The Nation*, Vol. CII, p. 435, and *The Chicago Tribune*, August 13, 1916.

262 *The Weekly Iowa State Register* (Des Moines), September 30, 1892.

263 The *Weaver Scrap Book*, pp. 19, 43, 59, 95, 97; *The Weekly Iowa State Register* (Des Moines), September 30, 1892.

264 Quoted from the *Chicago Inter Ocean*, September 25, 1892, in *The Weekly Iowa State Register* (Des Moines), September 30, 1892.

265 The *Weaver Scrap Book*, p. 14.

266 The *Weaver Scrap Book*, pp. 11, 14, 36, 44, 50, 76, 85, 99, 113, 165. See Chapter IV of this volume for a discussion of this episode in Weaver's military record.

267 The *Weaver Scrap Book*, p. 14.

268 Statement by J. B. Weaver, Jr.; letter from Albion W. Tourgee, October 19, 1892, in the *Weaver Papers*.

269 Weaver's *A Call to Action*, pp. 5–7; the *Weaver Scrap Book*, p. 65; *Iowa Tribune* (Des Moines), April 1, 1891.

270 Dodd's *The Social and Economic Background of Woodrow Wilson* in *The Journal of Political Economy*, Vol. XXV, pp. 261–285.

271 *Appleton's Annual Cyclopaedia*, 1892, pp. 755, 756; McPherson's *A Hand-Book of Politics for 1894*, p. 272; McLaughlin and Hart's *Cyclopedia of American Government*, Vol. III, pp. 38, 39; *The Weekly Iowa State Register* (Des Moines), August 19, 1892.

272 Letter from A. M. West, September 11, 1892, in the *Weaver Papers*.

273 The *Weaver Scrap Book*, pp. 41, 103; *The Weekly Iowa State Register* (Des Moines), November 18, 1892.

274 The *Weaver Scrap Book*, p. 19; *Clinton Weekly Age*, November 18, 1892.

275 The *Weaver Scrap Book*, p. 72.

276 The *Weaver Scrap Book*, p. 39.

277 *The Weekly Iowa State Register* (Des Moines), December 2, 1892.

CHAPTER XVI

278 *Clinton Weekly Age*, December 16, 1892.

279 *The Weekly Iowa State Register* (Des Moines), February 3, 1893.

280 The *Weaver Scrap Book*, p. 73.

281 The *Weaver Scrap Book*, pp. 76, 103.

[282] *The Weekly Iowa State Register* (Des Moines), March 3, July 14, and August 4, 1893; *Clinton Weekly Age*, October 6, 1893.

[283] The *Weaver Scrap Book*, p. 111.

[284] *The Weekly Iowa State Register* (Des Moines), September 8, 1893.

[285] *Iowa Official Register*, 1894, pp. 106, 107.

[286] *The Weekly Iowa State Register* (Des Moines), May 4, 11, 1894; *Clinton Weekly Age*, May 4, 1894.

[287] Weaver's *The Commonweal Crusade* in *The Midland Monthly*, Vol. I, pp. 590–594.

[288] The phrase ''middle-of-the-road'' was used to describe those Populists ''who voted for Watson and were in favor of maintaining their own organization without alliance or fusion with any other party''. McKee in his *National Conventions and Platforms of All Political Parties 1789 to 1900* states that it is ''taken from the adjuration of Milton Park, of Texas, who led the bolt, to 'Keep in the middle of the road' '' at the Populist convention in St. Louis in 1896. It was used at least as early as 1892 as is shown by the following campaign verses printed in the *Rocky Mountain News* of Denver:

> Side tracks are rough, and they're hard to walk,
>   Keep in the middle of the road;
> Though we haven't got time to stop and talk
>   We keep in the middle of the road.
> Turn your backs on the goldbug men,
> And yell for silver now and then;
> If you want to beat Grover, also Ben,
>   Just stick to the middle of the road.
>
>
> Don't answer the call of goldbug tools,
>   But keep in the middle of the road;
> Prove that the West wasn't settled by fools,
>   And keep in the middle of the road.
> They've woven their plots, and woven them ill,

We want a Weaver who's got more skill,
And mostly we want a Silver Bill,
So we'll stay in the middle of the road.

— See McLaughlin and Hart's *Cyclopedia of American Government*, Vol. II, p. 757; McKee's *The National Conventions and Platforms of All Political Parties 1789 to 1900*, pp. 353, 354; the *Weaver Scrap Book*, pp. 52, 86 — clippings from *Rocky Mountain News*, July 17, 1892.

[289] *The Weekly Iowa State Register* (Des Moines), September 7, 1894.

[290] In July, 1894, Weaver resigned as editor of *The Iowa Farmers' Tribune*, published at Des Moines (with which he had been connected since its establishment in 1878) because of his nomination for Congress and his "purpose" to remove to Council Bluffs.— See *The Iowa Farmers' Tribune* (Des Moines), July 25, 1894.

[291] *Iowa Official Register*, 1895, pp. 186–190.

[292] *The Daily Iowa State Register* (Des Moines), August 9, 1894.

[293] The *Weaver Scrap Book*, pp. 16, 17, 37, 76, 79, 85, 91, 117.

[294] The *Weaver Scrap Book*, pp. 33, 36; *Iowa Official Register*, 1895, p. 190; *The Review of Reviews*, Vol. X, p. 624; letters from Samuel Gompers, September 28, 1894, and Eugene V. Debs, October 23, 1894, in the *Weaver Papers*.

[295] The *Weaver Scrap Book*, p. 36.

[296] McVey's *The Populist Movement* in *Economic Studies*, Vol. I, p. 197.

[297] *The Weekly Iowa State Register* (Des Moines), May 17, June 7, 14, 1895; *Clinton Weekly Age*, March 1, 1895.

[298] *The Weekly Iowa State Register* (Des Moines), June 14 and August 2, 1895.

[299] *Clinton Weekly Age*, August 9, 1895; *The Weekly Iowa State Register* (Des Moines), August 9, 1895.

[300] The *Weaver Scrap Book*, p. 34.

301 The *Weaver Scrap Book,* pp. 102, 143.

302 The *Weaver Scrap Book,* pp. 27, 30.

303 The *Weaver Scrap Book,* p. 37.

304 *The Weekly Iowa State Register* (Des Moines), April 24, 1896.

305 *The Review of Reviews,* Vol. XIV, p. 265; *The Weekly Iowa State Register* (Des Moines), July 24 and 31, 1896; *Clinton Weekly Age,* July 21 and 24, 1896.

306 Bryan's *The First Battle,* pp. 276–279; Bryan's *A Story of the Campaign of 1896* was dedicated to "the Three Pioneers", R. P. Bland, J. B. Weaver, and H. M. Teller. In the *Weaver Papers* there are letters from Bryan, dated December 5 and 10, 1896, asking for a copy of the nominating speech and for permission to use Weaver's name in the dedication. When he returned the speech of which he had made a copy he added: "For directness, logic, strength & diction it can hardly be surpassed. I am glad to have it in my book."

307 *The Weekly Iowa State Register* (Des Moines), August 14, 1896.

308 The *Weaver Scrap Book,* p. 18; *The Weekly Iowa State Register* (Des Moines), August 21, 1896.

CHAPTER XVII

309 The *Weaver Scrap Book,* pp. 18, 27, 34, 35.

310 *The Weekly Iowa State Register* (Des Moines), August 5, 1898; the *Weaver Scrap Book,* p. 31; *Iowa Official Register,* 1899, p. 232.

311 The *Weaver Papers.*

312 The *Weaver Scrap Book,* p. 110.

313 The *Weaver Scrap Book,* p. 85.

314 The *Weaver Scrap Book,* p. 112.

315 Letter from J. H. Edmisten, dated January 10, 1900, in the *Weaver Papers. The Weller Papers,* in the library of the

State Historical Society of Wisconsin, contain a printed address to the People's party and independent voters of the United States, giving an account of the controversies between the two factions and chiefly devoted to the meeting at Lincoln.

316 Letters from S. B. Crane, dated March 12, 1900, from Marion Butler, dated April 30, 1900, and from Geo. H. Shibley, dated May 2, 1900, in the *Weaver Papers*.

317 McKee's *The National Conventions and Platforms of All Political Parties 1789 to 1900*, pp. 347–355; McLaughlin and Hart's *Cyclopedia of American Government*, Vol. II, pp. 757, 758.

318 Letter from Geo. S. Canfield, May 16, 1900, in the *Weaver Papers*.

319 Letter from T. M. Patterson, May 22, 1900, in the *Weaver Papers*.

320 Letter from E. H. Gillette, June 28, 1900, in the *Weaver Papers*.

321 McKee's *The National Conventions and Platforms of All Political Parties 1789 to 1900*, pp. 330, 331.

322 The *Weaver Scrap Book*, p. 112.

323 The *Weaver Scrap Book*, p. 104.

324 *The Weekly Iowa State Register* (Des Moines), May 6, 1904; letter from W. W. Baldwin, May 6, 1904, in the *Weaver Papers;* the *Weaver Scrap Book*, pp. 38, 139.

325 The *Weaver Scrap Book*, pp. 46, 70, 114; letter from Daniel McComille, chairman of the speakers' bureau of Democratic national committee, October 21, 1904, and letter from John W. Kern, November 14, 1904, in the *Weaver Papers*.

326 The *Weaver Scrap Book*, p. 96; letters from M. J. Wade, John R. Clark, Leonard Brown, and A. Q. Wooster in the *Weaver Papers*.

327 Letter from John W. Kern, February 20, 1909, in the *Weaver Papers*.

328 Letter from E. H. Gillette, June 8, 1908, in the *Weaver Papers.*

329 *The Sioux City Tribune,* August 23, 1911.

330 The *Salt Lake Tribune,* September 10, 1911.

331 Letters from A. Van Wagenen, dated November 2, 6, and 8, 1911, in the *Weaver Papers.*

332 Letters from W. D. Jamieson, dated December 29, 1911, January 15 and 19, 1912, in the *Weaver Papers.*

333 The *Weaver Scrap Book,* p. 154.

CHAPTER XVIII

334 Letter from H. C. Evans, February 23, 1903, in the *Weaver Papers;* the *Weaver Scrap Book,* p. 112.

335 The *Weaver Scrap Book,* pp. 152, 153.

336 Harlan's *Honors for General Weaver* in *The Midwestern,* Vol. III, pp. 60–62 (March, 1909); *Journal of the House of Representatives,* 1909, p. 190; *The Register and Leader* (Des Moines), February 14 and 16, 1909; a typewritten report of the *Ceremony of the Historical Department of Iowa on Installing a Portrait by Charles A. Cumming, of General James B. Weaver* in the chamber of the House of Representatives, Capitol, February 15, 1909.

337 *The Register and Leader* (Des Moines), February 14 and 16, 1909; the *Weaver Scrap Book,* p. 154.

338 *Pioneer Lawmakers' Association,* 1909, pp. 72, 73.

339 *Letters of Friends of General James B. Weaver Expressing Views on his Life and Character and on the Placing of his Portrait in the Gallery of The Historical Department of Iowa,* February, 1909.

CHAPTER XIX

340 *The Register and Leader* (Des Moines), February 7, 1912.

341 *The Register and Leader* (Des Moines), February 9, 1912; a typewritten report of the *Funeral Services of General James*

B. Weaver in the *Weaver Papers; Des Moines News*, February 7, 1912; *Pioneer Lawmakers' Association*, 1913, pp. 90–93.

[342] *The Register and Leader* (Des Moines), February 8, 1912; *Des Moines News*, February 7, 1912.

[343] The *Weaver Scrap Book*, p. 161.

[344] *The Register and Leader* (Des Moines), February 8, 1912.

[345] The *Weaver Scrap Book*, p. 161.

[346] *The Sioux City Tribune*, February 7, 1912; other newspaper estimates reprinted in the *Pioneer Lawmakers' Association*, 1913, pp. 87–90.

[347] *Congressional Record*, 2nd Session, 62nd Congress, p. 1840.

[348] A typewritten report of the *Dedication of Weaver Park*, at Bloomfield, Iowa, August 18, 1915, in the *Weaver Papers; The Register and Leader* (Des Moines), July 26 and August 18 and 20, 1915.

[349] *The Des Moines Capital*, February 16, 1912.

[350] Statement from James B. Weaver, Jr. The quotation, he says, is from the Persian poet Hafiz.

INDEX

INDEX

477

MID-AMERICAN FRONTIER

An Arno Press Collection

Andreas, A[lfred] T[heodore]. **History of Chicago.** 3 volumes. 1884-1886

Andrews, C[hristopher] C[olumbus]. **Minnesota and Dacotah.** 1857

Atwater, Caleb. **Remarks Made on a Tour to Prairie du Chien:** Thence to Washington City, in 1829. 1831

Beck, Lewis C[aleb]. **A Gazetteer of the States of Illinois and Missouri.** 1823

Beckwith, Hiram W[illiams]. **The Illinois and Indiana Indians.** 1884

Blois, John T. **Gazetteer of the State of Michigan,** in Three Parts. 1838

Brown, Jesse and A. M. Willard. **The Black Hills Trails.** 1924

Brunson, Alfred. **A Western Pioneer: Or, Incidents of the Life and Times of Rev. Alfred Brunson.** 2 volumes in one. 1872

Burnet, Jacob. **Notes on the Early Settlement of the North-Western Territory.** 1847

Cass, Lewis. **Considerations on the Present State of the Indians,** and their Removal to the West of the Mississippi. 1828

Coggeshall, William T[urner]. **The Poets and Poetry of the West.** 1860

Darby, John F[letcher]. **Personal Recollections of Many Prominent People Whom I Have Known.** 1880

Eastman, Mary. **Dahcotah:** Or, Life and Legends of the Sioux Around Fort Snelling. 1849

Ebbutt, Percy G. **Emigrant Life in Kansas.** 1886

Edwards, Ninian W[irt]. **History of Illinois, From 1778 to 1833:** And Life and Times of Ninian Edwards. 1870

Ellsworth, Henry William. **Valley of the Upper Wabash, Indiana.** 1838

Esarey, Logan, ed. **Messages and Letters of William Henry Harrison.** 2 volumes. 1922

Flower, George. **The Errors of Emigrants.** [1841]

Hall, Baynard Rush (Robert Carlton, pseud.). **The New Purchase:** Or Seven and a Half Years in the Far West. 2 volumes in one. 1843

Haynes, Fred[erick] Emory. **James Baird Weaver.** 1919

Heilbron, Bertha L., ed. **With Pen and Pencil on the Frontier in 1851:** The Diary and Sketches of Frank Blackwell Mayer. 1932

Hinsdale, B[urke] A[aron]. **The Old Northwest:** The Beginnings of Our Colonial System. [1899]

Johnson, Harrison. **Johnson's History of Nebraska.** 1880

Lapham, I[ncrease] A[llen]. **Wisconsin:** Its Geography and Topography, History, Geology, and Mineralogy. 1846

Mansfield, Edward D. **Memoirs of the Life and Services of Daniel Drake.** 1855

Marshall, Thomas Maitland, ed. **The Life and Papers of Frederick Bates.** 2 volumes in one. 1926

McConnel, J[ohn] L[udlum.] **Western Characters:** Or, Types of Border Life in the Western States. 1853

Miller, Benjamin S. **Ranch Life in Southern Kansas and the Indian Territory.** 1896

Neill, Edward Duffield. **The History of Minnesota.** 1858

Parker, Nathan H[owe]. **The Minnesota Handbook, For 1856-7.** 1857

Peck, J[ohn] M[ason]. **A Guide for Emigrants.** 1831

Pelzer, Louis. **Marches of the Dragoons in the Mississippi Valley.** 1917

Perkins, William Rufus and Barthinius L. Wick. **History of the Amana Society.** 1891

Rister, Carl Coke. **Land Hunger:** David L. Payne and the Oklahoma Boomers. 1942

Schoolcraft, Henry R[owe]. **Personal Memoirs of a Residence of Thirty Years With the Indian Tribes on the American Frontiers.** 1851

Smalley, Eugene V. **History of the Northern Pacific Railroad.** 1883

[Smith, William Rudolph]. **Observations on the Wisconsin Territory.** 1838

Steele, [Eliza R.] **A Summer Journey in the West.** 1841

Streeter, Floyd Benjamin. **The Kaw:** The Heart of a Nation. 1941

[Switzler, William F.] **Switzler's Illustrated History of Missouri, From 1541 to 1877.** 1879

Tallent, Annie D. **The Black Hills.** 1899

Thwaites, Reuben Gold. **On the Storied Ohio.** 1903

Todd, Charles S[tewart] and Benjamin Drake. **Sketches of the Civil and Military Services of William Henry Harrison.** 1840

Wetmore, Alphonso, compiler. **Gazetteer of the State of Missouri.** 1837

Wilder, D[aniel] W[ebster]. **The Annals of Kansas.** 1886

Woollen, William Wesley. **Biographical and Historical Sketches of Early Indiana.** 1883

Wright, Robert M[arr]. **Dodge City.** 1913